Advance Praise for The New Health Economy

"*The New Health Economy* is a masterclass about how health care works—and doesn't work—in America." —**Bob Kocher, former special assistant to President Obama for health care and economic policy and partner at Venrock**

"*The New Health Economy* rightly focuses on one of the most critical issues facing US health care: rapidly escalating costs. The affordability crisis is real and, as the authors argue, will define social and economic vitality in the decade ahead. This is an essential read for leaders seeking to better understand the forces of change at play in health care, and how we can better manage them to reimagine the future of health in America." —**David Cordani, president and CEO, Cigna**

"If the COVID-19 pandemic was the catalyst for the rapid change our health system needs, *The New Health Economy* is the guidebook for leaders intent on bringing value to American patients, purchasers, and policymakers. This authoritative book belongs on the desk of every current and future health company CEO." —**Ceci Connolly, president and CEO, Alliance of Community Health Plans**

"In clinical medicine, the 'crisis' is the point in the course of an illness where the patient either dies or gets better. In health care management and health care systems, neither has happened. *The New Health Economy* breaks out of the model of crisis and instead identifies leadership as the key element for improvement." —**Mark V. Pauly, Bendheim Professor in the Department of Health Care Management, The Wharton School, University of Pennsylvania**

"*The New Health Economy* is a primer for industry leaders in the postpandemic world." —**Michael A. Mussallem, chairman and CEO, Edwards Lifesciences**

"*The New Health Economy* reflects how important it is for health care leaders to understand the relationship between politics, health policy, delivery networks, and the consumer. The leaders who understand these forces will implement the changes in health care that will close the current gaps." —**Mark E. Miller, executive vice president of health care, Arnold Ventures**

"The transformation in American health care is happening now. Success will depend on effective leadership, management, and governance. Engaged and informed board members are critical as health systems, health insurers, and medical groups grow in scale and complexity. At the same time digitization and new entrants are upending what's possible. They are changing the rules of the game with the resources to back it up. Board members and all emerging health care leaders will greatly benefit from the timely insights and hard-won knowledge shared in *The New Health Economy*." —**John Koster, board member, Banner Health**

"*The New Health Economy* is a rich source of insight into health care politics, policy, providers, and personalization that helps lift the fog to reveal a new framework for the future of health care." —**Greg Carpenter, Harold T. Martin Professor of Marketing, Kellogg School of Management, Northwestern University**

The New Health Economy

THE
NEW HEALTH
ECONOMY

Ground Rules for Leaders

GARY BISBEE JR.
DONALD TRIGG
SANJULA JAIN

Georgetown University Press / Washington, DC

The publisher is not responsible for third-party websites or their content. URL links were active at time of publication.

Library of Congress Cataloging-in-Publication Data

Names: Bisbee, Gary, Jr., author. | Trigg, Donald, author. | Jain, Sanjula, author.
Title: The new health economy : ground rules for leaders / Gary Bisbee, Jr.,
    Donald Trigg, Sanjula Jain.
Description: Washington, DC : Georgetown University Press, 2022. | Includes
    bibliographical references and index.
Identifiers: LCCN 2021037748 (print) | LCCN 2021037749 (ebook) |
    ISBN 9781647122539 (hardcover) | ISBN 9781647122546 (paperback) |
    ISBN 9781647122553 (ebook)
Subjects: LCSH: Medical economics—United States. | Medical policy—Economic
    aspects—United States. | Medical care, Cost of—United States. | Medical policy—
    United States. | COVID-19 (Disease) | COVID-19 Pandemic, 2020–
Classification: LCC RA410.53 .B57 2022 (print) | LCC RA410.53 (ebook) |
    DDC 338.4/73621—dc23
LC record available at https://lccn.loc.gov/2021037748
LC ebook record available at https://lccn.loc.gov/2021037749

♾ This paper meets the requirements of ANSI/NISO Z39.48-1992 (Permanence of Paper).

23 22   9 8 7 6 5 4 3 2   First printing

Printed in the United States of America

Cover design by Erin Kirk
Interior design by BookComp, Inc.

Contents

PART III: PROVIDER NETWORKS

PART IV: DATA-DRIVEN PERSONALIZATION

Foreword

The US health care ecosystem is moving into a new era of uncertainty and possibility. In the postpandemic world, change is not just accelerating but also changing direction. While the quest for scale and consolidation continues, the bigger shift is toward more fundamental systemic changes: reconfiguring relationships, adding new players, and changing the very definitions of efficiency, equity, and quality. This means that the determinants of future success in the US health care system will be qualitatively different from those of the past.

Modern health care is often framed as a nexus of interactions spanning patients, providers, and payers. Surrounding this are the worlds of politics, finance, and regulation, which themselves are shaped by the changing context of societal expectations and technological possibility. To this already complicated ecosystem, we now introduce new technologies, new data possibilities, new models of provision and payment, and new sources of capital. Today's health economy is more complex, but it also holds more potential for productive change.

For decades, everyone who has looked at the US health care system has concluded that deep change is inevitable. This is as true in 2022 as it was in 2001 and in 1981. Inevitability should not be confused with immediacy. It should by now be clear to all that the challenge is not just in finding a better blueprint but also in strategizing a transition from where we are to where we want to go. Reform is hard because we do not have the luxury of creating a new health care system from scratch. The work in transitioning ecosystems is in recognizing the critical pieces for whom change will be a negative and finding a way to shift the conditions such that critical actors will nonetheless have motivation to transition; hopeful reformers who depend on likely losers to support change are usually disappointed.

Despite complexity, there is genuine reason for optimism—conditions post–COVID-19 really are different. Pressures are higher, and enablers are more robust and more accessible. But leveraging these conditions productively depends on understanding the forces that underlie how the current ecosystem came to be and how it can evolve from here. Navigating this changing landscape requires broadening our approach to strategy. The need to deploy a wider lens that can explicitly account for the co-innovation and adoption chain challenges that confront reformers in the health care ecosystem is greater than ever.

The New Health Economy: Ground Rules for Leaders answers this call. The authors of this volume are exceptional guides to understanding and shaping the landscape. Their collective experience within the health care context is deep and is magnified by the insights brought to light in leadership cases that connect the big issues to the critical decisions and to the individual decision makers who took action. The combination has given rise to a truly unique volume.

Within this book, we can find the precedents that have created the system with which we confront the current challenges as well as possibilities for change in a multitude of dimensions that will define a better health care future. The authors' 4Ps of the new health care economy—health care politics, health policy, provider networks, and data-driven personalization—present a holistic perspective for understanding interactions in the health care sphere that overcomes the limitations of many prior treatments.

For newcomers to the health care context, this book will offer an essential entry point, a thoughtful overview of thirty years of evolution in a setting that is only becoming more important to the economy and to society at large. For veterans, the book offers a repository of critical decisions and perspectives that have given shape to the health care system and that anyone hoping to reshape the system must consider in depth. For all readers, increased clarity about the system and its underlying rules will magnify individuals' effectiveness in and impact on this crucial and fascinating setting.

—Ron Adner, PhD
Professor of Strategy and Entrepreneurship,
Tuck School of Business, Dartmouth College,
and author of *Winning the Right Game: How to Disrupt,
Defend, and Deliver in a Changing World*

Preface

The late health care information technology entrepreneur and dynamic leader Neal Patterson often said in his closing days that "health care ultimately becomes personal." The reach of health care is wide and deep. It is, in the end, deeply personal. As we learned during the coronavirus pandemic (COVID-19), the health of the population and the health of the economy are inextricably linked. GDP, the broadest definition of national economic output, decreased 3.5 percent in 2020.[1] It was the lowest growth rate since 1946.[2] Moreover, according to the Bureau of Labor Statistics, the number of unemployed individuals increased during the peak of the pandemic from 7.1 million in March 2020 to 23 million at the start of May 2020.[3] And tragically, the Johns Hopkins Coronavirus Resource Center reports that as of September 2021, more than 685,000 Americans had died from COVID-19. The numbers tell the story of a staggering societal toll.

In one of the great feats of modern medicine through a public/private partnership, vaccines were introduced in late December 2020. According to the Centers for Disease Control and Prevention, by August 2021, 77 percent of the population eighteen years of age and older had received at least one dose of vaccine, and 93 percent of those persons age sixty-five and older had received at least one dose. The United States began its recovery with pace from there aided by fiscal stimulus, monetary stimulus, and rising consumer confidence that the pandemic fight-back was finally taking hold. In the years to come the health economy will seek a "new normal," as identified by Duke University professor Dr. Mark McClellan, former Food and Drug Administration commissioner and Center for Medicare and Medicaid Services administrator. And as Purdue University president and former Indiana governor Mitch Daniels said, it will not look exactly the same as it did before. The shock and disruption of COVID-19 will bring inevitable change to the health economy. One of the reasons we undertook writing this book was to advance a strategic framework for leaders to better anticipate and manage that change.

Health care represents 18 percent of GDP and was the largest item in the federal budget at 25 percent. Washington's role in the health economy is a large and growing one. The defining trends of the 2010s fundamentally altered traditional health care dynamics. Indeed, many leaders have argued that across the longer arc of history, the 2010s will be viewed as the most important in health care since the passage of Medicare and Medicaid in 1965. Today amid the accelerating forces of the COVID-19 pandemic, this book seeks to share with the reader our considered view that the decade unfolding may well become even more consequential than the last. Time—and the collective impact of health care leaders—will tell.

In our view, the challenge of a coordinated crisis response is a microcosm of the tough intersectional forces that define the US health economy in the 2020s. Furthermore, the shift from crisis response to durable recovery within the context of the new normal still to come will fully expose the intersectional forces that health care leaders must manage in the decade ahead. This shift will demand that leaders challenge sharpening *political* orthodoxies to advance new bipartisan *policy*, will accelerate changes in the *provision* of care including teleservices and the home as venue, and will offer a stark reminder that health care is *personal* and that the individual is the ultimate decision maker, which will be an essential part of any systemic approach to changing health care.

Why did we undertake the tough task of writing this book? A quarter century ago, one of us cofounded a health care industry collaborative called The Health Management Academy. One of us served as head of research, and another of us was an active executive participant and voice for key areas of industry and leadership collaboration. In our various roles, we have organized and facilitated leadership development programs for thousands of health care executives. Two of us have held faculty positions in graduate programs in health administration and policy, and one of us is currently on a medical school faculty. One of us has trained hundreds of leaders in a commercial setting. We have learned from firsthand experience the importance to leaders of a learning framework that incorporates the health care and economic realities of the health economy and its many intersectional forces.

Of course, just like the leap from an entrepreneurial idea to an active company, the decision to jump into the manuscript was one that came over the course of many months as we actively listened to hundreds of leaders from across health care. They were telling us that health care is changing at an ever-faster pace. They found it necessary to formulate and understand direction and pace of change. They were requesting a decision-making framework in areas such as setting strategy and managing operations.

This book is intentionally written as a resource for leaders (regardless of their background within health care) to develop a foundation that will guide strategy development and enhanced decision making at a time of accelerating change. Through our professional roles, we have facilitated seminars for health system and health insurance executives; commercial company leaders in the supplier, pharmaceutical, and medical device businesses; health policy decision makers; and graduate students in masters and PhD programs and medical schools.

Our collective learning is that health care is too important and complex for traditional academic or health care silos. In addition to traditional health care companies providing health care products and services, new entrants ranging from big cap companies such as Amazon, Walmart, Google, and Apple to early-stage and start-up companies (e.g., interviews in the book include Walmart's Marcus Osborne and Tia's Carolyn Witte) at the entrepreneurial forest floor.

As a result, the business of health care is not only the province of health care educational programs. In our conversations with the faculty and directors of leading health care management and public health programs, every program director has expressed a need to have a contemporary text to help their students understand why the industry has evolved as it has and how that translates into the practical realities of what is to come. As a result, the courses in these schools and respective programs are looking to equip their graduates (who ultimately are on the path to be leaders) with the tools for understanding how to approach their career role whether it be in health policy, politics, provider and financing systems, or personalization.

One of us currently serves on the faculty of a medical school and has been asked to teach classes that include graduate students and experienced executives enrolled across the cross section of the School of Medicine, the School of Public Health, and the Business School. The leading academic institutions are encouraging more and more faculty to build classes that have an applied, industry perspective, and thus the importance of writing this book now.

Our dialogue with industry leaders offers important validation of that larger trend. Speaking with executives in our various roles has convincingly revealed for us that knowledge of health politics and policy, developing provider and health insurance models, and the personalization of health care is a requirement for leadership in the new health economy. And as COVID-19 shifted more of those conversations to a virtual form, we nonetheless heard from leaders a narrative around the intersectional forces of change afoot. Politics has influenced policy in testing, mask wearing, and vaccine development/administration in both the Donald Trump and Joe Biden administrations. Leaders in health systems, health insurance, and pharmaceutical companies have been required to make decisions multiple times a day that tested their understanding and knowledge of politics, policy, and personalization and their intersection.

We use the term *leader* in the broader sense. Leaders include a member of the C-suite with multiple billions of dollars of responsibility, a physician with several physician peers, the chief medical officer of a health system or insurance company with hundreds of physician direct reports, a nurse with a patient care unit or operating room staff, and a social worker with responsibility for a food center. Individuals may also want to learn about leadership and the health economy to feel more in control of their environment. We designed the book to serve each of these leaders as they enhance their understanding of health care, its history and future.

The importance of COVID-19 to the health economy in terms of public health and economic cost has been virtually unmeasurable. As of early 2021, $4 trillion has been taken out of the federal treasury or borrowed by the federal government alone, without reference to what state governments have spent. With the added cost due to COVID-19 for the Veterans Administration, Department of Defense, and interest on borrowed monies, the public health and financial consequences of the coronavirus pandemic in the United States are huge, and its impact will be felt for generations.

On the positive side, the public/private partnership to develop vaccines in one year instead of the typical seven years will accelerate both science cycles and leadership decision cycles. The addition of telehealth as a formal diagnostic and therapeutic capability expands the potential for home as venue. Gaps of health equity and affordability are already causing change in health financing and delivery. Other effects include the privacy issues regarding vaccines and testing that are being debated and will have consequences. References are being made today to changes that occurred in response to the 1918 virus. One imagines that a hundred years from now, reference to lessons learned from the COVID-19 pandemic will be equally common. Dr. Mark McClellan's new normal is already under way.

We considered how to best convey the dynamic impact of COVID-19 on the delivery and financing of health care as it evolved from January 2020. We had a rich primary source of information from organized interviews that we conducted. We chose thirteen cases out of the more than eighty in-depth interviews to best convey the status of COVID-19 at a particular point in time and the dynamic effect it was having on communities, patients, physicians, and other frontline caregivers and employees. Concern was high among leaders over the possibility of PTSD acquired by frontline caregivers. Terms such as "battle," "fear," and "heroes" were routinely used.

The reader will be able to track the progression of COVID-19, understand more fully the impact on health organizations, and read how leaders were being faced with the necessity to make first-time decisions, frequently with little data.

For example, we make references to leaders such as Dr. Steven Corwin, who led the response at the outbreak epicenter in New York City and saw this event as unlike any other in his career (compared to the AIDS pandemic, the September 11 attacks, and other defining events) and also saw how going forward, New York-Presbyterian will have to make different types of decisions.

Each case study has been shaped to present the topics relevant to a particular section of the book. We included a range of organization and leader profiles to provide depth and richness describing the impact of COVID-19. The reader will learn from CEOs of health systems and health insurers, former federal and state government officials, CEOs of pharmaceutical companies that developed vaccines, an entrepreneur building a patient care business, and former governors.

We use quotes liberally to provide the reader with a "from the front lines" feel for the cases that we discuss. There are quotes integrated into the text to support the conclusions of the authors and quotes in call-out boxes that characterize the general themes of the section or chapter. The interviews are cited by date in the "COVID-19 interviews" chapters where they are featured: chapters 2, 5, 8, and 11. When these key leaders are quoted elsewhere in the book, there are no additional citations of interview dates; we refer the reader to those core chapters. We do provide interview citations for the other leaders we interviewed who are quoted throughout the text.

We organized the book around the 4Ps—health care politics, health policy, provider networks, and data-driven personalization—with a section devoted to each, within which are three parallel chapters. The first chapter in each section frames the P with the historical background, trends, and review of the issues to best provide the foundation for the future. We fully subscribe to the quote attributed to Winston Churchill: "The longer you can look back, the farther you can look forward."[4] In our quarter century working with health care leaders, it is our observation that the past is an undervalued guidepost to navigating the health care complexities of today and tomorrow. The second chapter in each section contains a set of cases based on individual interviews that provide the real-world effect of COVID-19 and its influence on the trends and background discussed in the first chapter in each section. At the request of many leaders who have participated in our seminars and our work across the industry, we included summary information about individuals and organizations—a decision supported by some of the peer reviewers of this manuscript selected by Georgetown University Press.

The third chapter in each section contains lessons for leaders and a ground rule that incorporate the information in the first and second chapters and the authors' synthesis. The purpose of the ground rules is to provide swim lanes for how a leader can approach each of the 4Ps and how to navigate the intersections between them. Our personal experience and that reported by the many leaders we have interviewed and interacted with is that the intersections between the 4Ps can be difficult because there are no roadmaps or texts that describe how to navigate the intersections. Leaders bemoan that while they have domain experts within their organization in one of these areas, there is no framework to bring them together to make the sum of that expertise greater than its parts. We note that the literature is sparse in terms of the influence of COVID-19 on politics, policy, delivery models, and personalization, taken as a whole. Intersections matter.

The experienced and aspiring leaders with whom we work daily are struggling to navigate intersectional forces of change in the effort to conceive, create, and implement the solutions that the business of US health care so desperately needs. Informed by hundreds of conversations with frontline leaders throughout the pandemic, we have seen the COVID-19 crisis accelerate the cycle time for medical science. The creation of the vaccine tells the story. Development cycle times of seven years were compressed to one year by Pfizer, Moderna, and Johnson & Johnson. Our conclusion is that cycle time for health care financing and delivery progress will speed up commensurately to keep pace.

While there are many books in the field that consider one angle (and have been deeply formative for all three of us), we've not seen a 360-degree view of the health economy represented here. We apply the 4Ps framework in the context of the coronavirus crisis and contend that many of the trends taking hold before COVID-19 were emphasized during the pandemic and will accelerate transformation after COVID-19. Our collaboration shines a light on health care change derived from our real-time work with organizations and executive leadership teams across the industry.

The New Health Economy looks (with admitted ambition) to bring together the best thinking in each of the 4Ps, infuse them with emerging leadership insights from the COVID-19 crisis, and set out the essential ground rules required for postpandemic impact.

Today's highly talented, educated, and dynamic leaders inspire confidence that they will rise to and exceed the challenges of understanding the health economy, with its complex and tough intersections. Success in the dynamic period of disruptive change to come will demand our best thinkers and leaders.

Indeed, the winds of change set in motion in the last decade and accelerated by COVID-19 will be transformative in the 2020s. This decade demands a different model. The effective leader must deeply understand the intersectional forces of change that are unfolding and craft holistic strategies to influence them. And in the end, it is our obligation as leaders to invest the required energies for understanding and improving a health economy that is too important to stay the same.

—Gary, Don, and Sanjula

Notes

1. Harriett Torry, "U.S. Economy Shrank in 2020 Despite Fourth-Quarter Growth," *Wall Street Journal* (January 28, 2021), https://www.wsj.com/articles/us-gdp-economic-growth-fourth-quarter-2020-11611802382.
2. Torry, "U.S. Economy Shrank."
3. Bureau of Labor Statistics, "Employment Situation News Release."
4. This is the correct version of a quote that has often been phrased incorrectly, according to the International Churchill Society, founded in 1968, which describes itself as "the world's preeminent member organisation dedicated to preserving the historic legacy of Sir Winston Churchill." International Churchill Society, "About the Society."

Introduction

The US Health Economy

As the COVID-19 pandemic ground into the winter months of 2020, people around the world spoke of the fatiguing forced march of the coronavirus. Trended numbers filled the COVID-19 dashboards and drove banner headlines. We surveyed the daily counts of confirmed cases, watched rising hospitalization levels, and searched for even a hint of positive trend in the case fatality rates.

For leaders on the front lines of the COVID-19 crisis, every bit of data told a story. Dr. Jim Linder, CEO at Nebraska Medicine, described preparing the biometric unit for the first patient from the *Diamond Princess* cruise ship when the diagnosis of the then still-novel coronavirus was unknown. Dr. Laura Forese, chief operating officer at New York-Presbyterian, recalled loved ones watching their relatives die on FaceTime because they could not be next to them in the intensive care unit (ICU). Wright Lassiter, president and CEO at Henry Ford Health System, worried about the potential for PTSD in his caregivers as they struggled with almost 250 patient lives lost in just a three-week period.

In COVID-19 hotspots starting in the spring of 2020 and continuing with multiple surges (driven by multiple variants) in the months that followed, ICU and medical-surgical beds overflowed with patients of every profile, initially with an overweighting of older and immunocompromised patients. Staffing demands were unrelenting. By year's end, few health providers and the communities they care for were left unchanged by the virus.

All told, by June 2020 COVID-19 had taken more American lives than the Korean War, the Vietnam War, and all subsequent US-fought wars combined.[1] Beyond the loss of life, the health, economic, and social welfare impact of the pandemic will be generational in scope and reach. We will grapple with the before, during, and after of COVID-19 for decades to come.

Somewhat paradoxically, amid the massive complexities and challenges of COVID-19, the best leaders also saw possibilities. COVID-19 accelerated forces of health care change that had already begun playing out through the prior decades. The crisis catalyzed leaders—both within and outside health care—to challenge fundamental assumptions of health care supply and demand and offered the promise of a new health economy after COVID-19 that was far better than the one before it.

Our use of the term *health economy* is an important one. We define the demand side of the health economy as comprising aggregators of risk and purchasers of health and care services. Government, employers, and individuals are the predominant funding sources of the health economy. They are the payers for health care. We define the supply of the health economy as providers of services ranging from hospitals to physician practices to retail pharmacies to telehealth services. Health insurers are intermediaries between the payers and providers.

The coronavirus pandemic is the latest catalyst for change in the health economy. Next steps will rely on leaders mastering the complicated intersectional forces that recognize that the *person* is the ultimate decision maker, the *provision* of care and its financing will evolve steadily through this decade, and bipartisan *policy* will challenge *political* orthodoxy.

We wrote this book in part because of health care's history in the decades before COVID-19 and the gaps identified by the pandemic. We see this decade as one of great evolution. As we have spoken with hundreds of executives, they have increasingly noted that the growing pace of change in health care requires a new framework for decision making. We believe there are four foundational pillars of the health economy: health care politics, health policy, provider networks, and data-driven personalization, or the 4Ps. The book frames the historical progression of each of the 4Ps, offers some early primary research on the challenges and opportunities presented by COVID-19 in the pre–delta variant window, and outlines a strategic pathway forward, which we call "ground rules for leaders."

We intend this book to be a resource for leaders, regardless of their background in health care. This book was written for the many leaders across all sectors of health care with whom we have interacted for three decades. Whether a member of the C-suite, a member of the board of directors, a practicing physician, nurse or other frontline caregiver, or a graduate student, current and aspiring leaders are driven by an ambition to have a deeper understanding of the health economy and play an active role in building a new and better one.

The First US COVID-19 Patient

Headquartered in Seattle, Washington, Providence, one of the largest health systems, was ground zero for COVID-19 in January 2020. The patient who presented at a Providence Medical Center urgent care facility noted to a nurse practitioner that he had a cough. She would learn, through the documentation process, that he had recently returned from an overseas trip to Wuhan, China. He was tested for the novel coronavirus and, a day later, admitted.[2]

The footprint of Providence extends well beyond Seattle. The health system has more than fifty hospitals across five western states and counts 120,000 caregivers amid its ranks. The longtime leader and CEO, Dr. Rod Hochman, talks of delivering the best health care model for the future—today.[3] Dr. Hochman is unabashed that Providence must be a voice for not only the poor and vulnerable but also needed reforms in health care.

As Providence sought to respond to COVID-19 at scale, the organization drew heavily on its procedural learning from severe acute respiratory syndrome, or SARS, in 2003 and the Ebola virus in 2014. But the size and scale of COVID-19 was massively greater than previous pandemics.[4] In the spring of 2020, Hochman was thrown into a leadership challenge like no other he had experienced in his career in health care. Still today, the impact on Dr. Hochman is palpable.

Strikingly, even amid the throes of surge response, Dr. Hochman pushed himself and his team to think beyond just crisis response. He challenged his leaders to contemplate durable recovery beyond the crisis and, most importantly, to ask how the crisis could be a catalyst for rethinking the health economy itself.

Hochman tells the story of a whiteboard in his Seattle office. At the top of it, he wrote three acronyms spread evenly across the length of the board: BC (Before COVID-19), DC (During COVID-19), and AC (After COVID-19). This, in Dr. Hochman's mind, was the pivotal lens through which to look at the triad of clinical, operational, and financial challenges facing Providence and indeed US health care. This was his effort to simplify the complex and his push to drive strategic clarity amid the crisis.

Over the course of hundreds and hundreds of conversations we had with leaders across all facets of health care in 2020 and 2021, Dr. Hochman's strategic framework stuck with us. And in the end, drawing on Dr. Ron Adner's *The Wide Lens*, that framework became a key part of the health care ecosystem underlying *The New Health Economy: Ground Rules for Leaders*.

Before COVID-19:
A Consequential Decade for US Health Care

Before the COVID-19 pandemic upended global health care, a decades-long foundation of future disruption was afoot. Three major secular forces of change played out in the 2010s: digitization, Democratic-led reform, and demographics.

First, as the Great Recession unfolded in the late 2000s and early 2010s, the Barack Obama–era federal stimulus package included tens of billions of dollars for the Health Information Technology for Economic and Clinical Health (HITECH) Act.[5] The "Meaningful Use" regulations it spawned in 2010 drove pervasive electronic health record (EHR) adoption.[6] A decade later, the paper-based medical record had largely been digitized. The second- and third-order impacts of that digitization in the 2020s will be profound.

Second, the Democratic-led Affordable Care Act (ACA) fundamentally addressed access to health care coverage, which had been the paramount health policy issue since World War II. Among its key provisions, the ACA extended Medicaid to nonelderly adults with incomes up to 138% of the federal poverty line and offered an enhanced federal match. Political battleground Arizona was one such Medicaid expansion state. As Tom Betlach, the former director of Arizona Medicaid for more than a quarter century, noted, the federal match allowed the state to broaden coverage without trading off K–12 education and other key budgetary line items. With thirty-nine states having embraced expansion, Medicaid covers one in four Americans and is growing.[7]

The demographic aspect of change has been at least as profound as the impacts of digitization and coverage reform. In 2011 the first baby boomers turned sixty-five, making ten thousand seniors eligible for Medicare each day. This demographic shift—what the late Peter Peterson called the Gray Dawn more than two decades ago[8]—means that the number of Medicare enrollees who are baby boomers will increase by 43 percent, from 51 million to 73 million, by 2030.[9]

Before COVID-19, the 2010s meaningfully altered US health politics, health policy, provider networks, and personalization. There was a vastly different health economy at the beginning of 2020 before the coronavirus pandemic took hold.

During COVID-19:
Acceleration of Secular Forces of Change

On February 3, 2020, Health and Human Services (HHS) secretary Alex Azar declared a public health emergency in the United States. In the weeks and months that followed, the public learned the three criteria that define a global pandemic: "illness resulting in death, sustained person-to-person spread, and worldwide contagion."[10] By March 2020, COVID-19 met all three.

In that same month as COVID-19 emerged in hotspots from Seattle to New York, former Center for Medicare and Medicaid Services (CMS) administrator and Food and Drug Administration (FDA) commissioner Dr. Mark McClellan described the idea of a "new normal" beyond the crisis. A seasoned public servant, Dr. McClellan was not naive about the public health highs and lows to come. However, like Providence's Dr. Hochman, Dr. McClellan saw the potential of organizational realignment and a health care tomorrow that was better than today.

Setting aside the election-year politics and social media soundings that dominated 2020, the health economy delivered sustained moments of transformative impact over the course of the year. Alex Gorsky, Former CEO at Johnson & Johnson (J&J), described the COVID-19 crisis in May 2020 as "an opportunity to rethink the way that we do everything." The success of the pharmaceutical industry in the research, development, and manufacturing of the COVID-19 vaccine stands as one of the great medical innovations of the modern era.

As with any crisis, there also were disappointments. The absence of better and more pervasive diagnostic testing was an early flash point. Dr. Julie Gerberding, former director of the Centers for Disease Control and Prevention (CDC), talked to us in early March 2020 about the value of testing for understanding how to make better decisions for the individual and also how to implement smarter interventions at a community level.

The forward and backward steps during COVID-19 offer a meaningful body of primary research that can be foundational for building a better health economy. Not all of the insights are big and bold. They often represent a thousand small steps and require, as Dr. Gerberding said, an objective acknowledgment that "we learn as we go."

As Patrick Collison and Tyler Cowen have compellingly written, we like to talk of moonshots. However, progress is often about the Apollo-era epiphany of small steps in pursuit of big ideas. The frontline learning during COVID-19, to borrow from Collison and Cowen, "merits sustained and coordinated inquiry."[11] It is one piece of the essential understanding required to know where the health economy must head in the decade to come.

After COVID-19:
Shifting Opportunities and Challenges

Crisis is a demanding instructor. It asks us as leaders to grapple with the opportunities after COVID-19 as we simultaneously navigate crisis demands during and following COVID-19. As we write, we continue to grapple with the onward march of vaccine administration and variant mutations. Crisis remains the task at hand.

Former Obama White House veteran Nancy-Ann DeParle observed that "the pandemic laid bare the systemic strengths and weakness" of our health economy.[12] While some forces of change will prove to be cyclical, much of what has played out is secular. These secular forces of change have been accelerated by the pandemic.

Before COVID-19, demographic-driven Medicare growth, coupled with the expansion of Medicaid, placed Washington, D.C., in a new role. The federal government was now both the top regulator *and* the top payer for US health care. COVID-19 has accelerated the dominant voice of the federal government in health care.

The implications of a growing health care role for Washington are made more complex as a result of the highly partisan statutory fights surrounding Hillarycare, the ACA, and repeal and replace. Straight party-line passage of the ACA, followed by an equivalent Republican-only push to repeal and replace it, made health care fully political during the 2010s.

The politics of health care, in turn, define the art of the possible in health care policy. The improvement in health insurance access shifted the health policy lens to affordability. As the rebranding from the original name "Patient Protection and Affordable Care Act" to simply "Affordable Care Act" connotes, affordability was the top issue facing national policymakers as the decade closed. Now, the growing crisis of affordability has been deeply accelerated by COVID-19 dislocations.

The provider side of the US health economy responded aggressively to passage of the ACA. The anticipated shift to value-based care, coupled with declining reimbursement, drove significant consolidation. Hospital acquisitions consistently exceeded a hundred transactions per year starting in 2014. Moreover, in addition to horizontal integration, hospitals consolidated physician practices. This vertical integration within local markets was driven by the assumption that value-based care models within the ACA would become core to the health system's business model. At the end of the decade, the average size of the nation's top one hundred health systems was over $7 billion, and forty not-for-profit health systems were large enough to qualify for the *Fortune* 500 if they were listed companies.

As COVID-19 advanced, providers of care struggled with the cancellation of traditional fee-for-service (FFS) procedures. Volume still mattered to the bottom line more than value-based care. At the same time, traditional health insurance companies benefited from lower hospital utilization, leading to record profitability. Importantly, leaders in both industry segments, from Dr. Marc Harrison, CEO at Intermountain Healthcare, to Dr. Craig Samitt, former CEO at

Blue Cross Blue Shield of Minnesota, framed the same payment model failure points and called for a reinvention following the gaps in coverage identified during COVID-19.

Finally, a whole-person (patient, member, caregiver, consumer) shift inched forward in the 2010s. Rising costs caused consumers to seek a new value equation. Traditional retail expectations around cost, convenience, and service were increasingly visible. As the United States grappled with the pandemic response, the essential role of the person in public health efforts reminded us of what former Nebraska governor Bob Kerrey described as the importance of enlisting "the willingness of the people themselves." In the end, the person is the most influential decision maker in health and care.

Health politics. Health policy. Provider networks. Data-driven personalization. The 2010s laid the foundation for a level of change not seen since the passage of Medicare and Medicaid in 1965. And as these winds of change were strengthening, the gale force disruption of COVID-19 accelerated them.

The Intersectionality of the New Health Economy

In the years to come, successful change will require leaders to deeply understand the intersection of health politics, health policy, provider networks, and data-driven personalization. Yet, we believe that few leaders seeking to shape the US health economy today have a fully nuanced command of the dynamic change playing out across the intersection of these four critical areas. Absent that deeper intersectional understanding, they run the risk of missing the opportunity to be a voice of change in the growing postpandemic national conversation on health care.

The New Health Economy: Ground Rules for Leaders seeks to play a small role in helping current and aspiring leaders fully comprehend, frame, and advance the post–COVID-19 solutions that US health care demands.

The first section of the book begins by looking at the politics of health care along the historic progression of Hillarycare, Obamacare, and repeal and replace. Washington's role as the largest payer and regulator, which accelerated during COVID-19, is critical to understanding our current state of the health economy. In the second section, we delve into health policy with a heavy focus on the still-evolving space of health care finance and the shift toward value-based care. In the third section, we look at the provider networks during a period of the most significant consolidation and pursuit of systemness since the early 1990s. Also in this section, we include the insurers who are inextricably linked to providers and have gone through twenty years of consolidation that redefined the business of health insurance. In the fourth section, we examine data-driven

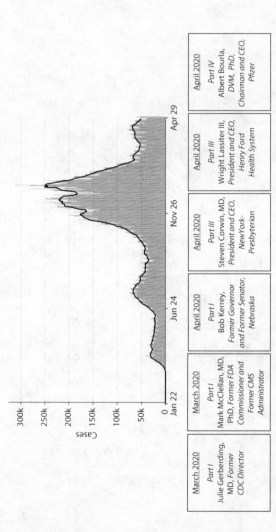

Figure I.1. Featured case study interviews in the context of seven-day COVID-19 case average in the United States, January 2020 to April 2021. Source: Data from Centers for Disease Control and Prevention, 2021. Figures are updated as of May 1, 2021, from the COVID Data Tracker and underlying data set available at https://covid.cdc.gov /covid-data-tracker/#datatracker-home.

personalization and explore whole-person consumer trends both inside and outside of health care.

Each of the sections follows a similar flow. We begin with a historical framing of the key dynamics that shaped the environment. Our experience in working with leaders is that the past is undervalued as a tool for understanding the future. From that foundation, we then look at a curated collection of conversations with leaders that have taken place during the first year of the COVID-19 pandemic (see figure I.1). Our objective is to not only offer readers a point-in-time view of leadership thinking during the pandemic, but also frame a historic timeline of milestone events (see the appendix for a COVID-19 timeline).

The third chapter in each section enumerates what we believe the applied learnings should be. These chapters, which provide lessons for leaders, each present a ground rule that we think of as a roadmap for the future and that represent our collective view of what leaders need to understand across the intersection of health care politics, health policy, provider networks, and data-driven personalization. The formation of the new health economy will flow from the sum of these parts.

The postpandemic years to come will necessitate even greater health care leadership than we saw at the best and brightest moments of the crisis. *The New Health Economy* brings together the best thinking from each of these four areas, infuse it with emerging leadership insights from the crisis, and set out the essential rules following the disruption of COVID-19 that leaders will demand. We hope that these building blocks will allow leaders to be a voice for change in their organizations, in their communities, and in the corridors of decision making in Washington, D.C.

Notes

1. Lance Lambert, "The Coronavirus Has Now Killed More Americans Than Every War since the Start of the Korean War—Combined," *Fortune*, June 12, 2020, fortune.com/2020/06/10/coronavirus-deaths-us-covid-19-killed-more-americans-korean-war-vietnam-iraq-persian-gulf-combined-how-many-died/.
2. Robison, Bass, and Langreth, "Seattle's Patient Zero."
3. Rod Hochman, interview with author Gary Bisbee via phone, January 22, 2020.
4. Callaway et al., "The Coronavirus Pandemic in Five Powerful Charts," 482–83.
5. The regulations surrounding the HITECH Act required providers to meaningfully use the technology as a prerequisite for receipt of federal dollars. As a result, the industry vernacular surrounding the investment led to it being described as "Meaningful Use."
6. Office of the National Coordinator for Health Information Technology, "Office-Based Physician Electronic Health Record Adoption."
7. Kaiser Family Foundation, "Health Insurance Coverage of the Total Population."

8. Peterson, "Gray Dawn."
9. Centers for Medicare and Medicaid Services, "National Health Expenditure Data."
10. Kelly, "The Classical Definition of a Pandemic Is Not Elusive."
11. Patrick Collison and Tyler Cowen, "We Need a New Science of Progress," *The Atlantic*, July 13, 2019, https://www.theatlantic.com/science/archive/2019/07/we-need-new-science-progress/594946/.
12. Nancy-Ann DeParle, interview with Gary Bisbee, January 2021.

PART I

Health Care Politics

1

Health Care Is Fully Political

Background

The late Speaker of the House of Representatives Thomas "Tip" O'Neill is frequently cited as the originator of the phrase "All politics is local."[1] Notwithstanding the progression of telemedicine and a wide swath of virtual health offerings during the COVID-19 pandemic, health care too is decidedly local. Consumers rely on local caregivers, friends, and neighbors for critical guidance on the best strategies for health and care. Moreover, the local voices of health care providers not only were a fixture of the COVID-19 crisis but also emerged from the pandemic with unprecedented levels of public trust.[2]

But if health care is local in its personal decision-making and provider orientation, health care financing has never been more fully federal in its sourcing. Medicare and Medicaid benefits now cover nearly 40 percent of the population.[3] Health care is the single largest item in the federal budget.[4] Medicaid benefits, likewise, are one of the largest line items in state budgets nationwide.[5]

As a result, health care participates in the ebbs and flows of the political calendar like never before in the post–World War II era. And unfortunately, the same partisanship that is omnipresent in our elections has also enveloped the national conversation around health and care. As Jarrett Lewis at Public Opinion Strategies framed in a post-2020 reflection with us, "The health care 'wedge' issues of politics past have now become chasms."[6]

There is an oft-cited adage in Washington, D.C.: understand politics, but do not play them. This sage advice nicely captures the inextricable link between health care politics and health care policy. The failure to navigate that tricky intersection has generated some of the greatest health care stumbles in the last quarter century.

We are consistently amazed in our conversations with health care leaders at the failure to look back at past health care events as an essential guide to future-state opportunities and challenges. Successful health care leaders simply can't understand what lies ahead without reviewing the contours of modern health care politics from Hillarycare to the pandemic-shaped defeat of President Donald J. Trump.

Hillarycare

No single example is more illustrative of the power of the intersection between health care politics and health care policy than the infamous journey of Hillary Rodham Clinton and Bill Clinton to reform US health care. Before there was Obamacare, there was Hillarycare.

In the fall of 1993, first-term president Bill Clinton stood before a joint session of Congress to unveil his plan for comprehensive health care reform. The policy goals of the legislation were threefold: drive universal access, tackle the rate of health care cost growth, and establish a statutory and regulatory framework to drive public and private collaboration.[7] It is a list that we could imagine featuring in the public policy framing of President Joe Biden (or even his successor) as the decade unfolds.

With great aplomb, President Clinton held up a health security card that was a paean to President Franklin Delano Roosevelt and the Social Security Act signed in 1935. The legislative titling of the bill, the Health Security Act, further reinforced the argument. In typical Clinton fashion, the forty-second president was not content with a "rule of three" rhetorical framing. He instead enumerated six core themes to animate his statutory push: security, simplicity, savings, choice, quality, and responsibility. Once again, one could imagine bipartisan positioning around many if not all of the same attributes today.

Clinton also acknowledged, amid the noise over the Ira Magaziner–led National Task Force for Health Care Reform launched in the first one hundred days and headed by First Lady Hillary Clinton, that the politics of health care can be contentious.[8] This reform journey, he framed to Democratic House and Senate majorities that autumn, "will have rough spots and honest disagreements about how we should proceed."[9]

A year later, Senate majority leader George Mitchell (D-ME) delivered the news to the forty-second president that his proposed Health Security Act of 1993, informally known as Hillarycare, was dead after failing to even come to a vote on the Senate floor. It was an amazing turn of events. Health care politics, meet health care policy. You two are sure to be fast friends.

A confluence of political factors contributed to the undoing of the Health Security Act. In business, we often frame the idea of "win the inside, win the outside," a chance for leaders to cleverly manage the intersectional dynamics between the two. A strong culture inside can build a durable brand outside. Compelling thought leadership on the outside can drive alignment on the inside for key organizational initiatives. These outside and inside dynamics also can be seen in US politics. And in the postmortem on Hillarycare, the Clinton team struggled with both.

Beyond the Capital Beltway, the Clinton team never found its footing. The 1992 campaign and its vaunted War Room led by George Stephanopoulos and James Carville inspired front-page stories and documentary movies. Clinton's first presidential campaign became the bellwether for modern campaign response.

The early work on Hillarycare showed little evidence of those innovations.[10] The team driving production of a detailed plan provided limited access to the media amid numerous working groups and hundreds of task force meetings. They were seen to be at arm's length with special interests such as traditional insurers. They also were far less aggressive in their response to rising criticism.

The impact of special interest advertising is illustrative of the failure to "win the outside." As Darrell M. West, Diane Heith, and Chris Goodwin concluded in the cleverly titled *Harry and Louise Go to Washington*, "ads directed against the Clinton plan played a crucial role in the public's attaching negative connotations to some of its key elements."[11] In an era before the internet browser and social media, these ads were widely viewed and influential.

In addition to their "win the outside" breakdown, the Clinton team also struggled to win the inside game. As the Harry and Louise narrative bemoaning the complexity of the mammoth 1,342-page bill filled the airwaves, noise was growing inside the beltway. US House partisans such as Texas congressman Dick Armey were creating glossaries of unknown terms. US Senate voices such as Pennsylvania senator Arlen Specter were creating complex charts decrying a phalanx of new federal bureaucracy.[12]

More troubling, Capitol Hill insiders who should have rallied in support of Hillarycare were slow to do so. Many health care historians and political prognosticators have speculated that one reason may have been the fact that the bill was not generated through the legislative process. Capitol Hill veterans understand that one benefit of our often lumbering, phase-gate legislative process is that it creates an iterative understanding of core provisions. In the case of Hillarycare, it is certainly arguable that few members were willing to defend legislative details they didn't draft.

In addition to lacking legislative involvement, the bill also suffered from timing, one of the essential ingredients in getting anything done in Washington. In politics as in business, the art is often in the timing. A long, quarrelsome budget process coupled with a separate effort to attain ratification of the North American Free Trade Agreement (NAFTA) pushed the launch of health care reform into the fall of 1993.[13] The subsequent legislative deliberations occurred in a midterm election year.

As we saw with the Biden first-term agenda, the first one hundred days— and the first year of a first term—is a critical legislative window. It requires the discipline to understand the short-list policy opportunities of the moment and smart political strategies to advance them (as reflected by the passage of a series of multitrillion-dollar COVID-19 relief packages).

The 1994 off-year elections that followed were a political tsunami. The GOP picked up fifty-four seats in the US House and gained eight seats in the US Senate. The party also saw meaningful gains in governorships and state legislators. In an evening punctuated by high-profile, unexpected defeats such as that of House Speaker Tom Foley, Richard Berke at the *New York Times* characterized it as a Republican tide.[14]

The policy promise and ultimately the political perils of Hillarycare made an indelible impact on the Clinton presidency and also shaped the politics (and policy) of health care for years to come. It would take more than a decade and a half for a renewed push for comprehensive health care reform. And like Hillarycare, it would prove no less contentious.

Obamacare

Walmart's Sam Walton (who, like Bill Clinton, hailed from Arkansas) frequently observed that the best way to find a niche in business is to head in the exact opposite direction.[15] An understanding of the failure of Hillarycare is a necessary predicate for exploring Obamacare, because President Barack Obama did just that.

In 2009, President Obama (and Vice President Joe Biden) inherited a complicated post–financial crisis economy. Obama passed a large stimulus package that notably included funding for the first-time digitization of health care through creation of the Meaningful Use program.[16] Like Clinton, Obama then turned his attention to a set of big swing domestic agenda items to include health care.

At the policy level, there were significant commonalities between Hillarycare and Obamacare, formally known as the Affordable Care Act. Both efforts sought to increase access to health insurance, establish a standard benefits package that included coverage for preexisting conditions, and enact a set of policies (such as the so-called Cadillac Tax, a 40 percent tax on high-end insurance plans) to reduce health care costs.[17]

If the policy ambitions were similar, however, the political push was decidedly different. Failure is, it is said, always the best and most important teacher. Obama and a set of Clinton veterans in his White House weren't interested in repeating the sins of the past. They wanted to make modern health policy history.

The differences in political approach were evident from the outset. As opposed to an extended task force deliberation and voluminous draft bill, Obama framed key principles and left the technical details to Congress and the legislative process.

With that overarching framework in place, Obama and his team sought to manage outside opposition. Drawing from the lessons of Hillarycare, they would strive to win the outside. Obama and his White House inner circle worked to co-opt the insurance companies, and their advocacy arm, America's Health Insurance Plans, with the promise of millions of additional customers due to the mandated insurance provisions.[18] The West Wing meetings with key special interests were high-profile, visible ones as opposed to closed-door or off-the-record discussions.

Later it was learned that the insurers funneled large amounts of money to other third-party advocacy groups because of opposition to the cap on the medical loss ratio (MLR). However, the insurers were not overtly funding Harry-and-Louise–style campaigns to torpedo the ACA legislation as we saw with their Clinton-era opposition.[19] Their role was a more muted one.

Finally, while attempting to shape the outside game, Obama and his team also managed congressional insiders with senior staff who knew the ins and outs of Capitol Hill. White House chief of staff and former congressman Rahm Emanuel and deputy chief of staff and former Health Care Finance Administration head Nancy-Ann DeParle were seasoned pros. They were looking to change health care, not change Washington.

"Was the ACA law perfect? No, but it was a step forward toward goals that, on a bipartisan basis, all the people that I spoke with shared, which was getting everybody covered and bringing the rate of health care cost growth down."

—Nancy-Ann DeParle, former assistant to the president and deputy chief of staff for policy for the Obama administration (2011–13)

The march for legislative passage was nonetheless messy. Following the death of Massachusetts senator Ted Kennedy, Democrats no longer had the filibuster-proof majority of sixty votes they needed to leverage regular order. They turned to a budget reconciliation process that required just fifty-one votes.[20] Ironically, it was an option that was available during the Clinton push for the Health Security Act. It was not, however, one that would be countenanced at the time by Senator Robert Byrd (D-WV), dean of the Senate.

After passage by the upper chamber, the House would follow less than two weeks later with a vote of 219 to 212 that found all Republicans voting in opposition. And then on March 23, 2010, President Obama signed what became known as the ACA, with Vice President Biden reminding him just prior to the signing ceremony that passage of Obamacare was quite a big deal.[21]

We would learn several years later that Obama knew that the politics of this health policy decision would be tough. Washington insiders John Heilemann and Mark Halperin tell the story of Obama talking to White House political director (and later ambassador to South Africa) Patrick Gaspard in their book *Double Down: Game Change 2012.* With champagne in hand, Obama turned to Gaspard and said, "You know, they are going to kick our ass over this one."[22]

The political backlash, presaged by the surprise win of Republican Scott Brown in a January 2010 special election to fill the late Senator Kennedy's seat in Massachusetts, was a sizable one. In November, Republicans won sixty-three seats in the US House and gained six seats in the US Senate. The House totals, for historical perspective, eclipsed the numbers in 1994 following the defeat of Hillarycare.

While the economy was at the top of voters' minds as they went to the ballot box, health care also was a key factor in election day voting. In particular, health care played an outsized role in several dozen swing House districts and likewise a select number of red-state Senate races. As with any electoral outcome, the causal factors behind voter intensity are always widely scrutinized and debated. In our conversations with Republican pollster Bill McInturff, he has consistently contended that the ACA had a meaningful impact in key races.[23]

At the same time, the debate over how important Obamacare was to the Tea Party revolt in 2010 obscures a much larger takeaway for health care leaders. Health care is a bipartisan topic, a deeply personal issue that touches every American independent of party affiliation. Notably, speed to federal health policy impact typically correlates to its level of bipartisan backing at adoption. Medicaid expansion is one of several examples. Its growth and impact across the country has been profound. At the same time, it has been highly litigated and debated, leading to a rate of adoption that has been slower than advocates would have hoped when the ACA became law in the spring of 2010.

While recounts and the winter COVID-19 surge made postelection 2020 somewhat ahistorical, the weeks that follow an election typically bring reflection in Washington. It is a rare moment when party elders—and the media—look to glean lessons learned. It is also the window in which White House and congressional insiders look to frame the legislative session to come.

Following the success of the 2010 off-year election, Republicans became committed to rolling back Obamacare. Their 2010 gains would trigger a multiyear push for what came to be called repeal and replace. It was a fight that consumed big pieces of GOP mindshare for multiple legislative sessions and would make Obamacare a feature of at least five election cycles from 2010 to 2018.

Repeal and Replace

In November 2016, Donald J. Trump was elected the forty-fifth president of the United States. Trump won the electoral college vote 304 to 227 but lost the popular vote. This made Trump only the fifth candidate in history to lose the popular vote yet ascend to the presidency.

Trump came to office focused on delivering on the agenda of his core supporters. He championed tax and regulatory relief to spur new job creation and wage growth. He sought to impact the profile of the federal courts. He opened new fronts on fair trade and made a major push to strengthen immigration enforcement on the nation's southern border.

At times, these policy initiatives were at odds with the Paul Ryan– and Mitch McConnell–led Congress. Moreover, Trump also could seem flummoxed by the Madisonian realities of checks and balances that frequently complicated his efforts to advance his first-term agenda at a businessman's pace.[24]

As the 115th Congress played out, the American Health Care Act would emerge as an area of significant policy focus for Republicans.[25] Arguably, with the exception of tax reform, the legislative call to "*repeal* Obamacare and *replace* it with patient-centered care" was the most dominant legislative topic of the session.

The House moved first, passing the American Health Care Act narrowly in the spring of 2017. The Senate then moved in fits and starts, beginning with a large working group created by Senate majority leader Mitch McConnell. This later gave way to a block grant scheme advanced by Senators Bill Cassidy (R-LA) and Lindsey Graham (R-SC).[26]

Notably, one of the constituencies arguing in favor of maintaining Obamacare in this pivotal window was a collection of Republican governors who had made the decision to expand Medicaid. Their decisions came after the US Supreme Court, in *National Federation of Independent Business v. Sebelius*, held that the federal government could not compel states to do so.[27] In all, "eleven

Republican governors chose to expand [and then] lobbied to keep billions of dollars of federal Medicaid money flowing."[28] Their advocacy highlights what is always a central dimension of health care policy and politics: the states are essential laboratories of reform and important voices on the workable realities of health care delivery and finance at the federal level.

As GOP hopes for repeal and replace faded, Republicans arrived at the same flash point that Clinton and Obama had faced. Did they want to attempt to make a major change to health policy through a simple-majority budget reconciliation process? In the end, Republicans made the decision to proceed. However, the use of reconciliation and the broader push for repeal and replace fell short of the fifty-vote threshold in the US Senate.

Once again, the simple-majority, partisan push elicited a harsh electoral reaction in the fall of 2018. In the US House, Democrats needed twenty-three seats to take back the gavel. They won forty. In the Senate, Democrats faced a tough electoral map: they held twenty-six of the thirty-five seats being contested. Thus, Democrats had to win twenty-eight of thirty-five seats, or 80 percent of all the contested races, to win the Senate.

This structural advantage allowed the GOP to add two seats to their slim margin of fifty-one to forty-nine but also brought less upside than many nonpartisan pundits predicted at the outset of the election cycle. As University of Virginia's Larry Sabato argues, Senate races are about not just who wins the chamber in any single cycle but also which party positions itself for success in the subsequent cycle.[29]

The history of repeal and replace frames an important takeaway for health care leaders: the politics of health and care are dynamic, and ever-changing. GOP leaders failed to fully recognize and effectively respond to the shifting politics of the ACA. By 2017, core elements of the ACA were engrained with the electorate including popular protections for preexisting conditions. The politics that animated the original 2010 midterm revolt had shifted. The GOP not only failed to interpret the changing playing field but also struggled to fashion policy prescriptions around ACA pain points such as declining health care affordability.

The ACA repeal effort also reaffirmed the complexity of working to enact health policy without bipartisan consensus. While President Trump and Republicans in Congress supported repeal and replace, a thin majority in the Senate meant that the ability to drive a sixty-vote change was impossible. Democratic lawmakers were unanimous in their opposition.

The divided government ushered in by the 2018 election relegated meaningful health care policy change to the federal courts. In 2019, the Trump administration and eighteen state attorneys general challenged Obamacare as unconstitutional once again on a new legal front. Their core contention was that once the Trump tax bill zeroed out the penalties associated with the individual mandate, then the mandate was no longer constitutional. Oral arguments occurred after the 2020 general election.[30]

Pre-COVID-19 Election 2020

The 2020 election was, in its early months, marked by what Amy Walters at the Cook Political Report described as twin (and often assumed to be oppositional) dynamics: chaos and consistency.[31] There seemed to be very little, Walters wrote, from the chaos of impeachment to various threatened and actual government shutdowns that could change the contours of the 2020 campaign.

The first consistent feature of the pre–COVID-19 political landscape was the economy. The US economy performed exceedingly well during the first three-plus years of President Trump's term. As Jon Hilsenrath wrote in the *Wall Street Journal*, it might be debatable if it was the best economy ever, as former president Trump liked to claim in this political window, but "it was without question good."[32]

The 2019 Federal Reserve's "Report on the Economic Well-Being of U.S. Households" told the story of the before COVID-19 window: "A large majority of individuals report that, financially, they are doing okay or living comfortably."[33] Moreover, the researchers went on to note, "Overall economic well-being has improved substantially since the survey began in 2013."[34] If the data weren't generated by Jay Powell's Federal Reserve, we might well have seen these verbatims streaming through the Trump Twitter feed (which, at the time, was still a critical part of his omnichannel communication efforts).

At the same time, record-low unemployment and solid GDP growth were only part of the story. The same Federal Reserve report went on to detail that nearly 40 percent of Americans would struggle to cover an unexpected expense of $400 such as out-of-pocket costs associated with an unforeseen medical issue. "Relatively small, unexpected expenses," the researchers wrote, "can be a hardship for many families without adequate savings."[35] These anxieties were particularly present in key swing states such as Wisconsin, Michigan, and Pennsylvania that were central to Trump's 2016 victory and were a core piece of the electoral battleground in the 2020 presidential election.

In the months before COVID-19, the base case for the Trump reelection was simple. It began with an economy that was on track thanks to his work on regulatory relief and tax policy. Solid economic indicators, a booming stock market, and an unemployment rate at a near fifty-year low were the preferred presidential data points. An ongoing focus on the forgotten middle class would be the unfinished business of a second term.

The polling data suggested in July 2019 that the reelection narrative of President Trump was a strong one.[36] At the time, more than two-thirds of voters held a positive view on the state of the economy. In addition, more than half believed that Trump had done well in his efforts to manage it.

Beyond the polling, the state of the US economy (GDP, unemployment) is typically predictive in our quadrennial presidential process. The "bread and peace" model advanced by former Harvard professor Doug Hibbs is illustrative, contending that an incumbent president tends to be a statistically significant beneficiary of "increased bread," or positive economic trends.[37]

Finally, in addition to a solid electoral base and a strong economy, pundits in the months before COVID-19 began to define the 2020 cycle and also extolled the advantages of incumbency. Since the end of World War II, commentators noted, just three incumbent presidents had lost their reelection bids. Gerald Ford, Jimmy Carter, and George H. W. Bush in 1976, 1980, and 1992, respectively, had all been plagued (among other liabilities) by tough economies. These dynamics led many prognosticators to speculate that a president who had come to office without a popular vote majority was well positioned to win reelection.

COVID-19 Defines the 2020 Race

In early February 2020, HHS secretary Alex Azar declared a public health emergency for the entire United States to aid the nation's health care community in responding to the novel coronavirus.[38]

"Public health emergencies are a foundation for the President and political leaders getting out there and working together. The government can bring to bear more resources faster and enable responses that under normal circumstances would be blocked by usual regulations. The regulations are there for good reasons, but the whole cost-benefit analysis shifts substantially in circumstances like this."

—Mark McClellan, MD, PhD, former CMS administrator (2004–6) and FDA commissioner (2002–4)

As Azar and other federal officials were communicating a public health emergency, President Trump seemed unclear about what tone to strike with the American people surrounding the growing crisis. His inconsistent narrative around the magnitude of the public health challenge would become a core feature of the 2020 election.

On February 27, 2020, at a White House meeting, Trump said of the novel coronavirus, "One day—it's like a miracle—it will disappear."[39] He went on to say, "We'll see what happens. Nobody really knows."[40] In the summer months, Trump frequently took issue with COVID-19 prevalence data. He argued that positive rates were high because US testing capabilities were far superior to those of other countries. He alternatively posited that "many of those cases were young people that would heal in a day."[41] In the post–Labor Day window, it was revealed that Trump had admitted to legendary journalist Bob Woodward in a March 19, 2020, interview for Woodward's forthcoming book, *Rage*, that he had intentionally dismissed the risk: "'I wanted to always play it down,' the president said.'I still like playing it down, because I don't want to create a panic.'"[42] It was hardly an end-of-campaign mea culpa. In the same window as the *Washington Post* piece, Trump would opine to a rally in Ohio that the coronavirus "affects virtually nobody."[43]

Beyond the struggle to determine the right presidential tone, Trump also struggled with core elements of the public health response. The politics of diagnostic testing were the first in a series of flash points. As we will explore in deeper detail in chapter 2, the CDC struggled with faulty test kits. The absence of quality testing, in turn, made it difficult for public officials to advance data-driven management of local hotspots as they arose.

The politics, for their part, were toxic. During the debate over the ACA, President Obama was lambasted for his claim that "if you like your plan, you can keep your plan" (in reference to the health insurance network design changes contemplated under the ACA).[44] Now, in the spring of 2020, Trump would make a similar definitive statement that the public struggled to reconcile to the diagnostic testing realities of the moment. In early March he would say, "Anybody that wants a test [for COVID-19] can get a test."[45]

Over the course of 2020 and into 2021, it would become clear that regulatory red tape made ramping up national testing challenging for the United States. This would have seemed, on its face, to be a tailor-made political opportunity for Trump. The administration would later enlist public labs, universities, and private-sector organizations in the effort to develop and distribute tests. And indeed, the travails around testing may have been formative for Operation Warp Speed and the approach taken on the COVID-19 vaccine. However, in the early weeks and months of the crisis when public views were forming on

Trump's COVID-19 response, the testing issue proved damaging for the president's reelection prospects.

The issue of public health response also became a defining political issue for the 2020 election. Interestingly, early in the campaign, some rough consensus existed around key public health strategies. In early polling from Pew Research in the late first and early second quarter of 2020, "two-thirds of Americans—including majorities in both parties and across all major demographic groups—saw COVID-19 as a significant crisis."[46] Moreover, there also was a mostly shared view on the need for travel restrictions and other necessary public health steps to address the outbreak.

However, as 2020 progressed, these issues took on increasingly partisan contours. In 2016, Trump's political ascent had been defined by his deft use of social media and his large and raucous rallies. In the early spring of 2020, Trump discontinued his rallies amid the growing public health crisis. Then as the second quarter of 2020 played out, he and his allies would plan a Tulsa, Oklahoma, rally that would be his first foray back into large public gatherings. The rally would lead to a number of positive tests among campaign staffers, the high-profile loss of life of former presidential candidate (and pizza entrepreneur) Herman Cain, and, amid it all, less attendance than anticipated (which campaign officials would attribute to national news coverage criticizing the decision to hold the event). This was a visible punctuation point that the early consensus on public health response had evaporated. COVID-19 was now fully political as the Trump and Biden campaigns moved into the summer and fall months of the election.

In addition to public gathering, masks also became a flash point for the growing political divide. Some governors moved to issue statewide requirements for masks. Other governors were reluctant to mandate mask requirements, openly challenging their public health benefit or deferring to the localities to set their policies as officials deemed appropriate. Biden would say that if he were elected, he would "do everything possible to make it required" to wear a mask in public.[47] Trump, for his part, would wear a mask for the first time in public in a trip to visit Walter Reed Medical Center, where he met with wounded soldiers and health care workers. It was July 2020—months after the public health declaration from Azar and countless admonitions from the National Institutes of Health's Dr. Anthony Fauci and other public health officials on the value of masks in public settings.

Arguably, the penultimate preelection COVID-19 moment for the Trump reelection was in early October when it was announced that the president and the first lady tested positive for the coronavirus. Over the course of modern presidential campaigns, there has always been talk of an October surprise. While this news was slightly different than the historic "gotcha" opposition framing, it was nonetheless a massive surprise in the closing days of the campaign. Trump and the first lady were not alone, as multiple members of the White House and the Trump campaign tested positive. And while less than two weeks later the president would be back on the campaign trail, his positive test and subsequent hospitalization would be a fitting reminder that the virus was the defining issue of the 2020 election as mail-in ballots were being sent and in-person voting was set to commence on November 3.

Election 2020 Outcome

While the weeks and months that followed the November election were contentious, the result was known when Joe Biden was elected the forty-sixth president after his victory in Pennsylvania put him above the 270 electoral college votes required under the US Constitution. In total, he would secure more than 300 electoral college votes and over 51 percent of the popular vote.[48]

Despite the complexities of a global pandemic, Americans voted in record numbers. According to the nonpartisan Pew Research, over 150 million ballots were cast. These represented more than "six-in-ten people of voting age and nearly two-thirds of estimated eligible voters."[49]

After a bitterly contested election that reinforced partisan divisions, there was perhaps one thing that both sides could agree on. A preelection survey from Pew found that "a record share" of registered voters (83 percent) said it "really matters" who won.[50]

The governing challenge for President Biden was one that he understood and attempted to begin to address from the outset. He pledged, in his first remarks, to be a unifier who would "work with all my heart to win the confidence of the whole people."[51]

Notes

1. O'Neill and Novak, *Man of the House.*
2. A joint Public Opinion Strategies and Jarrard Phillips Cate & Hancock National Survey of one thousand US adults, conducted April 16–20, 2020, found that the percent of trust placed in providers—nurses and physicians (89%) and hospitals (86%)—reached its highest level since July 2000. This represents an approximate 70 percent increase from trust levels before the COVID-19 outbreak. Respondents were asked to evaluate provider trust in the context of other relevant health care stakeholders ranging from employers and the media to federal health agencies.
3. Congressional Research Service, "U.S. Health Care Coverage and Spending 2020."
4. Center on Budget and Policy Priorities, "Policy Basics."

5. Medicaid and CHIP Payment and Access Commission, "Medicaid's Share of State Budgets."

6. Jarrett Ramos Lewis (partner, Public Opinion Strategies), in discussion with author Donald Trigg, November 2020.

7. Wellstone and Shaffer, "The American Health Security Act."

8. National Archives, "Health Care Task Force Records."

9. "Clinton's Health Plan; Transcript of President's Address to Congress on Health Care," New York Times, September 23, 1993, https://www.nytimes.com/1993/09/23/us/clinton-s-health-plan-transcript-president-s-address-congress-health-care.html.

10. Adam Clymer, Robert Pear, and Robin Toner, "The Health Care Debate: What Went Wrong? How the Health Care Campaign Collapsed—A Special Report; For Health Care, Times Was A Killer," New York Times, August 29, 1994, https://www.nytimes.com/1994/08/29/us/health-care-debate-what-went-wrong-health-care-campaign-collapsed-special-report.html.

11. West, Heith, and Goodwin, "Harry and Louise Go to Washington."

12. Senator Arlen Specter, a Pennsylvania Republican (who years later would switch affiliation to the Democratic Party), presented a series of charts to the Senate as a way to depict the complexity of the proposed Clinton plan for health reform. The charts were visibly complicated, with some White House officials saying that they looked more like the "the New York subway system than any health care plan they knew." Pete Leffler, "Specter Defending Convolutions of His Clinton Health Plan Chart," The Morning Call, January 28, 1994, https://www.mcall.com/news/mc-xpm-1994-01-28-2965666-story.html.

13. Blendon, Brodie, and Benson, "What Happened to Americans' Support for the Clinton Health Plan?"

14. Richard L. Berke, "Party Chairman Attacks 4 Democrats Who Failed," New York Times, May 26, 1994, https://www.nytimes.com/1994/05/26/us/party-chairman-attacks-4-democrats-who-failed.html.

15. "Sam Walton in His Own Words," Fortune, June 29, 1992, https://archive.fortune.com/magazines/fortune/fortune_archive/1992/06/29/76578/index.htm.

16. The HITECH Act, enacted as part of the American Recovery and Reinvestment Act of 2009, was signed into law on February 17, 2009, to promote the adoption and meaningful use of health information technology. Additional context on the reform is provided in chapters 4 and 6.

17. The Cadillac Tax was established to help pay for the ACA's provisions and to reduce health care costs by limiting the income tax exclusion for employer-sponsored insurance. The Cadillac Tax would require coverage providers to pay a 40 percent excise tax levied on "excess benefits," or the value of health insurance benefits surpassing approximately $11,200 for individuals and $30,150 for families. The tax has been delayed on several occasions but is currently scheduled to be enacted in 2022.

18. Oberlander, "Long Time Coming."

19. Harry-and-Louise–style campaigns refer to the multimillion-dollar yearlong television advertising campaign funded by the predecessor of the current America's Health Insurance Plans—a health insurance industry lobbying arm—that ran in opposition to President Bill Clinton's proposed health care plan in 1993–94. The ads were featured on television and radio and in print formats depicting a suburban middle-class

married couple (named Harry and Louise) troubled by aspects of the proposed plan with the intent of demobilizing public support for Hillarycare.

20. Created by the Congressional Budget Act of 1974, reconciliation allows for expedited consideration of certain tax, spending, and debt limit legislation. The process of reconciliation allows legislation to pass without necessitating the sixty-vote threshold and unlimited floor debate that is required for most legislation in the US Senate.

21. Department of Health and Human Services, "What Is the Affordable Care Act?"

22. Halperin and Heilemann, *Double Down.*

23. Bill McInturff is a longtime colleague of coauthors Gary Bisbee and Donald Trigg. Bisbee most recently spoke at length with McInturff in February 2021.

24. The term "Madisonian" refers to the structure of government proposed by James Madison (fourth president of the United States) in which the powers of the government are separated into three branches: executive, legislative, and judicial. This governmental scheme was intended to ensure balance in power and influence across the three branches.

25. The American Health Care Act of 2017 was a leading proposal in the first half of 2017 by House Republicans to repeal and replace the ACA.

26. The Graham-Cassidy bill (an approach to repeal and replace the ACA) proposed ending Medicaid expansion and federal subsidies for health insurance exchanges in 2020 and replace them with a short-term block grant to states that would cut about $200 billion from current spending levels between 2020 and 2026.

27. *National Federation of Independent Business v. Sebelius* was a US Supreme Court case regarding the individual mandate and Medicaid expansion provisions of the ACA. Under the provisions in question, the ACA required most individuals to maintain minimum health insurance coverage and required states to expand their Medicaid programs or else lose federal Medicaid funds. The court upheld the individual mandate as a legitimate exercise of Congress's Article 1 taxing power and found that state participation in the Medicaid expansion program was voluntary.

28. Castele, "Meet the Republican Governors."

29. Sabato, Kondik, and Skelley, eds. *Trumped.*

30. On November 10, 2020, the US Supreme Court heard about two hours of oral argument over the constitutionality of the individual mandate and the fate of the entire ACA. The lawsuit, initially fashioned as *Texas v. United States,* was filed in February 2018 by twenty Republican state attorneys general and Republican governors. The plaintiffs want to revisit *National Federation of Independent Businesses v. Sebelius,* where the Supreme Court, in a 5 to 4 vote, upheld the mandate as constitutional. In that decision from 2012, Chief Justice John Roberts construed the mandate as a tax, concluding that it was valid under Congress's authority to tax and spend.

31. Walter, "Will Impeachment Reshape the 2020 Race?"

32. Jon Hilsenrath, "The Verdict on Trump's Economic Stewardship, before Covid and after," *Wall Street Journal,* October 14, 2020, https://www.wsj.com/articles/trumps-economic-record-is-divided-before-covid-and-after-11602684180.

33. Federal Reserve, "Report on the Economic Well-Being of U.S. Households."

34. Federal Reserve.

35. Federal Reserve.

36. Cox, "Trump Is on His Way."

37. Hibbs, "Bread and Peace Voting." The bread and peace model, developed by political economist Douglas Hibbs, predicts the two-party popular vote based on just two fundamental variables that systematically affected postwar aggregate votes for president: weighted-average growth of per capita real disposable personal income over the term and cumulative US military fatalities due to unprovoked, hostile deployments of American armed forces in foreign wars.

38. Aubrey, "Trump Declares Coronavirus a Public Health Emergency and Restricts Travel from China."

39. Donald Trump, February 27, 2020, statement at the White House as quoted by many sources reproducing timelines of his statements about the virus. See MSNBC, "Trump."

40. Summers, "Timeline."

41. "Transcript: 'Fox News Sunday' Interview with President Trump," *Fox News Sunday*, July 19, 2020, https://www.foxnews.com/politics/transcript-fox-news-sunday-interview-with-president-trump.

42. Robert Costa and Philip Rucker, "Woodward Book: Trump Says He Knew Coronavirus Was 'Deadly' and Worse Than the Flu While Intentionally Misleading Americans," *Washington Post*, September 9, 2020, https://www.washingtonpost.com/politics/bob-woodward-rage-book-trump/2020/09/09/0368fe3c-efd2-11ea-b4bc-3a2098fc73d4_story.html?no_nav=true&arc404=true.

43. Timothy Bella, "'It Affects Virtually Nobody': Trump Incorrectly Claims Covid-19 Isn't a Risk for Young People," *Washington Post*, September 22, 2021, https://www.washingtonpost.com/nation/2020/09/22/trump-coronavirus-young-people/.

44. Yglesias, "It's Good That You Can't Keep Your Insurance Plan."

45. Valverde, "Donald Trump's Wrong Claim."

46. Deane, Parker, and Gramlich, "A Year of US Public Opinion on the Coronavirus Pandemic."

47. Matt Viser, "Joe Biden Says He Would Require Americans to Wear Masks in Public," *Washington Post*, June 26, 2020, https://www.washingtonpost.com/politics/joe-biden-says-he-would-require-americans-to-wear-masks-in-public/2020/06/26/8c430db8-b75d-11ea-a8da-693df3d7674a_story.html.

48. National Archives, "2020 Electoral College Results."

49. DeSilver, "Turnout Soared in 2020."

50. Pew Research Center, "Election 2020."

51. Matt Stevens, "Read Joe Biden's President-Elect Acceptance Speech: Full Transcript," *New York Times*, November 9, 2020, https://www.nytimes.com/article/biden-speech-transcript.html.

2

Chaos from Testing to Vaccines

Interviews

As chapter 1 detailed, the first quarter of 2020 saw an election cycle–changing shift in the Donald Trump reelection calculus as the COVID-19 crisis advanced. In early March, Dr. Nancy Messonnier of the CDC echoed HHS secretary Alex Azar, saying it was "not so much a question of if this [broader community-based transmission in the United States] will happen anymore, but rather more a question of exactly when."[1] And at the same time, public health officials were also working to rally the public in a fight back against the virus. World Health Organization (WHO) Director General Tedros Adhanom Ghebreyesus implored, "We can push this virus back."[2]

The comments from the WHO director would come as hospital bed capacity in early hotspots such as Seattle, Detroit, and New York City (and the surrounding tristate area) were rapidly worsening. And as the national media covered provider organizations struggling with crisis surge response, public fears were increasing as a national outbreak seemed to be, as Dr. Messonnier had framed, an increasing eventuality.

The challenge of a coordinated response was a microcosm of the tough intersectional forces that define US health care in the 2020s. Health care, as we saw through the travails of Hillarycare, Obamacare, repeal and replace, and then the 2020 election, is now wholly political. The right health policy strategies, even amid a global pandemic, often challenge those same political orthodoxies. COVID-19 was no exception.

While there were aspects of the COVID-19 pandemic that were unique to the crisis, many of the complexities were ones that a review of health care history would describe as Pareto analysis probabilities. They were a collection of Donald Rumsfeld's "known knowns" (with a handful of known unknowns).[3]

The federal agencies were a critical linchpin of what it looked like to deliver the planning, funding, and resourcing that an effective multistate response required.

The earlier-framed challenges of the CDC when the crisis first exploded included distribution of test kits with faulty negative controls caused by contaminated reagents. Labs that received the test kits with negative controls had to ship their samples back to the CDC for testing.[4] Dr. Julie Gerberding, Merck executive and former CDC director, said in a discussion with us several weeks after the CDC shipped the faulty tests that she was saddened and mystified at the slip-up and viewed it as an exception after a decades-long history of fine CDC performance.

> "The CDC is all about health science and the science of public health. This should not be political. The CDC should always be able to talk candidly and truthfully about what's going on. That has to be the backbone of any effective public health response. I think we've seen examples where that's worked brilliantly, and we've seen examples where it was not so great."
>
> **—Julie Gerberding, MD, executive vice president and chief patient officer, Merck, and former director (2002–9), CDC**

The lack of reliable testing prevented local officials from taking a crucial first step in coping with a possible outbreak, called surveillance testing.[5] The snafu would be a dominant national narrative in the early spring 2020 window. Further, there were a limited number of test kits distributed across all fifty states, leaving an insufficient number of test kits in the hotspots where they were immediately needed. As Peter Fine, president and CEO of Banner Health, recalled, "Early on, the CDC mishaps of not getting useful tests out into the market cost us three weeks which turned out to be significant. Regardless of the mistakes that were made, you've got to count on the CDC to be that source of truth and to fund it in a manner that will allow it to be ahead of a crisis like COVID-19 instead of trying to play catch-up all the time."[6]

The Trump team would course-correct, allowing university and commercial labs to perform their own tests, but the politics of the testing issue would come to be seen in its most charitable form as "too little, too late."[7]

The testing issue illuminated the second major challenge of the spring 2020 window: a tension between Washington, D.C. and the states. As Jennifer Selin at the

Brookings Institution framed it, "The COVID-19 pandemic brought increasing attention to our federalist form of government."[8] It has long been held, as
US Supreme Court justice Sandra Day O'Connor wrote, that this inherent
tension between the federal government and the states "offers the promise of
liberty."[9] Amid the COVID-19 outbreak, however, the subtleties of who does
what could be unclear. In this critical early spring window, they got lost.

The early weeks and months of COVID-19 saw the emergence of a third
challenge that would be foundational for the fall 2020 election. It was, in simple
terms, the tension between public health, economic health, and individual rights.
In any era, this is a challenging first-principles issue set. In an era when health
care is fully political, it is a supreme challenge for any leader.

As we worked through 2020 with surges ebbing and flowing by urban areas
and regions, the Trump administration focused on developing vaccines with its
Operation Warp Speed created in May 2020. In the summer months and early
fall, there was media speculation that early clinical trial success might bring a
vaccine outcome before the November election. In July Trump said, "We'll end
up with a cure. We are very close to a vaccine—I think we are going to have
some very good results."[10]

Initially funded with $10 billion drawn from the Provider Relief Fund,
support was provided to six pharmaceutical companies to tool up manufacturing if or when their vaccine was approved by the FDA under a process called
Emergency Use Authorization (EUA). In addition, the Trump administration
reserved at least nine hundred million doses from the companies in anticipation
that some of the vaccines would be approved.

There were two fundamental technologies being tested. The Pfizer/
BioNTech and Moderna vaccines were based on the mRNA technology, while
the J&J and AstraZeneca vaccines used the viral vector technology. In general
terms, the mRNA technology was new and had not been used to formulate a
vaccine, while the viral vector technology had been used successfully in the past,
for example, for Ebola. Operation Warp Speed did not know which technology would work or, for that matter, whether either one would work. Thus, the
program hedged its bet by reserving the right to purchase both technologies if
approved.

The bet made by Operation Warp Speed paid off. On December 11, 2020,
the Pfizer/BioNTech vaccine received EUA from the FDA, followed closely by
the Moderna vaccine on December 18, 2020. The J&J vaccine received approval
on February 27, 2021, and was shortly thereafter met with a temporary pause
in administration approval (see the appendix for a detailed timeline of events).

The politics of the 2020s cause every single health issue to be viewed
through a partisan lens. It is the legacy of Hillarycare, Obamacare, and repeal

and replace. Having said that, Operation Warp Speed assisted in vaccines being developed and readied for distribution in one year. As Alex Gorsky of J&J and Dr. Albert Bourla of Pfizer both indicated, the typical time was seven years. It was a true marvel of modern science. Once the vaccines were approved, the Joe Biden administration was single-minded in distributing it. And while the politics of the moment don't allow for much in the way of bipartisan recognition, both administrations (to include the nonpartisan civil servants at key federal agencies such as the CDC and the FDA) made significant contributions to get the public vaccinated.

COVID-19 Interviews

In the case discussions that follow, you will have the opportunity to hear from four health care leaders who offered real-time thoughts over the course of 2020 on the COVID-19 crisis and their implications for health care politics. First, Dr. Julie Gerberding has the vantage point of being a former CDC director and current Merck executive. Merck is partnering with J&J to assist J&J in manufacturing its vaccine to accelerate its distribution. Dr. Gerberding has also been president of Merck's Vaccine Division. She is familiar with health care politics from both the public and private sectors.

Dr. Mark McClellan, currently a Duke University professor, has been FDA commissioner and CMS director. Dr. McClellan is well-versed in health care politics, having held leadership positions in both the FDA and the CMS. Between Dr. Gerberding and Dr. McClellan, we have provided the reader with the opportunity to hear directly from a leader of the three critical agencies leading the federal government's response to the pandemic.

Governor Bob Kerrey is no stranger to health care, as he is a trained pharmacologist. We were interested in speaking with former governor Kerrey to dig into the relationship between the states and the federal government in a crisis. When COVID-19 first exploded in early 2020, personal protective equipment (PPE) was in short supply almost immediately because of the just-in-time inventory models that had been adopted for efficiency purposes. PPE was being sourced globally, and the supply chain broke down. Health systems were competing with health systems and states were competing with states for the short supplies. We were interested in Kerrey's viewpoint, since he had been both a governor and a senator from Nebraska.

Finally, Operation Warp Speed was one of the most important strategies for, to paraphrase the WHO's Ghebreyesus, pushing back the virus. The timing surrounding its approval, manufacture, and distribution had massive implications

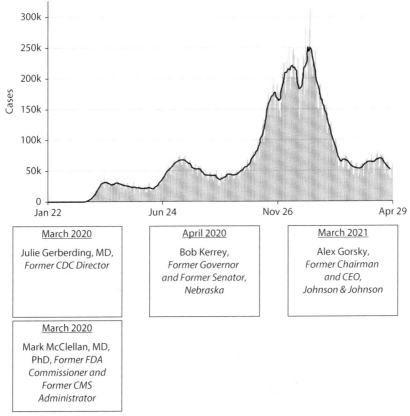

Figure 2.1. Featured case study interviews from a politics lens. *Source:* Data from Centers for Disease Control and Prevention, 2021. Figures are updated as of May 1, 2021, from the COVID Data Tracker and underlying data set available at https://covid .cdc.gov/covid-data-tracker/#datatracker-home.

in determining who would occupy the White House in 2021. Amid the omnipresent and oppressive partisanship of 2020, leaders such as Alex Gorsky, former chairman of the board and CEO of J&J, sought an opportunity to engage in nonpartisan efforts to tackle one of the greatest public health crises of the post–World War II period.

Amid hundreds of conversations with top leaders in 2020, these issues stood out to us in looking at the intersection between health politics and health policy. What did we learn about health care politics from the challenge that the esteemed CDC faced around diagnostic testing? How were the best thinkers grappling with the definition of the post–COVID-19 new normal even at the earliest days of the crisis? How should health care leaders (and aspiring leaders) think about federal, state, and local interactions on essential topics surrounding health and care? What does the success of Operation Warp Speed tell us about the opportunities to drive successful health strategies even amid the highest level of political polarization in our lifetime?

We are deep believers in the power of questions. The cases that follow here will be important to understanding and leading in the postpandemic health economy to come.

The CDC Walks a Political Tightrope

The science of public health should not be political. That's why inclusion of those leaders frontline in the care delivery environment and faithful exchange of information is critical.

—Julie Gerberding, MD, executive vice president and chief patient officer, Merck, and former director, CDC

When we spoke with Dr. Gerberding in March 2020, the surge had exploded in large urban areas, led by the New York region but also including Detroit and Seattle. There was growing realization that the surge was highly regional, and there were also pending questions about transmission, testing, and how to control the spread. Given the highly uncertain nature of the disease, advice by the CDC and other agencies was referred to as interim.

Escalating tensions among the scientists and agency leaders inside the walls of the CDC shed light on the unprecedented political interference in public health policy, as many of the world's top public health leaders were reminded just how political health care really is. We spoke to Dr. Gerberding again in April 2021 about progress at the CDC and vaccine manufacturing and distribution.

Julie Gerberding, MD

Dr. Gerberding's background as an infectious disease expert, former CDC director, and past leader of Merck's Vaccine Division made her a highly knowledgeable and relevant interviewee. As former president of Merck's Vaccine Division, she was responsible for planning the introduction of vaccines from the company's pipeline and accelerating Merck's ongoing efforts to broaden access to its vaccines in the developing world.

As the former director of the CDC under the George W. Bush adminis-tration (2002–9), Dr. Gerberding was responsible for coordinating more than forty emergency response initiatives as she led the agency through several public health crises including SARS, West Nile, Ebola, Zika, and H1N1. We inter-viewed her on March 17, 2020, shortly after the CDC botched test kits incident became public.

The Centers for Disease Control and Prevention

Since its founding in 1946, the CDC has been the premier public health agency for the United States. Although unique in that it is among the few large federal agencies whose headquarters are not located in the nation's capital, the CDC is far from immune from political pressures inside the Beltway.

As a beacon for trusted, evidence-based public health information, the CDC has had a long-standing history of effectively responding, communicating, and leading the United States through several public health emergencies and infec-tious disease outbreaks from Anthrax to Ebola. Despite this track record, the CDC found itself walking a tightrope between leading with science and tackling unprecedented political interference as the COVID-19 pandemic unfolded.

Public Health versus Politicians

According to Dr. Gerberding, the CDC's role in managing the health of the country hinges upon testing as a core competency but also the agency's exper-tise in disease surveillance and issuing critical guidelines and education prac-tices. Whether it is in the context of developing a test for a new pathogen or a new vaccine, she notes that effective public health decisions must calibrate both speed and safety. The CDC's focus on the science of public health "has to be the backbone of any effective public health response," she said.[11] Even though the CDC has quarantine authority for the country, both public health and political leaders ideally had to find ways to slow down the spread of dis-ease while also keeping essential health and civil services running. These prin-ciples, according to the former CDC director, served the agency well leading up to COVID-19.

The CDC's credibility in making the appropriate decisions for the health and safety of Americans was first called into question as a result of the faulty COVID-19 tests early in the pandemic. As part of the agency's initial response, the CDC opted to first create its own testing kit, which led to several faulty and inconclusive results, and then also limited how many people could receive tests.

"Worse than having no tests is having wrong tests," Dr. Gerberding said, "and so we do need to make sure that the performance is carefully calibrated so that when we get a result, we have confidence that we can make clinical decisions based on it but also public health decisions."

Although it remains a mystery to Dr. Gerberding as to how the CDC released ineffective testing kits, she wondered if complacency had set in following the 2009 H1N1 epidemic. Compounding the problem, the CDC had also issued guidelines that hospitals and health systems couldn't use their own in-house tests in lieu of the CDC's faulty kit, so alternative test results had to be certified by a centralized CDC lab. In time, the agency corrected its tests and expanded its testing criteria, but the CDC leadership's lack of transparency to the public and constantly changing testing guidelines laid the foundation for mistrust and confusion.

Fast-forwarding a few months to the summer, the COVID-19 hospitalization data that historically had been centrally reported to the CDC to ensure access to health departments and academics seeking to better understand the pandemic disappeared from its site and switched over to oversight by a third-party contractor. Along the way, various guidelines issued by the CDC such as those pertaining to reopening schools and testing people only with symptoms were highly disputed and questioned by other public health experts. In many of these instances, it was apparent that the Trump administration had pressured the CDC to require its guidelines despite discordance with the factual realities of the disease's progression.

Beyond Politics

In the early 2000s, Congress had appropriated nearly $2 billion to invest in the CDC based on the underlying assumption that the risks to the country posed by infectious disease were significant and that when the time came the agency would need to be prepared in order to have the capacity to effectively respond and lead. When those moments came over the next twenty years, from Anthrax to SARS to H1N1 influenza, the CDC time and time again upheld the gold standard for public health response. The agency's pre–COVID-19 legacy stands in sharp contrast to its failures in the face of COVID-19, from the inability to facilitate widespread testing diagnostics to fostering miscommunication to failed advocacy within the states and at the highest levels to value and listen to trusted and credible scientific and health experts. During COVID-19 we began to question the role of the government during a crisis. Beyond the political pressures, the pandemic highlighted the importance and the lack of centralized, trusted data to make real-time decisions that could have been used to make more targeted, region-specific decisions.

Postpandemic Lessons for Leaders

Efforts to undermine the credibility of the CDC also jeopardize the public's trust in a COVID-19 vaccine and any other public interventions needed to protect the health and safety of Americans. Both science and politics play a role during a public health crisis, and this is a delicate dynamic that leaders on both sides must learn to manage. Politicians were in a tough spot, having to indicate that much was unknown and to dispense hard messages about social distancing, masks, and economic shutdowns. Meanwhile, the absence of evidence-based information created an opening for politically motivated actions. As the nation heals beyond the pandemic, the first priority will be for the agency to regain the trust and confidence of the public. As Dr. Gerberding reminds us, local physicians and public health physicians are the most trusted during a crisis. People turn first to their own doctors and local caregivers for information and advice, and the CDC is an extension of local knowledge and trust.

"Initially, I was perplexed because the people who are responsible for the CDC response to this pandemic included people I worked closely with during my tenure. We know the caliber of the scientists and we know what they're capable of. I had enormous confidence in their ability to be a strong pillar of response in the coronavirus pandemic, but that didn't happen. If you know it's not the people, then you have to ask, what's changed? The surround sound is what changed in this situation.

The CDC was undermined, advice was overridden, and the politics overlaid the good science that the agency was intending to promulgate.

There are three categories of issues. One is that there were some very specific performance issues; the testing is one of them. There is a second issue that relates to politics and the suppression of science or the ignoring science, replacing it with politics in many cases. Then a third issue relates to the chronic underinvestment in the CDC and the public health system.

> The agency is basically operating with the same real dollars it was operating on ten years ago or before. There's no flexibility in the budget, and the crisis funding that does come is reactive and is only one-time funding. We rev up when there's a crisis, and then when the acuity resolves, the funding goes away and everybody lapses into a false sense of security, and that characterizes the CDC budget as much as anything else in our government."
>
> —Julie Gerberding, MD

A New Normal

There's going to be a new normal after this. That involves having to provide more services outside the hospital and at home because the risk of infection is going to be with us for a while. The silver lining is that this is an opportunity to pursue a strategy that you were waiting to try.

—Mark McClellan, MD, PhD, professor and director,
Duke-Margolis Center for Health Policy, and former
FDA commissioner and CMS administrator

Dr. Mark McClellan was the ideal expert to interview in March 2020.[12] The COVID-19 crisis had exploded, and there was a shortage of information about the transmission, testing, and longevity of the disease. We were interested in his view of how the private sector and governmental agencies were handling the crisis and what would be the next steps.

Mark McClellan, MD, PhD

Dr. Mark McClellan is a professor of business, medicine, and policy and the founding director of the Duke-Margolis Center for Health Policy. His research and teaching focus on value-based payment, global health policy, and real-world evidence and is informed by his rich experience, both as FDA commissioner from 2002 to 2004 and as CMS administrator from 2004 to 2006. Dr. McClellan has served in both Democratic and Republican administrations, first as deputy assistant secretary for economic policy in Bill Clinton's Department of the Treasury and then as a member of the Council of Economic Advisers and senior director for health care policy at the White House under George W. Bush.

Dr. McClellan has also held roles as a senior fellow at Brookings and as a faculty member at Stanford University.

Federal Drug Administration and Centers for Medicare and Medicaid Services

The purview of the FDA has expanded dramatically since its inception in the early 1900s with a focus on ensuring food and drug safety. Its role now encompasses regulatory approval and supervision of not only food and pharmaceuticals but also vaccines, supplements, transfusions, medical devices, and much more. Another operating division under HHS, the CMS, administers the Medicare program and partners with state governments to administer Medicaid and the Children's Health Insurance Program. Together and in concert with other divisions within HHS, these agencies fulfill a crucial role in guiding public health and setting health policy for Americans. In 2020, the agencies encountered a challenge unlike any other in modern times: a once-in-a-century pandemic accompanied by political pressures but also new capabilities.

The Government Role in a Crisis

When we spoke with Dr. McClellan in late March 2020, the surge of COVID-19 cases had exploded in large urban areas, primarily in New York City and the surrounding region but also in Detroit and Seattle. Dr. McClellan identified that this would be "a regional phenomenon" in the coming weeks, and experiences would vary significantly across the country. In some "worrisome spots" such as New Orleans, he noted, there was not yet a huge increase in detected cases, but there were plenty of reasons to suspect that the situation would worsen. While the focus of the government and health systems at that point was on dealing with the case surges effectively in the short term, Dr. McClellan predicted that COVID-19 would be with us in some form for longer, so "we need to also be thinking ahead now to the extent we can about how we make this a more manageable condition for getting ahead of future outbreaks over the coming year."

The federal actions needed to cope with a drawn-out pandemic could be informed by the experiences with past outbreaks such as H1N1 flu and SARS, which took place during Dr. McClellan's tenure as FDA commissioner. Those crises had taught him that the first stage of response tends to focus on non-medical interventions such as social distancing and closing schools, then moves into ramping up testing and surveillance followed eventually by advancing the availability of therapies to treat or prevent the disease and finally, a vaccine.

"When those kinds of steps are in place, it becomes feasible to start relaxing these nonmedical interventions that are so important and so disruptive right now," Dr. McClellan said.

The Politics of a National Emergency

Dr. McClellan emphasized the importance of President Trump's declaration of a national emergency on March 13 as the pandemic was escalating. Not only does this designation free up more resources for the government to mobilize its response and eliminate some of the regulatory red tape that could otherwise hinder a rapid reaction, but the declaration of a national emergency "is also important for adding focus and momentum to the response" and for emphasizing to the public the seriousness of the situation. The public health emergency gave the president and political leaders a mandate to work together on addressing supply chain issues, helping frontline providers, and other components of the pandemic response.

The national emergency also set the tone for dictating the scope of legislative response to the effects of COVID-19 on the overall economy. Dr. McClellan praised the passage of relief legislation that provided funding for COVID-19 testing and treatment, which ensured that cost would not present a barrier to care for the uninsured—a crucial step in the context of a contagious disease. In addition, congressional funding provided support for economic recovery, including enhanced unemployment payments and targeted assistance for more vulnerable populations, which Dr. McClellan called "very typical for a major national emergency—economic or public health."

The FDA is a critical part of the response to a public health emergency, as Dr. McClellan had seen during the agency's work on bioterrorism threats in the post-9/11 setting during his tenure as commissioner. In the particular context of the COVID-19 emergency, the FDA had to shift into overdrive its capacity for expediting the development and regulation of diagnostics and treatments. "The challenge that FDA has is that it has to ramp up these activities, and then the production and availability of the treatments that look like they're going to work to a much larger scale and much faster given how intensive this outbreak has been," Dr. McClellan said.

Beyond Politics

Another area where unprecedented steps were taken was in the payment space, as the CMS approved waivers to provide more flexibility in reimbursing for telemedicine amid the necessity of keeping patients at home as well as relaxing requirements around health care providers' state of licensure. The use of tele-medicine, especially in alternative payment models and primary care medical homes, is an example of how organizations can move toward a more sustainable business model instead of being bound to reimbursable services in the traditional FFS model.

Dr. McClellan noted the importance of long-term thinking about realigning organizations to deliver more services virtually, which can be less costly and more convenient for patients. The advances in virtual medicine can also enable organizations to step up their population health tracking capabilities to gather more data on patients after they leave the hospital and can even expand these data to encompass all the individuals in the community so they will be better positioned to deal with public health crises, including future surges of COVID-19 cases, he said.

Postpandemic Lessons for Leaders

"Leaders and health care organizations shouldn't just be thinking about how to get through the next four weeks and get back to normal after the surge," Dr. McClellan said, "because there's going to be a new normal after this." More and more health care leaders are realizing that certain patients can be managed virtually and locally instead of needing to come to the office, and staff have adapted quickly to using telemedicine. A final component of the new normal will be an increased emphasis on proactively reaching out to high-risk patients instead of waiting for them to present with symptoms. "These are permanent changes that I think are coming in our health care system," Dr. McClellan concluded. "While we absolutely have to focus on the short-term surge response, first and foremost, we also have to look ahead to what is going to be changing after that."

> "It is so challenging to be a leader today dealing with this pandemic, and you do have to focus first and foremost not on reimbursement for all of this but on what do I actually need to do to respond to the epidemic? That starts with the safety and well-being of the workforce. Paying close attention to strategies around redesigning care not just for the next month of the surge but for the longer term of increasing telemedicine and providing care that doesn't need to be given in the hospital out of the hospital. But for the longer term, this is going to be with us in some ways for months to come.

More emphasis should be placed on managing the whole population, not just COVID-19. Conducting testing on patients who say that they may be at risk but being able to look in your community to identify who is at risk and reach out to them and get them into appropriate triage management. These are permanent changes that I think are coming in our health care system. While we absolutely have to focus on the short-term surge response, first and foremost, we also have to look ahead to what is going to be changing after that."

—Mark McClellan, MD, PhD

Balance of State/Federal Power in a Crisis

If the president nationalizes the National Guard, all of a sudden, the president of the United States, as commander in chief, has full authority. So, in most disasters, there is a significant amount of automatic coordination between states and federal agencies.

—Bob Kerrey, former governor of and former
US senator from Nebraska

We sat down with Governor Bob Kerrey toward the end of April 2020 to discuss a governor's relationship with the federal government and the key roles that governors play in a crisis.[13] At the time, PPE was in dramatically short supply, and states were competing with each other to find sparse PPE and questioning the role of the federal government.

Governor Bob Kerrey

Bob Kerrey served as the thirty-fifth governor of Nebraska from 1983 to 1987 and as a US senator from Nebraska from 1989 to 2001. Kerrey has a wide range of experiences, including being an officer for SEAL Team One during the Vietnam War and receiving the National Defense Medal of Honor. He serves as lead director of Tenet, one of the largest investor-owned health systems in the country.

Nebraska

Nebraska is a midwestern state with nearly two million people. It was admitted to the union in 1867, shortly after the American Civil War ended. Nebraska's legislature is unique among other states, as it is unicameral. That is, its legislators are elected without reference to a political party.

The Role That Governors Play during a Crisis

We were interested in asking Kerrey about the role that governors play during a crisis. During his tenure as governor, he came to realize that governors have moral and social authority and responsibility. Constituents tend to "typically grant a governor moral authority to help them understand what's going on." He believes that this is a unique opportunity to lead.

He observed that the governor may not have statutory authority over employers, but the employers will grant the governor authority in exchange for the opportunity to communicate to the governor what they need during a crisis.

During his time as governor, Kerrey managed several crises and made sure that he listened to people, talked to experts, and understood the problem. When he had as much information as he could gather, he developed a solution that would address what is always a primary desire of constituents, which is to provide a better life for their children and grandchildren.

As Kerrey discussed in a *Wall Street Journal* op-ed in April 2020, most public officials live in fear of not doing enough because they often find themselves in a position where there is no right answer.[14] Kerrey tells us that these moments carry extreme weight, and sometimes one must choose the well-intended decision over the least costly one.

In the *Wall Street Journal* op-ed, Kerrey discussed the importance of balancing the health of the people and the vitality of the economy. He explained that a governor's success is directly connected to the willingness of the people to help each other get through challenges. There will be heroic people willing to run a considerable risk to help, which every leader counts on.

Governors' Relationship to the Federal Government during a Crisis

Kerrey commented that beginning with the creation of the US Constitution in 1787, the states have maintained a substantial amount of authority over decision making, from education to certain parts of health care. When considering Medicare and Medicaid, there is recognition by governors that the federal government is the largest payer and regulator. Governors meet among themselves regularly and count on sharing information and learning from each other.

Conflict arose around the acquisition of PPE, which highlighted challenges during a crisis. Governors generally believed that the federal government has responsibility to acquire and distribute PPE. In this case, that responsibility was left to the states and put governors in a position of competing with each other. Kerrey believes that the root cause of the problem is that we need to develop a reliable supply chain for PPE, similar to that developed by the Department of Defense.

The 9/11 Crisis versus the COVID-19 Crisis

Kerrey described the parallels between 9/11 and the ongoing COVID-19 crisis. He was one of the ten members appointed to the National Commission on Terrorist Attacks upon the United States, also known as the 9/11 Commission. He explained that the time following 9/11 was incredibly partisan, resulting in the creation of the 9/11 Commission that was cochaired by a Democrat, Lee Hamilton, and a Republican, Tom Kean. This commission was defined by the notion of unity during a time of extreme division and provided a nonpartisan space for discussion.

In comparison, Kerrey believes that putting a commission together during the pandemic is not a good idea. The virus is entirely different, you "cannot declare war on it," and we are not going to "defeat it." Instead, we are going to have to figure out how to live with it. Therefore, a commission will be more effective in a year or so when the cases have gone down and we have gotten a better hold on the virus. There is widespread understanding that health care is fully political.

Postpandemic Lessons for Leaders

Kerrey spoke about parallels between leadership by a CEO and a governor and noted that each deals with a much different constituency. A governor is elected, and a CEO is appointed. Governors don't tell people what to do and must persuade them. A governor can't be a benevolent dictator. When it comes to the characteristics of a CEO, it is much easier to lead with control.

Kerrey commented that the first responsibility of a health care leader during a crisis is to abide by the legal standard of the duty of care. For a member of the board of directors, he explained that a director meets the legal standard by asking the right questions of the CEO and making a judgment about whether the CEO is doing well. The top priority for discussions with the CEO is how the health care organization is supporting caregivers, employees, and the community.

Kerrey reviewed four key characteristics that constitute a successful leader in a crisis regardless of the sector in which the person is leading. A successful leader should inspire respect and confidence among employees to believe that they will successfully get through the crisis, be prepared to make mistakes and be honest when a mistake is made, lead the way in communicating truthfully, and listen for the multiple perspectives of employees, constituents, and the community.

"The hardest thing in politics to do is when somebody gets up in a town hall meeting and says, here's a problem. What are you going to do about it? And maybe the most difficult answer is nothing. Because there are times when nothing is the right answer. If the questions focus on what's the government going to do, it is possible that the government can make it worse. I think banning elective surgery is a good example of a very well-intended decision, not by bad people. But it was a well-intended decision that was a costly one. The cost-benefit ratio is decidedly against the benefit.

If I'm the governor of Nebraska and my hospitals tell me we don't have enough personal protective equipment or we don't have enough testing supplies, I'm going to do everything I can to get whatever I need in order to give my hospitals, my medical community, what they need to test and protect themselves when they're caring for people. You're just doing your job."

—Bob Kerrey

A Moonshot: COVID-19 Vaccine Development

When we're talking about developing a vaccine in an abbreviated period of time that could be administered to billions of people around the world, there should be a level of transparency and expectations around our data.

—Alex Gorsky, former chairman and CEO, Johnson & Johnson

We interviewed Alex Gorsky on March 8, 2021, eight days after Johnson & Johnson (J&J) received EUA from the FDA.[15] J&J had already shipped nearly four million doses in anticipation of FDA approval. The J&J vaccine was a single shot with no extraordinary refrigeration requirements like the other two approved products from Moderna and Pfizer. In the United States, the J&J vaccine was expected to be particularly useful in rural areas and with populations where it would be difficult to arrange a second shot. We spoke about challenges of developing the vaccine in months when it normally takes years, how he viewed relationships with the pharmaceutical industry and the federal government, and the intense politics that surrounded the development and distribution of the vaccine.

Alex Gorsky

Alex Gorsky is former chairman of the board and CEO of J&J. He was only the seventh chairman and CEO in J&J's 135-year history, having been appointed CEO in 2012. Gorsky is a West Point graduate, has an MBA from the Wharton School of the University of Pennsylvania, and is active in military affairs and veterans' groups.

Johnson & Johnson

J&J is the most valuable health care company in the world, with a market capitalization of $400 billion as of April 2021. The company has three operating lines of business: pharmaceuticals, medical devices, and consumer goods. J&J has had a successful history in vaccine research in areas such as HIV, Ebola, and Zika. The J&J scientists began working in mid-January 2020 to assess the characteristics of the coronavirus, and approximately fourteen months later its vaccine was being administered.

Developing a Vaccine in a Public "Fish Bowl"

Scientists from J&J in late January and early February 2020 obtained genomic sequencing information and, building on the J&J vaccine platform used for Ebola and HIV in which the company had invested billions over the years, were able to develop multiple potential vaccines, or constructs, and narrow them down with characteristics to maximize safety, efficacy, and producibility.

At that point, the clinical trials began. Gorsky referred to his pride in the willingness of pharmaceutical companies to collaborate in the interests of developing a coronavirus vaccine. They were committed to sharing information, research, data, and other resources designed to speed development.

The federal government geared up to assist in production of a vaccine by providing funding and encouraging the pharmaceutical industry to work closely with the FDA and other agencies. There was a commitment to data transparency and the rigor of study. There was sensitivity on all sides to ensure that all regulatory requirements were met.

Gorsky shared his hope that the partnerships with other pharmaceutical companies and the federal government would continue as other crises occur or other medical challenges arise.

In referencing the political partisanship that existed during the development process, Gorsky indicated that it is a very political time when "every comment and aspect" is scrutinized. In his mind, because this is a global pandemic, the challenge and opportunity to vaccinate people around the world balanced the political pressures.

Gorsky indicated that J&J was thinking about not only capacity of production but cost to the system. Therefore, the company worked to produce the vaccine on a not-for-profit basis so that price did not interfere with demand.

Vaccine hesitation requires a strong commitment to educate, share data, and be fully transparent. If 10 percent of the population will never take a vaccine and 20 percent are in the wait-and-see category, the latter group is the one that we should focus on with full effort now, Gorsky said.

Building a Reliable Supply Chain

We had previously interviewed Gorsky on May 20, 2020, shortly after the COVID-19 crisis had peaked in New York City and was still under way in many parts of the country. We discussed his view of the US supply chain and the shortage of PPE.

Gorsky drew on J&J's experience in developing a global reliable supply chain. His view is that it will take public-private partnerships and that neither side has the ability to do it alone. There will be certain components of the health care supply chain system that should be more centralized or standardized and done at the federal level, just as you would expect a company such as J&J to do. Gorsky indicated that centralized function needs to be balanced with the right amount of agility, flexibility, accountability, and responsibility at the local level so as to provide supplies for the unique needs of a particular entity or customer at any given time.

In the preparation stage around stockpiling, Gorsky thought that the federal government could play an important role rather than individual suppliers. The local level is important for ensuring that real-time need is being matched with real-time supply and should not be encumbered with what could be a paralyzing bureaucracy or other impediments that would prevent a particular hospital or company from getting exactly what it needs at a certain time.

Postpandemic Lessons for Leaders

As a leader, Gorsky is constantly monitoring the pace of J&J and his team. When things are going too fast, he needs to slow the pace down. When things are going too slowly, he needs to cause the pace to speed up.

In a crisis, Gorsky has found that he needs to stay focused on the data and the facts and not be distracted by real-time, fast-moving activity. He believes in having a diverse team to prevent tunnel vision and having a culture whereby the team can challenge openly and disagree. It is necessary to create a vision where there is "light at the end of the tunnel" and a plan to get there.

> "I don't think anybody has the ability to do it alone. It's going to take a lot of public-private partnerships; there will be certain components of the supply chain health care system that should be more centralized or standardized or done at the federal level, just as you would expect us in a company like J&J to do. On the other hand, you want the right amount of agility, flexibility, accountability, and responsibility at the local level so that people can respond based upon the unique needs of that particular unit or customer at any given time.
>
> Out of every crisis, there comes an opportunity to rethink the way that we do everything. Coming out of this, a few changes that will actually be good for us as a society and as a country would be a reprioritization of public health policy. We clearly are gaining an understanding that without a strong public health policy and outcomes, we can't have a strong economy, we can't have strong security, and we can't have a strong society. Making those appropriate investments and keeping them consistent going forward is going to be more important than ever."
>
> —Alex Gorsky

Notes

1. Centers for Disease Control and Prevention, "Transcript for the CDC Telebriefing Update on COVID-19."
2. United Nations, "Launch of Global Humanitarian Response Plan for COVID-19 Secretary-General."
3. "There are known knowns" is a phrase from a response that US Secretary of Defense Donald Rumsfeld gave to a question at a US Department of Defense briefing on February 12, 2002, about the lack of evidence linking the government of Iraq with the supply of weapons of mass destruction. Rumsfield's expanded response was as follows: "As we know, there are known knowns; there are things we know we know."
4. Patel, "Why the CDC Botched Its Coronavirus Testing."

5. Chen et al., "Key Missteps at the CDC."
6. Fireside Chat with Gary Bisbee, Ph.D., "Episode 56."
7. Pradhan, "CDC Coronavirus Testing Decision."
8. Selin, "How the Constitution's Federalist Framework Is Being Tested by COVID-19."
9. Legal Information Institute, "Gregory v. Ashcroft, 501 U.S. 452 (1991)."
10. Cancryn, "Is Trump on Track for an October Vaccine Surprise?"
11. The content of this case study was gleaned from Julie Gerberding's interview with author Gary Bisbee on March 17, 2020. For a longer excerpt of the interview, see Fireside Chat with Gary Bisbee, Ph.D., "Episode 8."
12. The content of this case study was gleaned from Mark McClellan's interview with author Gary Bisbee on March 21, 2020. For a longer excerpt of the interview, see Fireside Chat with Gary Bisbee, Ph.D., "Episode 9."
13. The content of this case study was gleaned from Bob Kerrey's interview with author Gary Bisbee on April 21, 2020. For a longer excerpt of the interview, see Fireside Chat with Gary Bisbee, Ph.D., "Episode 24."
14. Bob Kerrey, "'Elective' Surgery Saves Lives," Wall Street Journal, April 20, 2020, https://www.wsj.com/articles/elective-surgery-saves-lives-11587400926.
15. The content of this case study was gleaned from Alex Gorsky's interviews with author Gary Bisbee on May 20, 2020, and March 8, 2021. For a longer excerpt of the first interview, see Fireside Chat with Gary Bisbee, Ph.D., "Episode 33."

3

Develop Incremental and Bipartisan Agendas

Lessons for Leaders

As the 2020 election concluded, it was hard for health care leaders not to recall the title of the book by political writers Jules Witcover and Jack Germond, *Wake Us When It's Over*. For all of the partisan fervor and elevated voter participation rates, the sentiment that we heard most frequently from health care leaders in the post–Labor Day 2020 window was fatigue.[1] As they weathered the COVID-19 crisis, focused on durable recovery, and, in the wee hours of any given morning, contemplated a larger system-level rethink, the frontline realities of needed health care reform were mostly missing in the days leading up to November 3, 2020 (and the chaotic weeks and months that followed).

In his inaugural speech in late January, President Joe Biden seemed highly attuned to a nation that was languishing from the aftereffects of a visceral, polarized election and from the ongoing impositions of COVID-19. In his remarks, he declared that we must come together as one nation. "We have much to repair, much to restore, much to build, much to heal—and to gain." Biden would say that his singular purpose as president was "bringing America together."[2]

The First One Hundred Days

In the first one hundred days of the Biden term, the president was squarely focused on three things: setting a healing tone for the nation, effectively leading in regard to the COVID-19 crisis response, and taking steps to bolster the US economy. It was the vital few list of work to be done in the early months of the Biden presidency.

Biden's COVID-19 response centered predominantly on vaccine administration. And as framed in chapter 2, the progress was material. The early goals for distribution and administration of the vaccine were exceeded. And while there were setbacks such as the temporary decision to halt administration of the J&J vaccine (due to an adverse event concern with blood clotting), President Biden and his team received praise for its competence.

Along with the COVID-19 response, Biden also focused in the first one hundred days on economic recovery. The crisis fell disproportionately hard on Americans who did not have jobs that could be conducted virtually, did not see the benefits of ascending home prices, and were not beneficiaries of a rising stock market. These Americans had been a bipartisan focus of the relief packages that passed in the preelection window and remained a centerpiece of the relief strategies that were pursued in the early months of Biden's first term.

These twin efforts to drive the COVID-19 response and economic recovery were reflected most meaningfully in the signature legislative outcome of the first one hundred days: passage of the $1.9 trillion COVID-19 relief bill. The bill, called the American Rescue Plan, was passed and then signed in early March. It provided funding for a new round of stimulus checks, offered help for small business, and provided additional aid for the unemployed.

Notably, the bill did not garner bipartisan support. Senate minority leader Mitch McConnell's (R-KY) response was illustrative of the criticism: "This isn't a pandemic rescue package. It's a parade of left-wing pet projects that they are ramming through during a pandemic."[3] It was a harbinger of a shifting tone to come as Congress and the president increasingly reverted to the modern political equivalent of "regular order."

But in his remarks to a joint session of Congress in late April, Biden continued to strike a bipartisan tone. As the remarks occurred, more than half of Americans in an NBC News poll had a favorable view of the president.[4] While those ratings were lower than those for Barack Obama and George W. Bush, they were notably better than those of Donald J. Trump. Moreover, almost seven in ten Americans in the same poll approved of Biden's response to the pandemic.

Buoyed by across-the-board support for his efforts on COVID-19, Biden continued to push for legislative changes that he positioned as central to ongoing recovery and American leadership in the decades to come. "Thanks to the help of all of you, we're marshalling—with your help, everyone's help—we're marshalling every federal resource."[5] Biden seemed to softly imply the boldness of his efforts with the repetitive use of the verb "marshalling." It appeared, at least to us, to be a soft and favorable acknowledgment of the European Recovery Plan of 1948 pushed by US Secretary of State George Marshall that would come to be called the Marshall Plan.

There is, of course, a difference between political rhetoric and policy realities. The distinction is a critical one for navigating the intersectional forces of change in the decade ahead. It is true that the contours of what Duke University's Dr. Mark McClellan called the postpandemic "new normal" increasingly can be seen.[6] At the same time, so too can we see the forces of health care policy and health care politics colliding on Capitol Hill.

The first one hundred days, in many ways, tells the story of smart incrementalism with a dash of bipartisan aspiration. It is perhaps not surprising given a president who knows Capitol Hill as well as any commander-in-chief since Lyndon B. Johnson.

Myriad executive orders were signed in the early weeks of the Biden administration. No action from Congress was needed. A significant number of the executive orders focused on health care. Biden pushed to protect Medicaid and the ACA, making "high-quality care accessible and affordable for every American."[7] Second-order actions included moves by the CMS to create a special enrollment period to increase insurance signups on the HealthCare.gov marketplace.

Beyond executive orders, Biden also seemed to sense an opportunity in the first one hundred days for incremental and bipartisan progress on medical research. Late in the second term of President Obama, Congress passed the 21st Century Cures Act with massive bipartisan support. In his joint session remarks, Biden called on Congress to "end cancer as we know it."[8] It was an emotional moment in the speech, as lawmakers understood the connection that Biden had to the issue, having lost his son Beau to brain cancer in 2015.

President Biden called for the creation of an equivalent to the Defense Advanced Research Projects Agency. It would be housed within the National Institutes of Health and, in the president's view, create momentum for a new round of biomedical research.

As health care leaders begin to think about health policy progress beyond regulatory actions at the health agencies and targeted legislative strategies such as the proposed Advanced Research Projects Agency for Health, they need to understand the phasing of health care reform to come and the ground rules that will shape it. Partisan realities will make it hard to undertake sweeping health policy reform in the current Congress even with the health care–related policy tailwinds driven by COVID-19. For the foreseeable future, the postpandemic health economy will operate within the statutory and regulatory framework of the ACA that Biden helped pass as vice president.

Three Stages of New Health Economy Reform

The ACA set in motion three distinct phases of reform that will continue to advance in the 2020s. The first shift was insurance reform represented by the core statutory components of the ACA. Access was its dominant focus. Indeed, on the ten-year anniversary of its signing, advocacy voices such as the Center for American Progress championed its transformative impact by noting that the bill expanded coverage for tens of millions of Americans. And indeed, the number of uninsured dropped by half, and Medicaid now has more total enrollees than Medicare.[9] Of course, the COVID-19 crisis disrupted coverage, and as those persons who are vaccinated grow and the economy recovers, coverage will grow to before COVID-19 levels.

The second phase of health care reform triggered by the ACA is payment reform. As Dr. McClellan noted, the "reimbursement system has been a huge problem in this country. It needs to be changed because we know it doesn't work."[10] There is bipartisan consensus that the current FFS payment model no longer aligns providers, insurers, consumers, and employers.

The third and final phase of reform will ensue once we see a meaningful change in how health care is paid for. This phase will involve a transformation of how health and care happen within the new incentive structure. The shift will drive a redesign of how care is delivered, paid for, and consumed and also will bring a new role for how the person operates within the larger postpandemic health economy.

In the wake of the COVID-19 crisis, the when—not if—realities of payment model change, and larger health economy reforms have been accelerated. Critical sectors, from higher education to health care to brick-and-mortar retail, were indelibly impacted. And as former Indiana governor Mitch Daniels rightly predicted during the height of the COVID-19 crisis, it "will not look just the same when [the pandemic] is over."[11]

As leaders look to effectively navigate the health care landscape post–COVID-19, the starting point for impact begins with health care politics, which is the first of four sections, followed by health policy, provider networks, and data-driven personalization. Chapter 1 provided the background, trends and review of key issues. Chapter 2 brought the voice of leaders in responding to COVID-19 and its influence on the issues discussed in chapter 1. This chapter

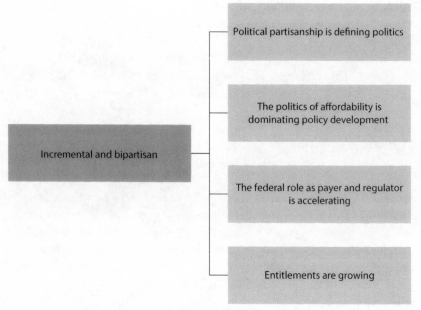

Figure 3.1. Ground rules for health care politics.

synthesizes the findings of the first two chapters and directs them toward lessons for leaders (see figure 3.1) that will define success throughout this decade.

Political Partisanship Is Defining Politics

Nothing is more important to our definition of well-being—or a greater potential source of anxiety—than our health. "Your health," as former Indiana governor Daniels noted in our dialogue with him during the spring 2020 COVID-19 surge, "is your first priority."[12]

At the political level, this reality means that health care issues will grab voter attention. They will only grow in their collective mindshare in the post-pandemic period. If it is an issue that commands universal attention independent of political affiliation, however, it is one that also has become fully political.

As Ron Brownstein wrote compellingly in *The Second Civil War: How Extreme Partisanship Has Paralyzed Washington and Polarized America*, "The political system has evolved to a point where the vast majority of elected officials feel comfortable only advancing ideas acceptable to their core supporters."[13] In framing the title of his book, Brownstein contends that political polarization is at its highest level since the American Civil War.

While Americans note a growing level of frustration with this elevated level of partisanship, nothing in the chaotic unfolding of the 2020 campaign season suggested to us that it will dissipate in the years to come. Former Nebraska governor Bob Kerrey agreed and commented that he did not see an end to the current politization. It is the tough paradox of the current era. Voters indicate time and again that they are fatigued by the divisiveness of our politics, and yet both Democrats and Republicans continue to be driven by partisans within their respective parties.

"It's important to understand that all the governor can do is connect to the willingness of the people themselves."

—**Bob Kerrey, former governor and former US senator, Nebraska**

Not surprisingly, the polar ends of the political health spectrum have begun to shape the national conversation on health care like never before. Early in the pandemic, the CDC emerged as a political lightning rod. Its struggle with effective activation of multistate diagnostic testing strategies notwithstanding, as Dr. Gerberding noted, the CDC has a long and storied history of fine performance and a national voice as a trusted broker and a collective voice of the physician. Unfortunately, the national politics of the moment cared very little about the long history of apolitical efforts to contain and mitigate new pathogens. The leaders at the CDC learned that health care is now fully political.

"This is a very tough environment for politicians, because they have to deliver really hard messages. And they're walking a tightrope. That's why I hope that we will hear more from the CDC and the state and local health officials and less from political leaders as this pandemic goes forward. Americans would like to hear from the CDC."

—**Julie Gerberding, MD, executive vice president and chief patient officer, Merck, and former director (2002–9), CDC**

The implications of these politicizations are profoundly important for health care leaders. Northwell Health CEO Michael Dowling talked about his early career work for New York governor Mario Cuomo, which reinforced for him "the importance of politics along with the key roles government should and should not play."[14] The effective health care leader brings that political lens to the tactics required to advance strategic plans.

The Politics of Affordability Are Dominating Policy Development

Robert Blendon and the Harvard T. H. Chan School of Public Health sought to understand the domestic policy priorities of the electorate leading up to the 2020 election. Prior to the onset of the COVID-19 crisis, they asked polling respondents to prioritize a list of more than twenty domestic policy areas. The findings are instructive on the issue of health care. The extremely or very important priorities spanning all political parties was "taking steps to lower the cost of health care." This was followed closely by tackling prescription drug prices.[15] As Blendon noted in framing the findings, "The poll results show ... the focus for the public is the pocketbook issue of lowering their health care costs and prescription drugs prices, not major health system reform."[16]

The increasing health care cost curve and declining levels of affordability brought an important shift in political sentiment during the COVID-19 crisis. The expansion of Medicaid by ballot initiative continued to be seen over the course of 2020 and extended into solid red states such as Oklahoma and Missouri. In total, six states passed Medicaid expansion by ballot initiative in what a longtime Clinton and Obama administration official called "the referendum strategy." This would have been an almost unimaginable outcome when the ACA was passed in the spring of 2010 and the political backlash described earlier in this section played out in the fall of that year. The crisis of affordability, coupled with the disruptive complexities of COVID-19, made "health care as a right" a national consensus issue at a time when political partisanship has never been higher.

At the political level, the winning political calculus for health care stakeholders will center on affordability in the 2020s. Amazingly, health care leaders seem to regularly miss the important political realities of health care affordability, concluding somehow that their larger mission makes them immune. It assuredly does not.

Surprise medical billing (and the larger issue of increased hospital price transparency) is an instructive contemporary example. Notwithstanding high levels of trust in their local markets (or perhaps because of it), US health systems were caught flat-footed in the 116th Congress by the bipartisan momentum on surprise medical billing. Likewise, they seemed oblivious to the politics of affordability when they launched a legal challenge to price transparency rules.[17] As the challenge wound through the courts, HHS secretary Alex Azar took each legal milestone to frame the politics (in an election year). "Especially when patients are seeking needed care during a public health emergency," Azar said, "it is more important than ever that they have ready access to the actual prices of health care services."[18]

The Federal Role as Payer and Regulator Is Accelerating

As we framed at the outset of this section, health care financing has never been more weighted toward the federal government. The University of Pennsylvania's Kevin Mahoney noted that so much is done by executive order that it is sometimes difficult to be heard in Washington. A range of factors before, during, and after COVID-19 underpin this trend.

First, there are seventy-three million baby boomers in the United States, and as of 2020 around fifty-one million were enrolled in Medicare. The remaining twenty-two million will become eligible by 2030. An increase of 44 percent in Medicare enrollees in ten years, particularly on the heels of the disruption caused by COVID-19, is a massive increase for the health care delivery and financing systems to accommodate. In addition, the number of individuals age eighty-five and older will quadruple, bringing increased intensity and expense of required medical care.[19]

At the other end of the demographic dynamic, the United States saw the fewest babies born in thirty years in 2017 as the US median age reached an all-time high. These demographic forces will obviously have major implications for health care delivery and financing.

Second, during the COVID-19 disruptions of 2020–21, widespread economic dislocation created significant growth in Medicaid. As the aforementioned state-level decisions for Medicaid expansion were advancing, we also saw a significant shift in payer mix as individuals and families with employer-based insurance lost their jobs. Notably, as health care leaders contemplate how long these increased levels of unemployment and underemployment will persist, the US economy did not see a return to baseline following the Great Recession of 2008–9 until 2014.

If we see a similar duration of the COVID-19–driven economic impacts, it will not be long before health care leaders are contemplating Medicare and Medicaid covering over half of all Americans. Moreover, in the absence of a set of tough statutory changes from policymakers on Capitol Hill, the current 25 percent of the federal budget consumed by health care will expand further. With that growth, the financial pressure on providers, insurers, and employers will accelerate commensurately.

What is the primary lesson for health care leaders during COVID-19 as they contemplate what health care politics will look like after the pandemic? Washington's role will only grow. Moreover, the graying of America into Medicare, coupled with the significant expansion in Medicaid, will inevitably challenge current entitlement structures.

In the end, as Bob Kerrey noted, rising deficits and the growing national debt are all financed with borrowed money. As COVID-19 vaccinations increase, herd immunity is realized, and the COVID-19 crisis winds down, we will move into a period of less accommodative monetary policy and rising interest rates. We will quickly see "interest on the national debt become the largest item in the budget."[20] It will bring hard choices for US policymakers, with unpopular politics looming on the other side of those decisions.

Entitlements Are Growing

At the outset of this section, we tracked the history of health care politics in the modern political era and demonstrated that in the pre-COVID-19 period, the electorate preferred bipartisan efforts on health care. The partisan push for Hillarycare led to sweeping Democratic defeats in the 1994 election. The passage of Obamacare on a straight party-line vote spurred the Tea Party revolt and the 2010 off-year election wave for Republicans. The equally partisan push to repeal and replace led to the Democratic wave in 2018. The lesson is clear, and the question is in what circumstances the political parties will rise above appealing to their respective partisan bases.

As the pandemic advanced, momentum for much-needed relief saw an inverse correlation between nonpartisan support and the remaining days until the November 3, 2020, elections. Even though partisanship increased as the remaining days in the legislative session decreased, the legislative story surrounding the Coronavirus Aid, Relief, and Economic Security (CARES) Act funding that became law during the crisis in December 2020 told a strong nonpartisan story.[21] Aspects of CARES included strong bipartisan packages providing over $175 million in relief funding for frontline provider organizations, which proved to be a critical lifeline for many organizations amid both the crisis surge and the corresponding disruption to non–COVID-19 surgeries.

The politics of the current era and its cacophonic social media amplifiers will push big and bold approaches to transform health care. The postpandemic realities, as always in health care, will favor bipartisanship. As Nancy-Ann DeParle said of Barack Obama, "He had studied history, and he knew that legislation with bipartisan support is stronger. It just is."[22]

Most change in Washington plays out incrementally over time as opposed to monumentally in one fell swoop. This simple insight is an important one for health care leaders and tracks the reality of health care policy in the post–World War II era. Durable, bipartisan, incremental change ultimately has greater speed to impact than ideological, sweeping reforms.

Following the vitriol of repeal and replace during the 115th Congress, the closing years of Obama's second term saw the passage of two major pieces of health care legislation. The first meaningful piece of legislation was the Medicare Access and CHIP Reauthorization (MACRA) in April 2015.[23] The second one was the 21st Century Cures Act in December 2016.[24] The former sought to end the sustainable growth rate formula that dated to the 1997 Budget Act and lay an expanded foundation for value-based care. The latter looked to eliminate impediments to product development and medical discovery.

Both bills passed the Senate with votes from over 90 percent of the chamber. When House Speaker John Boehner was asked about his collaboration with Minority Leader Nancy Pelosi on MACRA, Boehner said, "The door opened. I decided to walk in. As simple as that."[25]

Both MACRA and the Cures Act are foundational for big and important changes in how health care is paid for and how drug discoveries are advanced. And of course, legislative passage was just a step in the journey for far-reaching impact in health care. But both bills are a solid encapsulation of how incremental and bipartisan legislative progress can be made in Washington.

During the COVID-19 crisis, state and local governments emerged as both significant and largely trusted sources of information. The Associated Press–NORC Center/University of Chicago Survey in mid-April 2020 found that state and local governments were trusted a great deal or quite a bit by over half of Americans (third behind the CDC and a doctor or health care provider). Moreover, they also were the second most significant source of information after the news media. As Dr. Gerberding rightly framed in our discussions, "trust is always best at the local level."[26] In a nonemergent setting, those local efforts become foundational for a consensus that builds over time and then can catalyze action at the federal level.

While it is fashionable to talk of big swing reforms such as Medicare for All, the history of health care reform tells us that incremental (tethered to bipartisan) is the forward path for most health policy reforms. These incremental changes can be at the state and local level, building to a national consensus. They also can be statutory changes at the federal level such as we saw with payment reform in the closing days of the Obama administration.

In our conversation with Dr. McClellan, we asked why COVID-19 had proven to be a catalyst for long-contemplated change. "Why did it take such an emergency to make it happen? Well, the answer was focus," said Dr. McClellan. "We did what I call a 'tune out the static.' We stopped paying attention to noise that didn't matter and we only paid attention to noise that did."[27]

"As the trusted broker, the person they most want to get their health information from in a time of crisis is their local doctor, whether it's their personal physician or their local public health physician. That's why the cascade of exchange of information up and down the public health system needs to include the people who are on the front line in health care delivery."

—Julie Gerberding, MD, executive vice president and chief patient officer, Merck, and former director (2002–9), CDC

As the United States moves toward herd, or population, immunity and the economy continues its improvement, will the lessons of the COVID-19 crisis fade? Amid a true crisis of affordability, health care leaders have a unique opportunity in the postpandemic period to educate and an equally essential need to advocate. History tells us that payment and larger delivery reform will be a rhetorical, statutory, and regulatory journey. The time to mobilize to shape it is now.

Notes

1. Kevin Schaul, Kate Rabinowitz, and Ted Mellnick, "2020 Turnout Is the Highest in Over a Century," *Washington Post*, December 8, 2020, https://www.washingtonpost.com/graphics/2020/elections/voter-turnout/.
2. White House, "Inaugural Address by Joseph R. Biden Jr."
3. Pramuk, "Senate Passes $1.9 Trillion COVID Relief Bill."
4. Murray, "Poll."
5. White House, "Remarks by President Biden in Address to a Joint Session of Congress."
6. "New normal" refers to the post–COVID-19 realities of an evolving US health economy.
7. Jost, "President Biden Announces Priorities."
8. White House, "Remarks by President Biden in Address to a Joint Session of Congress."
9. Centers for Medicare and Medicaid Services, "National Health Expenditure Data."
10. Fireside Chat with Gary Bisbee, Ph.D., "Episode 9."
11. Fireside Chat with Gary Bisbee, Ph.D., "Episode 31."
12. Fireside Chat with Gary Bisbee, Ph.D., "Episode 31."
13. Brownstein, *The Second Civil War.*

14. Michael Dowling, interview with author Gary Bisbee, September 8, 2020.
15. Blendon and Benson, "Implications of the 2020 Election."
16. Blendon and Benson, "Implications of the 2020 Election."
17. Williams, "3 Legal Challenges."
18. Alonso-Zaldivar, "White House Wins Ruling."
19. Doherty, "Medicare's Time Bomb."
20. Fireside Chat with Gary Bisbee, Ph.D., "Episode 24."
21. President Trump signed the $2 trillion CARES Act in March 2020 (see the appendix for details) as Washington moved urgently to aid individuals and industries impacted by the global pandemic.
22. Nancy-Ann DeParle, interviews with authors Gary Bisbee and Sanjula Jain on September 25, 2020, and December 16, 2020.
23. The bipartisan legislation MACRA was signed into law on April 16, 2015. Under MACRA, the Quality Payment Program was established, which changed the way Medicare pays clinicians by repealing the sustainable growth rate formula and rewarding value over volume.
24. President Obama and the 114th Congress passed the 21st Century Cures Act in December 2016. The bill contained a number of provisions to hasten approval for new drugs and devices. It also contained new provisions on data blocking, attempting to address some of the interoperability limitations and lack of data sharing associated with meaningful use.
25. Paul Kane, "Republicans Heading for Whiplash on Partisan Budget, Bipartisan Health Bill," *Washington Post*, March 23, 2015, https://www.washingtonpost.com /politics/republicans-heading-for-whiplash-on-partisan-budget-bipartisan-health-bill /2015/03/22/32aef3a4-d0c5-11e4-8fce-3941fc548f1c_story.html.
26. Fireside Chat with Gary Bisbee, Ph.D., "Episode 8."
27. Fireside Chat with Gary Bisbee, Ph.D., "Episode 9."

PART II

Health Policy

4

Payment Is Policy

Background

When President Barack Obama took office as the forty-fourth president, inaugural observers from across the political spectrum spoke of a profound moment in American history. But on that crisp January day, few commentators foresaw a leader who would have the biggest impact on US health care since Lyndon Johnson.[1] Obama's core policy framework shaped the 2010s and brought forth the foundational pillars of US health policymaking for the decade ahead.[2]

In his January 2017 farewell address after two terms in office, a gray-haired, more seasoned President Obama trumpeted extending health insurance to tens of millions of Americans. He also noted that health care costs were rising at the slowest rate in fifty years.

The ACA was a massive force of change around access to care. The issue of access, which dominated the health care politics of the post–World War II period, was addressed materially during the Obama presidency.[3] His farewell phrasing offered a well-served bit of political offense in pursuit of defining his presidential legacy. The framing from Obama on a decreasing rate of cost increase also contained a hint of defense. For all its promotion of alternative payment structures and incubation of new delivery models, the ACA didn't systemically tackle a broken health care finance model.

As a result, the ACA didn't live up to its shortened naming convention, and that shortcoming all but ensured that a growing affordability crisis would be the new focal point for US health policy in the 2020s. From spiraling prescription drug prices to surprise medical bills for coverage out of a defined provider network, affordability in an era of escalating economic uncertainty rests at the core of the national conversation. This puts Washington's role as top payer and regulator on center stage.

Washington's Enlarging Payer and Policy Role

The origin story of the financial groundworks of US health care has been called a collection of accidents. From Baylor University offering public school teachers in Dallas a monthly insurance product that would become Blue Cross to the creation of employer-based insurance during World War II, the financial underpinnings of US health care would be unrecognizable to early generations of Americans.

The 2010s witnessed a set of consequential yet underappreciated changes in health care financing. At the outset of the decade, the ACA would be signed into law. As Nancy-Ann DeParle, then assistant to President Obama, shared, "Not a day goes by that I haven't wished we had Republican support for the law. It would have been so much stronger if it had been bipartisan." Among its key provisions, the legislation extended Medicaid to nonelderly adults and also offered enhanced federal matching funds.[4] Although Medicaid has operated as a jointly funded program, the ACA provided 100 percent federal funding for newly eligible Medicaid enrollees with a declining but still substantial level of subsidization.[5]

While participation in Medicaid in theory is optional, all states participate in the program. The Medicaid framework establishes a set of mandatory requirements for all beneficiaries, but the states can establish unique strategies around benefit design ranging from covered services to co-payment requirements.[6] It is the reason that Washington health policy leaders often say "If you have seen one Medicaid program, you have seen one Medicaid program."

The second major inflection point came in 2011. The first round of baby boomers turned sixty-five, making ten thousand seniors eligible for Medicare *each day*.[7] Notably, this growth in Medicare has been strongly oriented around Part C, so-called Medicare Advantage (MA) plans.[8] Boomers, comfortable with making decisions around health benefits as employees within commercial insurance plans, have flocked to MA, nearly doubling this decade alone.[9] Moreover, annual MA membership growth of 5 percent is expected through 2025.[10]

The growth in Medicare and Medicaid (see figure 4.1), in turn, placed Washington squarely in the role of the single largest payer for health care services. The implication for health care financing and delivery are underappreciated in their significance at a time when our tricameral federal system has never been less functional.

Defining the US Health Economy

One piece of health care strategy we see most consistently missed by leaders surrounds the realities of financing within the US health economy. Leaders looking to drive organizational and system-level impact must be aware of three

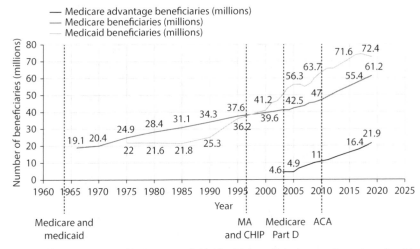

Figure 4.1. Growth in Medicare and Medicaid beneficiaries attributed to health reforms focused on increasing access. *Source:* Data analysis of Centers for Medicare and Medicaid data.

foundational policy elements within the larger health economy: who the key payers for services are, the underlying forces driving the rising cost curve, and key health care financing strategies being advanced by payers to tackle the crisis of affordability in US health care.

In its simplest form, the true definition of payer (as opposed to a third-party financial intermediary) is a source of funding for health and care services. In the United States, health care is paid for by one of three sources: the government, employers, or the individual.[11] Of total US health care expenditures, the largest spend is attributed to government payers.[12]

The involvement of the government and third-party intermediaries (most typically as an extension of the employer) has important implications for how consumer demand and provider supply operate within the health economy. Their involvement creates requirements for determining who is eligible, brings calculation around what health and care services are covered, creates a unique framework for how eligible providers are paid for their services, and shapes the requirements for how people need to consider their out-of-pocket costs.

Before COVID-19 Health Economy Headwinds

The issue of rising health care costs and defining affordability is not just one that was and will continue to be definitional for US health politics. It also will drive the health policy debate of the coming decade.

Spending on health care, as the Organisation for Economic Co-operation and Development and others have framed, has outpaced economic growth and been on a steady and "unsustainable ascent" for the last fifty years. The United States spends nearly twice as much as other high-income countries and performs less well on health outcomes and behaviors. As Federal Reserve chairman Jay Powell said at a press conference in 2018, "It's been true for a long time that with our uniquely expensive health care delivery system and the aging of our population, we've been on an unsustainable fiscal path for a long time."[13] US health care spending totaled $3.8 trillion in 2019, with the greatest growth in expenditures attributed to residual use and intensity of health care goods and services.[14]

As Powell notes, the "aging of our population" is indeed on the rise. The number of Americans over age sixty-five will more than double in the next thirty years, from forty million to eighty-eight million individuals. In addition, the number of individuals over age eighty-five will quadruple, bringing increased intensity and expense of required medical care (see figure 4.2).

At the other end of the demographic calculus, the United States saw the fewest babies born in thirty years, and median age reached an all-time high (see figure 4.3).[15] Suffice to say, these demographic forces have major implications for health care delivery and financing given that Medicare is financed through payroll taxes.

In addition to the graying of America, there also is a material growth in the chronic disease burden. According to the RAND Corporation, more than

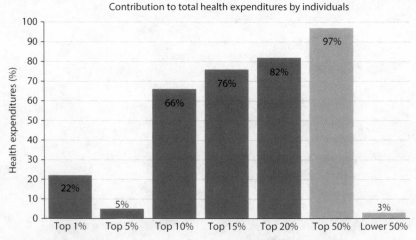

Figure 4.2. Contribution to total health expenditures by individuals. *Source:* Sanjula Jain, *2021 Trends Shaping the Post-Pandemic Health Economy* (Brentwood, TN: Trilliant Health, 2021).

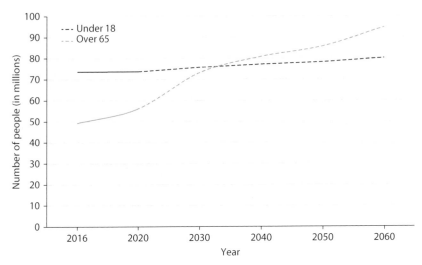

Figure 4.3. Population by age, 2016–60. *Source:* Data Sanjula Jain, *2021 Trends Shaping the Post-Pandemic Health Economy* (Brentwood, TN: Trilliant Health, 2021).

half of all Americans have at least one chronic condition. Moreover, more than 40 percent have multiple chronic conditions.[16] More importantly, it is also understood that Americans suffering from these conditions utilize more care. Indeed, Americans with five or more chronic conditions spend fourteen times more.[17]

Unfortunately, the current payment model does little to incentivize consumer demand and provider supply to deliver the highest possible quality of care at the lowest sustainable cost.[18] Consumers on the demand side of the health economy find the current payment model confusing, frequently receive bills that exceed their expectation, and struggle with escalating costs.[19] Providers on the supply side of the health economy struggle with the burdens of documentation for traditional payment models, incur substantial workforce costs to collect payments, and deal with payment time frames that are typically more than thirty days.[20]

During the Donald Trump administration, CMS administrator Seema Verma championed the Patients Over Paperwork initiative, taking on burdensome physician requirements and using her bully pulpit to call for changes to evaluation and management (E&M) documentation. The growing demands to document information, Verma said, have become "a serious distraction from patient care."[21] Moreover, "like the overall cost of the US health system as a whole, US administrative cost is number one in the world."

Before COVID-19 Health Economy Reforms

As we framed in part I, the first major health care policy initiative came in the early months of the Obama administration as the Great Recession ripped through the global economy. Obama proved particularly adroit at assembling a solid senior White House team including the seasoned Rahm Emanuel as chief of staff. The gruff Chicagoan would often say, "You never let a serious crisis go to waste."[22]

Amid the crisis, Obama pushed a $787 billion American Recovery and Reinvestment Act with three core components. It cut taxes, extended unemployment and health benefits, and, importantly for US health care, advanced $275 billion in job creation provisions that included the HITECH Act to encourage the adoption of EHRs and supporting technology.

In his inaugural address, Obama would offer a call to action that America must "wield technology's wonders to raise health care's quality and lower its cost."[23] The HITECH Act was the statutory manifestation of the rhetorical frame. The HITECH provisions would direct the Office of the National Coordinator, created by President George W. Bush, to promulgate a set of rules to promote the adoption and meaningful use of health information technology.

Against the heady benefit assessment, the meaningful use investment has met with some post-implementation critique over the course of the decade.[24] Health care providers bemoaned the workflow impositions on end users, decried the failure to drive more significant system interoperability, and lamented an insufficient focus on the technological needs of the patient.[25] As for the projected $81 billion in annual system-level savings, return on invested capital has been more incremental and modest.[26]

And yet, the transformative potential of health information technology is still to be realized.[27] And over the course of the 2020s, the second- and third-order impact of the meaningful use–driven digitization will be one of the profound forces of change in US health care.

Patient Protection and the Affordable Care Act

With the meaningful use framework on an accelerated forward path, Obama and his allies on Capitol Hill spent a core part of the first session of the 111th Congress fighting for the Patient Protection and Affordable Care Act (shortened over time to the Affordable Care Act, or ACA).

Among its many provisions, the paramount change driven by the ACA was a material increase in access to insurance coverage. The bill allowed young people to stay on parents' insurance until the age of twenty-six and prohibited insurance companies from denying coverage to individuals with preexisting conditions, which could make over fifty million people declinable for insurance. In addition, Medicaid expansion was a major driver of coverage expansion.[28] As noted, a legal challenge to these provisions, *National Federation of Independent Business v. Sebelius*, would leave federally subsidized expansion of Medicaid at state discretion.

In return for benefit of insurance coverage expansion, policymakers required a statutory tradeoff for payers: a cap on the MLR.[29] This was a material change.[30] The ACA not only required a supermajority of premium dollars go to health and care strategies, but it also limited the profitability of traditional insurance.

These three statutory forces—health- and age-based coverage expansion, a broadening of Medicaid eligibility, and a cap on medical loss—changed the US health policy landscape over the course of the decade. They worked in concert with each other to address the issue of access to coverage while simultaneously forcing traditional payers to rethink their historic business models. Efforts from consolidation in pursuit of scale to redirection of capital outside the core insurance business followed.

Insurance Reform, Not Payment Reform

In our minds, the ACA is best thought of as the first in the series of three phases of reform. In 2011, we framed that the initial stage of insurance reform would be followed by a second phase of aggressive, balanced budget–driven payment reform that felt akin to the Balanced Budget Act of 1997.[31] Then, with a new model of payment in place, we would see fundamental delivery system reform begin to slowly unfold.

While the White House and ACA authors did not use this same construct, the statutory experimentation in the legislation around payment and delivery reform clearly was a political and policy effort to lay a foundation for future waves of reform. One of the most visible ACA policy incubations was the creation of so-called accountable care organizations (ACOs).[32] These shared-savings programs were widely adopted, with results varying by geographic location and participating organization, and were seen as having mixed impact as we moved into the second half of the decade.[33]

The ACA also contained language to hasten the move from volume of service to value of care delivered with bundled payments. It would set a requirement for a five-year pilot on bundled payments for a range of medical conditions with time-based linkages to both preoperative (three days) and postoperative (thirty days after discharge) time frames.[34] While the legislative offered "the Secretary may" level of discretion for program expansion and extension, it stopped well short of any systemic shift in payment model. Beyond discrete statutory provisions, an additional force for payment reform experimentation contained within the ACA was the Center for Medicare and Medicaid Innovation, which was statutorily established and built out to explore new payment and delivery models.

Finally, it would be wrong to think about Medicaid expansion as simply about greater access. Broad shifts in the program framework coupled with Section 1115 waiver requirements have made these provisions a source of experimentation around payment and delivery reform. The Delivery System Reform Incentive Payment Program spanning multiple states is illustrative.[35]

Interestingly, amid the growing politicization of health care, the level of bipartisan consensus for moving from a health finance model focused on volume of services to one centered on value remained consistently strong throughout the 2010s. As Obama finished out his second term, he collaborated with a Republican Congress to pass MACRA in the spring of 2015. It would repeal the sustainable growth rate formula, streamline myriad quality programs, and "change the way that Medicare rewards clinicians for volume over value."[36] MACRA was widely reported to be something that the Obama administration had wanted to include in the ACA. Ultimately, the administration defaulted to a series of experiments. Five years later, the health politics of payment reform were still strong enough to support a new incremental, bipartisan round of policy.

Trump Era Reforms

In part I, we framed the idea that health care is now fully political and that for leaders incremental and bipartisan strategies are most effective. Both MACRA and the 21st Century Cures Act tell that story. At the same time, it is also true that the electorate—and, by extension, the members of Congress who represent it—is at a historic level of polarization.[37] As a result, a number of the most pressing policy issues in health care have not seen material statutory action since the partisan passage of the ACA more than a decade ago.

In the wake of repeal and replace, the Trump administration was left to advance its health care policy agenda through regulatory rulemaking. The sweeping breadth of the ACA provides a vast tool kit for regulatory change, including a number of funding mechanisms for payment model experimentation. Moreover, the same political complexities that made it hard to advance statutory policy changes in the Trump administration also made it difficult for Congress to provide aggressive, nonpartisan oversight of regulatory changes.

As the politics of health care affordability played out, drug pricing emerged as a focal point for federal rulemaking. Initiatives such as HHS secretary Alex Azar's American Patient First agenda led to a flood of press releases tied to hundred-day milestones and campaign-style progress.[38] By rulemaking, HHS sought to build a narrative around lowering out-of-pocket drug expenses and positioning new tools in areas such as MA that allow negotiating better drug pricing, pushing for increased drug competition, and creating new incentives for lower overall pricing (with efforts around increased transparency for price increases). The affordability crisis was front and center in this work as Americans grew frustrated with rising drug prices and looked to Washington for a solution.

With the growing level of participation in MA plans and the critical importance of voters aged sixty-five and older in the 2020 election, MA also was an important area of regulatory focus. In September 2020, the CMS would position important work to shape the program on the front end of the annual enrollment period. The CMS would trumpet a decline in premiums over the course of Trump's term, champion new plan choices, and herald new benefits. Affordability was front and center in the framing: "The Medicare Advantage average monthly premium will be the lowest in 14 years (since 2007) for the over 26 million Medicare beneficiaries projected to enroll in a Medicare Advantage plan for 2021."[39]

In addition to affordability efforts centered on drug pricing and MA, former CMS administrator Seema Verma also looked to the states as a critical activation node for the Trump health policy agenda.[40] US Supreme Court justice Louis Brandeis characterized the states as laboratories of reform where "if its citizens choose, [the states can] serve as a laboratory and try novel social and economic experiments without risk to the rest of the country."[41] "We are not," Verma said in 2017, "going to tell the states what their priorities are. They are going to come and tell us what their priorities are."[42]

This mindset, coupled with a majority Republican gubernatorial count across the fifty states, led to an active reform agenda around Medicaid. A combination of state plan amendments and Section 1115 waivers drove significant experimentation to include modest co-pays, work requirements, and associated school and job training conditions for participation.[43]

Across all of the Trump rulemaking, affordability was at the center of the regulatory agenda. The solutions to that growing problem, for their part, arguably were the same ones that had been used by employers to attempt to tackle quality, cost, and experience for their employees and dependents. They sought to increase transparency for consumers to help them understand and manage out-of-pocket expenses. They pushed to set market expectations for value of services provided (pay for value). They looked to leverage their size and scale to tackle the large cost drivers within the health care dollar.[44]

Employers as Health Economy Linchpins

It has long been theorized that one of the most powerful levers for health economy change was employers.[45] Over the last few decades, as health care costs continued to rise, employers had a clear incentive to rethink how the person and the provider interact, and employers' large aggregate spend made this a key stakeholder in the national conversation.

During the passage of Obamacare, one area of significant focus was the so-called Cadillac Tax. Specifically, the provision imposed a 40 percent excise tax on the value of employer-sponsored plans that exceed certain dollar values. The Cadillac Tax invoked strong opposition from traditional Democratic constituencies such as national labor unions who contended that the tax had become an excuse for employers to modify their health insurance offerings for workers in order to avoid these penalties.

In 2018, the Kaiser Family Foundation surveyed employers to understand how they were approaching the creation of or increase in the annual deductible for employees and dependents. They found that "annual deductibles had climbed about eight times as fast as wages over the course of the last decade."[46] The increase in out-of-pocket expense made health care the single largest non-wage benefit. As employees were being asked to spend more on health and care services, this increase also frames the tough politics of affordability at the intersectional center of health politics and policy.

As national employers advocated for bipartisan efforts to tackle rising health care costs (typically through associations such as the Business Roundtable and US Chamber of Commerce), they also continued a multiyear push around cost containment. In concert with increasing financial requirements for employees and dependents, employers also sought to provide new technologies for consumer engagement over the course of the decade. They sought to drive adoption of user-friendly services such as so-called transparency tools to ensure that employees understand what services cost. Employers also have sought to offer supplemental services to address administrative friction across the provider side of the health economy ranging from claims assistance to high-touch concierge services to second opinion services.

Finally, as employers have sought to place additional cost requirements on employees and provide them with the tools to be more active participants in strategies around their own health and care, they also have pushed efforts to redesign provider health networks and tackle high-cost procedures. As the National Business Group on Health has framed, "employer interest in alternative payment and delivery models including accountable care organizations (ACOs) and high-performance networks (HPNs) remains strong."[47]

The final leg of the health economy is the individual market, a significant area of focus for the ACA.[48] The bill sought to incentivize new market entrants, build a new marketplace where consumers could benefit from increased choice, and strengthen competition to drive down costs.[49] While the program struggles with a number of high-profile implementation issues,[50] these programmatic efforts drove significant enrollment increases over the course of the decade.[51]

However, during the Trump administration these gains in the individual markets plateaued and then began to decline.[52] There has been considerable political and policy speculation surrounding the declining trend of individual market participation during Trump's presidency (2017–21). Rising premiums for plans have been a significant political flash point.[53] In the before COVID-19 window, the US economy saw significant employment growth, giving individuals access to insurance through their employers. Finally, the Trump administration and congressional Republicans decided to zero out the penalty of the individual mandate for not having some form of ACA-compliant insurance.

For all of the uncertainties about the future of the individual insurance market, it is a critical health economy support for more than 13.8 million Americans.[54] The politics of affordability and associated health policy choices are on greater display for individuals who rely on this portion of the insurance market. The COVID-19 crisis and its associated economic impact led to a significant increase in enrollment on the exchanges for the first time during the Trump term.[55] This frames one of a collection of affordability policy flash points that will loom large in the decade ahead.

Notes

1. On July 30, 1965, President Lyndon B. Johnson signed into law legislation that established the Medicare and Medicaid programs. For more than fifty years, these programs have been protecting the health and well-being of millions of American families, saving lives, and improving the economic security of our nation.
2. President Obama's core health policy framework includes the HITECH Act, the ACA, MACRA, and the 21st Century Cures Act.
3. Since at least the passage of Medicare and Medicaid in 1965, the policy focus in the United States has been to increase access to health care. The health economist Jeff Goldsmith frames the policy reforms in health care over the last decade a mission accomplished. "Of the estimated 27.4 million uninsured in 2017, roughly 19 million were eligible for either Medicaid or publicly subsidized coverage on the ACA exchanges." As Goldsmith went on, "that is as close as we get." Goldsmith, "Relatively Modest Health Reform May Create More Value Than 'Medicare for All.'"
4. The ACA provides enhanced federal matching funds to states that expand Medicaid to nonelderly adults up to 138 percent of the federal poverty line ($17,236 per year for an individual in 2019). The ACA enhanced match (93 percent in 2019 and

90 percent in 2020 and thereafter) is substantially higher than states' traditional Medicaid matching rate. As a result, Medicaid covers one in five Americans according to data reported by the Kaiser Family Foundation in 2019. See Kaiser Family Foundation, "Health Insurance Coverage of the Total Population."

5. The Medicaid program is structured as a federal-state partnership. Subject to federal standards, states administer Medicaid programs and have flexibility to determine covered populations, covered services, health care delivery models, and methods for paying physicians and hospitals.

6. States can also obtain Section 1115 waivers to test and implement approaches that differ from what is required by federal statute, but the secretary of HHS determines advance program objectives. Given this flexibility, there is significant variation across state Medicaid programs.

7. Centers for Medicare and Medicaid Services, "National Health Expenditure Data." The total number of Medicare enrollees is now expected to double by 2040.

8. The Balanced Budget Act of 1997 created Part C within the Medicare program. It was known at inception as Medicare + Choice. As the program evolved after going into effect in 1999, it would become more commonly referred to as Medicare Advantage. These MA plans bring together a combination of Part A (hospital), Part B (physician services), Part D (drug coverage), and other coverage (vision, hearing, and dental).

9. According to data reported by the Kaiser Family Foundation in 2020, MA enrollment has nearly doubled this decade, reaching twenty-four million beneficiaries and a 36 percent penetration rate among all Medicare beneficiaries. See Freed, Damico, and Neuman, "A Dozen Facts about Medicare Advantage in 2020."

10. See Freed, Damico, and Neuman, "A Dozen Facts about Medicare Advantage in 2020."

11. First, the government provides payment through Medicare and Medicaid. Second, employers provide coverage for their employees and dependents typically through private health insurance plans. Third, individuals are a source of funds in the form of out-of-pocket expense based on the scope of their employer-based insurance, the purchase of a plan on the individual exchange, or direct purchase of services on an as-needed basis.

12. Of the total $3.5 trillion spent on health care in 2018 (or 18 percent of GDP), Medicare and Medicaid combined represent almost 40 percent, private health insurance represents about 35 percent, and individual out-of-pocket spending represents about 10 percent.

13. Statement by Powell at a press conference in response to a question by Yahoo Finance's Myles Udland, as reported by Wolff-Mann, "'Our Uniquely Expensive Healthcare' System."

14. Martin et al., "National Health Care Spending in 2019." The 2019 total US health care expenditures represent a 4.5 percent increase from 2018. In 2019 faster growth in spending for hospital care, physician and clinical services, and retail purchases of prescription drugs—which together accounted for 61 percent of total national health spending—was offset mainly by expenditures for the net cost of health insurance, which were lower because of the suspension of the health insurance tax in 2019.

15. Jeffrey, "U.S. Median Age Hits All-Time High of 38."

16. Buttorff, Ruder, and Bauman, "Multiple Chronic Conditions in the United States."

17. In addition to costs attributed to the increased consumption of care itself, indirect costs from poor health ranging from presenteeism to illness-related absence represent significant dollars in annual lost productivity. According to the CDC, these losses cost US employers approximately $1,685 per employee per year, or more than $225.8 billion annually.

18. Marc Harrison, interview by author Gary Bisbee, March 31, 2020.

19. Nearly half of all Americans are concerned about the high costs of health care and fear health-related bankruptcy, according to 2019 consumer opinion data captured by Gallup. Witters, "50% in U.S. Fear Bankruptcy Due to Major Health Event."

20. Friedberg et al., "Effects of Health Care Payment Models on Physician Practice."

21. Centers for Medicare and Medicaid Services, "Trump Administration Puts Patients over Paperwork."

22. As described in both the Health Care Politics and Health Policy sections, the colorful Emanuel was a powerful force for legislative change during the first term of the Obama administration. The former congressman and White House chief of staff made reference to this statement, which is widely believed to have been said by Winston Churchill during World War II. White House Archives, "Barack Obama's Inaugural Address."

23. White House Archives, "Barack Obama's Inaugural Address."

24. Hillestad et al., "Can Electronic Medical Record Systems Transform Health Care?"

25. Kellerman and Jones, "What It Will Take."

26. Hillestad et al., "Can Electronic Medical Record Systems Transform Health Care?"

27. Kellerman and Jones, "What It Will Take."

28. By the end of the decade, more than two-thirds of all states and the District of Columbia had made the decision to expand. Today, almost seventy-five million, or one in five, Americans receive their health coverage through Medicaid.

29. The MLR represents the amount of money that can go to administer health insurance coverage to a beneficiary, market and sell products to a potential beneficiary, and drive profitability of a plan offering once purchased. The ACA capped the MLR at no more than 20 percent for individuals and small groups and 15 percent for large groups.

30. While the ACA was statutorily architected to cap insurer profitability, a minimum MLR proved far murkier in its implementation and enforcement than the legislation's original intent. Multiple congressional committees have conducted hearings into the issue following record profits from the nation's largest health insurers. Many experts believe that a policy fight is looming between the not-for-profit providers of care (to individuals) and the for-profit insurers of those same lives.

31. The Balanced Budget Act signed into law on August 5, 1997, contains the largest reductions in federal Medicaid spending since 1981. Accompanying these spending reductions are provisions that represent the most significant set of structural changes. The legislation greatly expands the substantial discretion that states already enjoyed in administering their Medicaid programs; eliminates minimum payment standards that states must currently meet in setting reimbursement rates for hospitals, nursing homes, and community health centers; and allows states to require most Medicaid beneficiaries to enroll in managed care organizations that do business only with Medicaid.

32. ACOs are provider-led entities that seek to take collective responsibility for the health and wellness of a population. When an ACO succeeds both in delivering high-quality care and spending health care dollars more wisely, it will share in the savings it achieves for its respective payer contractor.

33. In December 2018 the Medicare Shared Savings Program was modified, resulting in a number of participants leaving the program. Among the changes, the CMS pushed to shorten the time for ACOs to begin to move to downside risk arrangements.

34. Bundled payments, also known as episode payment models, predetermine the total allowable acute and postacute expenditures (target price) for an episode of care. Providers share in any losses or savings that result from the difference between this target price and actual costs.

35. The Delivery System Reform Incentive Payment Program's initiatives are part of broader Section 1115 waiver programs and provide states with significant funding that can be used to support hospitals and other providers in changing how they provide care to Medicaid beneficiaries. The program leverages the triple aim of better care, better health, and reduced costs as a North Star of its design and seeks to tackle the silos of episodic care with a more integrated level of care coordination.

36. The Medicare sustainable growth rate was a method used by the CMS in the United States to control spending by Medicare on physician services.

37. Pew Research Center, "In a Politically Polarized Era."

38. HHS secretary Alex Azar was a Trump cabinet member with prior agency experience (under George W. Bush) and experience in the pharmaceutical space as an executive at Eli Lilly.

39. Centers for Medicare and Medicaid Services, "Trump Administration Announces Historically Low Medicare Advantage Premiums."

40. CMS administrator Seema Verma is renowned for her policy work at the state level. She worked closely to shape the health policy underlying Indiana's Healthy Indiana Plan with former governors Mitch Daniels and Mike Pence.

41. Legal Information Institute, "New State Ice Co. v. Liebmann."

42. Centers for Medicare and Medicaid Services, "Speech."

43. As federal requirements and state policies change over time, updates are made via state plan amendments. States can choose to submit plan amendments to make changes to their programs, such as changing a provider payment methodology or discontinuing coverage of an optional service.

44. It has been regarded that many of the Trump, Azar, and Verma policy strategies draw from the best thinking of private-sector innovators.

45. Employer health benefits tends to follow one of three designs: PPO, high-deductible health plan, and health maintenance organization (HMO). The most common plan type is the PPO. A PPO is a health plan that contracts with a network of providers with incentives for an individual or family to leverage that network for health and care services. The second common form of employer offering is a high-deductible health plan, which carries a larger deductible (the portion individuals pay out of pocket before their insurance can be used) than a PPO. High-deductible health plans are typically paired with a health savings account to pay for medical expenses in a given calendar year with dollars that are not subject to federal tax. Finally, a third variant of plan is HMOs, a collection of owned or contracted providers that comprise a health network. HMO coverage is confined to providers within group

of providers for any and all nonemergency care. Typically, these plans are offered to individuals who live within a given HMO service area and include a range of preventive and wellness strategies as a component part of the plan design.

46. Kaiser Family Foundation, "2019 Employer Health Benefits Survey."

47. Business Group on Health, "Large Employers Double Down."

48. In simple terms, the individual market offers the potential for coverage to any individual who is not covered by a public program or does not receive insurance through an employer.

49. Corlette, Blumberg, and Lucia, "The ACA's Effect."

50. Technology and Operations Management, "The Failed Launch of www.HealthCare .gov."

51. Corlette, Blumberg, and Lucia, "The ACA's Effect."

52. Gee, "Less Coverage and Higher Costs."

53. Gee.

54. Fehr, Cox, and Levitt, "Data Note." Total individual market enrollment, measured on an average monthly basis, increased from 10.6 million in 2013 to a peak of 17.4 million in 2015 before declining to 13.8 million in 2018.

55. Keith, "HealthCare.gov Enrollment Rises."

5

Flash Point on Disparities and Misaligned Incentives

Interviews

History tells us that health care policy changes are incremental. The policy framework put in place in the last decade represents a continuation of a multi-decade post–World War II push to increase access to health care. As part of this push for increased insurance coverage, the ACA put in place the early-inning foundation for a shift in the payment model that was advanced further under the HHS/CMS leadership team of President Donald Trump. The initial foundation established by increased access has now set up a second phase of reform centered on the US health care payment model as the country looks to better align the incentive models between person, payer, and provider to decrease cost and increase affordability. This shift in payment will lead to a third phase of reform as both person and provider begin to rethink how health and care are managed.

Before the COVID-19 crisis fundamentally shifted the contours of the 2020 election, three big health policy questions framed at least a piece of the national conversation. How will the country decide the question of health care is a right for all Americans versus a responsibility of the individual and the family? Will health care information technology investment in providers and the promise of data-driven personalization spawned by that digitization finally lower health economy costs? Will a bipartisan consensus on the affordability crisis and the role of paying for volume as opposed to value break the partisan stalemate on health reform?

During COVID-19, the United States has seen a material acceleration in the issues underlying all three health policy questions. Health equity became a flash point amid the pandemic on fail points ranging from access to diagnostic testing to priorities of vaccine administration. An overriding challenge is the complexities of a United States where employment is a centerpiece of the health economy funding and millions lost their jobs.

The pandemic also brought growing visibility to the misalignment of the incentive structures across the health economy. Insurer profitability skyrocketed.[1] Congress jumped in, with committees such as the House Energy and Commerce Committee announcing an investigation into health insurance business practices. While the ACA statutorily architected a cap on insurer profitability, a minimum MLR proved far murkier in its implementation and enforcement. During COVID-19 as providers are struggling for economic survival and on the front lines of surge response, the politics of low MLR offered new challenges.

Finally, Washington moved aggressively to respond to the disruptions and dislocations of the crisis. The US deficit soared to over $3 trillion as fiscal relief went up and federal tax receipts went down.[2] While the broad brushstrokes of this increased level of federal spending found bipartisan, bicameral support, a voice of concern for the long-term debt could also be heard. A range of nonpartisan stakeholders such as the Committee for a Responsible Budget noted that the failure to control rising costs of our health and retirement programs must be a policy focus after COVID-19.

The United States saw a material acceleration in the issues underlying all three of the aforementioned health policy questions. Many leaders on both sides of the political spectrum would speak of an out-year window in the coming decade when the bill for our deficit and debt will ultimately come due. The language recalled Michelle Wucker's 2016 book, *The Gray Rhino*. A Gray Rhino was, Wucker argued, a slow-moving yet highly foreseeable event. Its lumbering pace doesn't demand brute force response. Consequently, when it inevitably arrives, it overwhelms.

For leaders, the critical question is whether we can learn the consensus lessons from COVID-19 to build a new health economy that is more equitable and less costly in the decades ahead.

COVID-19 Interviews

In the case discussions that follow, you will hear from three leaders who offered real-time thoughts over the course of the pandemic on crisis response, durable recovery, and what it would take to reimagine key aspects of health policy and financing (see figure 5.1).

Dr. Rod Hochman spoke about moving financing toward shared accountability, what we refer to in this section as the "New Middle," and where

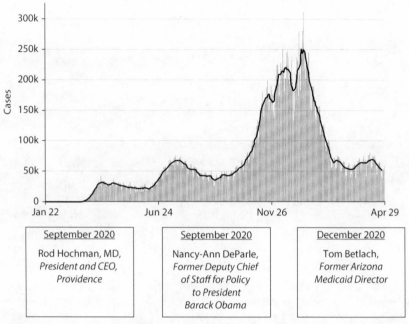

September 2020	September 2020	December 2020
Rod Hochman, MD, *President and CEO, Providence*	Nancy-Ann DeParle, *Former Deputy Chief of Staff for Policy to President Barack Obama*	Tom Betlach, *Former Arizona Medicaid Director*

Figure 5.1. Featured case study interviews from a health policy lens. *Source:* Data from Centers for Disease Control and Prevention, 2021. Figures are updated as of May 1, 2021, from the COVID Data Tracker and underlying data set available at https://covid .cdc.gov/covid-data-tracker/#datatracker-home.

telehealth ranks in importance over the next five years. He also challenged the health systems to spend more time in Washington educating decision makers.

Tom Betlach was the longest-tenured Medicaid director in the country, serving for twenty-seven years. He spoke about the fundamentals of the Medicaid budget, how Medicaid programs responded to COVID-19, and the next steps in Medicaid effectiveness employing social determinants of health (SDoH) programs.

Nancy-Ann DeParle, former deputy chief of staff to Barack Obama and architect of the ACA, shared her thoughts about the lessons learned from the political battle to get the act passed into legislation. She also provided advice to the Biden administration regarding next steps in increasing access and how to build on the ACA.

Shared Accountability for Costs and Outcomes

Unless this health insurance paradigm changes, that's going to be another crisis as we go forward. Unless the provider health community gets closer to being directly accountable for the premium and being part of that premium, we can't exist with this model long term.

—Rod Hochman, MD, president and CEO, Providence

A completely new paradigm was needed for the challenge Providence encountered on January 20, 2020. As noted in the introduction, the first known patient with COVID-19 in the United States received treatment at Providence Regional Medical Center in Everett, Washington, after returning from Wuhan, China. At that time, there was more unknown than known about COVID-19; its mode of transmission and optimal treatment protocols were still opaque.

With the first confirmed case, the United States had been thrown into the COVID-19 crisis, and Seattle would soon become ground zero of the COVID-19 outbreak in the United States before cases surged in New York City and other urban areas in the spring and then more broadly across the nation in the summer and late fall.

Rod Hochman, MD

Dr. Rod Hochman a rheumatologist by training, assumed the role of president and CEO of Providence in 2013 after Providence acquired Swedish Health Services; Providence then merged with St. Joseph Health in 2016. As the 2021 chair of the American Hospital Association and past chair of the Catholic Health Association, Dr. Hochman has interacted daily with decision makers in Washington about COVID-19, providing important guidance for the industry as the government's role as the largest payer and regulator grows, while providers move into the New Middle by carrying more risk in aligned payment structures.

Providence

Growing out of a network of hospitals, schools, and orphanages starting in 1856, Providence St. Joseph Health is currently one of the three largest not-for-profit health systems in the United States, encompassing 51 hospitals, 1,085 clinics, and 120,000 employees serving patients in seven states. The system also operates Providence Health Plan, which covers more than 375,000 members. Providence was no stranger to innovation, having built out several technology products through its Digital Innovation Group.

Providence on the Front Lines

Although our first conversation with Dr. Hochman on January 22, 2020, did not touch on COVID-19, elements of Providence's pandemic strategy could be seen in his descriptions of the innovative, fast-paced culture of the Pacific Northwest and his summary of his main lesson on leadership as being to "listen first, talk less."[3]

By the time of our next discussion on September 21, 2020, the world had changed. Not only had the COVID-19 pandemic spread across the country, but the patients served by Providence were also experiencing social isolation, environmental factors, and unrest around social justice. Dr. Hochman noted that Providence's scale of operations as one of the largest nonprofit health systems, its supply chain capabilities, and its close relationships with nearby technology companies enabled it to distribute key equipment and nimbly adapt to the telehealth environment. Providence's distinction as the first medical center to treat a patient with COVID-19 allowed it to organize quickly, Dr. Hochman said, praising Providence's "fantastic" response in terms of supply chain and capital and calling the crisis "the ultimate stress test."[4]

Even amid all this upheaval, Dr. Hochman kept an eye fixed on the future. He identified telehealth as the most profound driver of change over the next five years and provided caution about the possibility of more infectious disease outbreaks once we emerge from the current pandemic. The economic toll of COVID-19 will not be an easy hole to dig out from—for individuals, organizations, and the federal debt.

Moving Financing toward Shared Accountability

In our interview before COVID-19 erupted, we noted that "affordability" is a term being used more and more often, and Dr. Hochman emphasized that it is everyone's responsibility: insurers, pharmaceutical companies, hospitals, and the public. But with a shared responsibility must come shared accountability, with each component working with one another. Dr. Hochman highlighted the unsustainable status quo of payers and providers perpetually haggling over rates; instead, he said, "we need more partnerships [and] we need to really bring value-based health care together" such that providers are closer to being directly accountable for the premium and both parties share an incentive to reduce costs while improving health outcomes.

This is being accomplished through alliances between health systems and existing payers forming integrated systems on a small scale across the country, Dr. Hochman said, highlighting Providence's Heritage Medical Group in southern California, where the capitated model has been successful in keeping costs down while providing excellent care. However, broad change will require both the will of the health systems and the power of the federal government to change incentive structures. Capitating primary care and thus paying each primary care doctor at the beginning of the year to care for a defined panel of patients, Dr. Hochman said, would be "a first step that would revolutionize the way we do primary care in the United States." The government's role as the largest payer of health care presents enormous opportunities to do so but also frustrating challenges when policies are made without the input of those who do the work of caring for patients and understand how health care is delivered.

Beyond Policy

The best route to have the health system voice heard in policy decisions involves wielding the enormous political influence of public opinion, Dr. Hochman noted, considering that nurses and doctors are frequently ranked as the number one and number two most trusted constituencies by the public. "We don't talk about that enough, but that's the language that Washington, D.C., understands," he added. One of his goals as American Hospital Association chair was to amplify the hospital voice in the political process to a level on par with other industries.

Shifting toward capitation for primary care and ensuring access to comprehensive, affordable, cost-effective primary care would shake up provider delivery models in a way that Dr. Hochman described as a logical place to start solving the health care crisis. Primary care, including preventive medicine, is not necessarily the most expensive area to address, but doing so would have significant downstream benefits for the rest of health care, as it could prevent patients from ever needing to end up in the emergency department or ICU.

Another area of upstream intervention is SDoH, which Providence has addressed with a focus on housing and education. This commitment to population health and well-being reflects Providence's desire to broaden its definition of value to the community beyond simply diagnosing and treating patients inside the hospital walls.

In our first interview, Dr. Hochman highlighted Providence's work on the "4 D's"—digitizing, diversifying, deconstructing, and delivering—to address the challenges of before COVID-19. By the second interview, the pandemic had "changed a considerable number" of Providence's priorities, but Dr. Hochman pointed out several positive developments from its COVID-19 response, including the virtualization and digitization of health care services. Not only are patients receiving care via telehealth, but hospital boards have also become accustomed to meeting online, paving the way for more communication of real-time trends. He foresaw these changes persisting well into the postpandemic period, as "the way we think about health care is changing considerably based on COVID-19."

"Everyone agrees that we should get a better handle on prevention. When I look at health care, we've got to do a better job at the beginning of life and we've got to do a better job at the end of life. That's where a lot of our costs are, whether it's in the NICU or whether it's in the process of leaving this earth. We just need to do a better job with how we manage clinically those situations and then we've got to do a better job of preventing many of the chronic diseases that we have. And it must be through better health practices and providers need to be paid for health, not just the health care. These are general principles, and we need to work with the folks in the government so that they better understand that."

—Rod Hochman, MD

Increasing Dollars for Medicaid Means Fewer Dollars for K–12 Education

Affordability in Medicaid means the more money Medicaid consumes, the less money is available for K–12 education. That's the simple dynamics of where we're at right now.

—Tom Betlach, partner of Speire Health Care Strategies
and former Arizona Medicaid director

We sat down with Tom Betlach in December 2020 to gain his views on how Medicaid programs were affected by the COVID-19 crisis.[5] Medicaid, the joint state-federal program that funds health care for low-income populations, faces the challenge of working within limited state budgets to cover ever-increasing health care costs for a growing population, especially as more states expand Medicaid eligibility and in times of economic crisis. These pressures were amplified during the COVID-19 pandemic, which led to unemployment spikes and decreased tax revenues.

Tom Betlach

Tom Betlach is a nationally recognized consultant who shares his expertise with state Medicaid programs, industry, and think tanks. He is also the former director of the Arizona Health Care Cost Containment System, Arizona's state Medicaid agency. In that capacity, he led the department through steep cuts after the

Great Recession and oversaw expansion of the state's Medicaid program under the ACA's expansion of eligibility. His twenty-seven-year tenure working with Arizona's Medicaid program and his past experience as president of the National Association of Medicaid Directors make him uniquely qualified to lend insight into the intricate policy mechanisms of the state/federal Medicaid program.

Medicaid's Response to COVID-19

We spoke with Betlach just days after the FDA issued its first EUA for a vaccine against SARS-CoV-2. When asked about the key issues that Medicaid directors are thinking about, he mentioned health equity as a top-of-mind concern after the COVID-19 crisis had shone a light on the extent of disparities. Betlach predicted that we will see the federal government move to address disparities through the delivery system as a result, both through managed care at the payer level and through its expectations of large health care delivery systems.

Betlach also discussed the affordability concerns that worry Medicaid directors, considering that Medicaid is the second-largest item in the state budget after K–12 education. With the influx of unemployed individuals entering Medicaid during the initial months of the pandemic, the affordability concern became even more salient because "when Medicaid is consuming more dollars, it's coming at the expense of K–12 education," he said.

State Policy

Betlach predicted that the equity issues seen during COVID-19 would accelerate the move away from FFS toward managed care, a difficult task for state Medicaid directors equipped with only the existing FFS chassis but an area where some smaller states have been successful. He noted the "genuine interest" among congressional staff in better serving that population and said that "it keeps coming back to trying to get them into some managed care system that's really delivering care and financial efficiency for each individual."

The imbalance between the size of the federal government and the states is a concern for Betlach, who pointed out that the health care system will have to undergo significant readjustments when interest rates inevitably increase and the national debt is passed on to future generations. "That's clearly going to take a bipartisan answer to this," said Betlach.

States also wield less leverage than the federal government around sustainability because they are forced to balance their budgets; to do so, cutting rates to providers is often one of the only tools available to cut spending. While states have passed some bills targeting drug pricing, Congress controls the policymaking around it to a large extent. "Ultimately, it seems to me that there needs to be a broader debate around how does pharma fit into this affordability issue," Betlach noted.

Beyond Policy

As we outline in part I, health care legislation must be bipartisan to be broadly accepted by the population. Betlach sees programs for dual-eligible beneficiaries (individuals who are eligible for both Medicare and Medicaid benefits) as a potential area where the framework for a solution can be bipartisan. However, he also notes the difficulty of getting states to invest in these strategies in the present day when they know the savings will accrue to Medicare. A successful framework "to better incentivize states to help coordinate care for dual eligibles" is needed to realize this potential, he said.

Similarly, Betlach recognized the promise of programs to address social determinants in Medicaid and predicted that the federal government would provide more waivers such as those in North Carolina and Arizona, where the states have invested Medicaid dollars in rental housing subsidies. Payers including Medicaid programs may become more eager to coordinate and work with community-based organizations when they realize there's a potential return on investment to be made by broadening what is viewed as a medical expense to include social needs such as transportation, food, and housing. Though social determinants have been a topic of discussion for decades, the imperative to address them and realize these cost savings will expand as states begin to cover more of the adult population through the expansion of Medicaid, Betlach predicted.

One of the largest challenges to Medicaid at the moment is the completeness and quality of data, according to Betlach. Whereas Medicare is able to tap into the Social Security database to access more information, for Medicaid the onus is on individuals to identify their race, ethnicity, and language during the application process, leading to widespread data gaps. Betlach spoke of the need to better incentivize providers and plans to clean up their data and use them to close the gaps in health for vulnerable populations, including children, the elderly, and mothers.

Postpandemic Lessons for Leaders

When the United States inevitably contends with a fiscal reckoning due to unsustainable health spending, said Betlach, the changes will need to be incremental over time. He sees an opportunity to address end-of-life care, an area where the United States far outspends peer countries. There will need to be a broad bipartisan policy debate on how to grapple with these issues after comparing the performance of the United States to other countries, and Betlach acknowledged that it would be a difficult discussion. "Other countries spend a lot of time, effort, and energy on this topic and evaluating it," he said, "and we haven't gotten to that point because we're fearful of the policy debate and the political debate around the topic." Similar to how each dollar spent on Medicaid is a dollar that will not be spent on K–12 education in the state budget, end-of-life care is an area "where we consume resources at the expense of future generations."

"We'll have to wait and see where the solutions start landing. The framework can be bipartisan. Here's one of the challenging issues: States don't invest a lot on their strategies for dual eligible members because they know that the savings accrue to Medicare. It's hard because you have to devote resources in the Medicaid agency for people to learn Medicare and figure out your best ways to manage it. States need incentives to be able to do more, to better serve the dual eligible population. Look for proposals that try to build a framework to better incentivize states to help coordinate care for dual eligibles. States should get some enhanced match and try and really recognize the fact that third party studies have shown that you're going to save Medicare money.

When you're a state Medicaid director, you've got no great way to organize care; from a fee-for-service chassis, it's really difficult. Some smaller states have been successful moving away from fee-for-service. I've already had the opportunity to speak to congressional staff multiple times in the last couple of months. There's genuine interest in terms of trying to figure out better ways to serve that population. It keeps coming back to trying to get them into some managed care system that's really delivering care and financial efficiency for each individual."

—Tom Betlach

Assistance for Those Who Cannot Afford Health Care

Our approach was to form a bipartisan coalition to achieve objectives like lowering the cost of care, reforming the insurance markets, covering preexisting conditions, and if people can't afford it, get them assistance.

—Nancy-Ann DeParle, managing partner and cofounder, Consonance Capital Partners, and former deputy chief of staff to President Barack Obama

The ACA, which became law in 2010, was a next major step to increasing access to health care following the Medicare and Medicaid legislation of 1965. The purpose of the ACA was to increase access particularly for individuals and address the issue of health care affordability. The COVID-19 pandemic exposed gaps in access to health care for, among others, minorities and unemployed or partially employed workers. Broadening coverage under the ACA became a centerpiece of the Biden administration's health policy agenda. Nancy-Ann DeParle's intimate knowledge of federal health policy made her an ideal person to interview in April 2021 to explore her views on postpandemic lessons for leaders.[6]

Nancy-Ann DeParle

Nancy-Ann DeParle has been a remarkably successful leader in both the public and private sectors. Her public-sector experience in government agencies includes leading the Department of Human Services in Tennessee and the Health Care Financing Administration, forerunner of the CMS. As deputy chief of staff to President Obama, she led the development and passage of the ACA.

In the private sector, DeParle has practiced law and is currently managing partner and cofounder of Consonance Capital Partners, a firm providing financing to developing health care companies.

Director of the White House Office of Health Reform and, in 2011, Deputy Chief of Staff

As director of the White House Office of Health Reform for President Obama, DeParle led the ACA legislative initiative, which was passed into law in March 2010. Her federal and state experience administering health and social services programs and her deep knowledge of health care policy and the issues of payment and affordability made her an ideal leader of the ACA campaign.

Payment Is Policy

DeParle grew up in a coal-mining region of Tennessee, where her mother raised the family on her own. During DeParle's high school years, her mother was diagnosed with cancer and subsequently died. As DeParle shared her remembrances, she referred to her mother's concerns following her cancer diagnosis that she would lose her job and her health insurance and not be able to feed and care for her family. DeParle learned early on that "payment is policy," and ensuring affordability for all persons is one reason she devoted her public-sector energy to health care policy.

Leading the Department of Human Services for the State of Tennessee gave DeParle another view of the importance of "being close to what really matters to people." The Department of Human Services administered welfare payments and eligibility for Medicaid and developed programs for child and elder abuse, foster care, and adoption. In each case, she encountered people with everyday personal issues that related to governmental policy and payments.

The ACA

The development and passage of the ACA is a good example of where politics and health policy intersect. DeParle's experience leading health policy programs provided the understanding of health policy, and her discussions with politicians on both sides of the aisle created the outline of the legislative package. The signs of the current political hyperpartisanship were evident in her quest to gain Republican support for the bill. As she said, "I ruined a bunch of pairs of shoes traipsing the halls of the Capitol, meeting with anyone—Republican or Democrat—who would meet with me, and if there was a secret plan to do health reform without Republican support, I didn't get the memo."

DeParle believed that there was general agreement on covering preexisting conditions, with the development exchanges or marketplaces that would sell health plans underwritten by private companies, and though the notion of including a public plan was popular among some progressives, there was not a consensus even among Democrats to include it. She also thought that there was support for a bipartisan approach.

Addressing the fact that there were no Republican votes for the bill, DeParle said, "In the end, there were some hot button issues for them that were not included in the law, but a lot of their ideas were in it, and yet, they still couldn't vote for it. I still don't understand why." She shared that not a day goes by that she doesn't wish that it had been a bipartisan bill, because that would have been a stronger foundation. "I learned that politics can be ugly," she said.

States as Role Models for Federal Health Programs

States will continue to be role models for the development of federal health programs, just as Massachusetts, with its health reform bill passed in 2006, provided policymakers with a role model for the ACA.

DeParle advised the Biden administration during its first one hundred days to consider California a role model for further legislative regulatory initiatives. California was all in: it participated in Medicaid expansion and has been an active regulator and required any insurer interested in bidding on the Medi-Cal business to participate in the ACA marketplace for the uninsured. Additionally, California has committed resources to advertising to encourage people to sign up on the ACA exchanges. There are many insurers offering plans, and premium growth for 2021 was only 0.6 percent. Notably, there is no public plan. To capture DeParle's view, she told us, "There is a whole playbook from California on how to strengthen the ACA, and California has shown that the ACA can be effective in providing affordable coverage."

Postpandemic Lessons for Leaders

We have presented in this book the framework of politics, health policy, provider networks, and data-driven personalization as the foundation for understanding the complexity of health care. The intersections of these four pillars underlie the lessons for leaders in the postpandemic health economy.

No better example exists than the case of the ACA legislation. Policy-makers who designed the bill were building on decades of federal legislation increasing access to health care for the American people. And yet, policy differences interfered with bipartisan support for the most significant piece of health care legislation since Medicare and Medicaid was passed in 1965. Looking back, the legislative vote totals for the Medicare and Medicaid legislation were 313 to 115 in the US House of Representatives and 68 to 21 in the US Senate. Broad bipartisanship on major health legislation in the postpandemic health economy will be difficult to find, but if achieved it will result in more durable legislation.

The interview with DeParle highlighted the fact that when considering health care at the national level, at least three of the 4Ps are critical. Health care is both very personal and fully political, and payment is policy. The intersection between politics and health policy will influence legislation in the postpandemic health economy. Health care leaders will understand that payments will be under more scrutiny than historically.

Macroeconomists are cognizant that the federal government has pumped trillions of dollars into the economy and that the national debt doubled from 2020 to 2021. Jerome Powell, chairman of the Federal Reserve, spoke in mid-2021 about the strong recovery and health of the US economy. Postpandemic health care leaders will be alert to economic cycles and the effect on their investment income and payments from federal and state governments. "Payment is policy" will become ever more relevant in the postpandemic health economy.

"This pandemic has laid bare both systemic strengths and weaknesses in our health system. One of the strengths has been our hospitals. I and others like me have focused on making sure that we're paying the right amount, not too much, not too little, but not too much. We are all a little chastened by what's just happened. You need to have hospitals in rural areas that are solvent. You need critical infrastructure. You need hospitals to be incentivized to invest in proper equipment. We need a little slack in the system. We need to focus on what we are building here.

There is one silver lining even in the pandemic, which has been so challenging for everyone and especially for people whose health has been compromised by it. I think it's highlighted the importance of reliable, dependable, affordable health coverage. It's highlighted the importance of protection against preexisting condition exclusions. Having COVID-19 is a preexisting condition. We don't even know yet all the implications that flow from that, in terms of other disease burdens and long-term consequences.

As President Biden talks about building back better, there should be some element of building up our critical infrastructure in the health care system. Perhaps it's an offset for Medicare bad debt payments, payments to hospitals that are proxies for the additional investments they need to make, or an investment in social equity. Maybe there needs to be social determinants of health investment, maybe there needs to be a pandemic preparedness investment."

—Nancy-Ann DeParle

Notes

1. Reed Abelson, "Major U.S. Health Insurers Report Big Profits, Benefiting from the Pandemic," *New York Times*, August 5, 2020, https://www.nytimes.com/2020/08/05/health/covid-insurance-profits.html.

2. Michael Corkery, "Budget Deficit Hits Record $3.1 Trillion," *New York Times*, October 30, 2020, https://www.nytimes.com/live/2020/10/16/business/us-economy-coronavirus.

3. The content of this case study was gleaned from Rod Hochman's interviews with author Gary Bisbee on January 22, 2020, and March 30, 2020. A longer excerpt of the second interview appeared in Fireside Chat with Gary Bisbee, PhD., "Episode 13."

4. The content of this case study was gleaned from Rod Hochman's interviews with author Gary Bisbee on January 22, 2020.
5. The content of this case study was gleaned from Tom Betlach's interview with authors Gary Bisbee and Sanjula Jain on December 21, 2020.
6. The content of this case study was gleaned from Nancy-Ann DeParle's conversations with authors Gary Bisbee and Sanjula Jain on September 25, 2020, and December 16, 2020. A follow-up conversation was conducted as part of a longer excerpt of The Gary Bisbee Show, "Episode 3."

6

Anchor on Affordability

Lessons for Leaders

In the sixty-five years since 1946, when corporate health benefits were created during World War II, the United States has supported increasing access to health care through multiple legislative and regulatory initiatives.

At the outset of 2020 before COVID-19, the best estimates indicated that 90 percent of the 330 million people in the United States were covered by private insurance, government programs (e.g., Medicare, Medicaid, Department of Defense, Veterans Administration), or personal plans. Those not covered included students, those persons who were eligible for coverage but choose not to sign up, and those who fell through the cracks.

COVID-19 has shown in stark relief that during an economic downturn, people lose jobs and employer-based health insurance. Further, all insurance plans are not created equal, and there can be significant gaps in coverage, particularly among diverse populations. One substantial gap is termed "affordability," whereby people do not have access to coverage because they cannot afford it. Another is termed "health equity," whereby population groups, primarily minority groups, do not have access to care or insurance coverage.

The health priority by the US Congress for the last sixty-five years has been on increasing access to health care through legislation such as Medicare and Medicaid, Medicare Part D pharmaceutical insurance, and the ACA. The 2020s will see the focus turn to the cost of care and its traveling companion, affordability. Balancing coverage for all population groups, or health equity, will become understood as part of access and will gain attention and resources. Affordability for all, including diverse populations, will be addressed and improved throughout the decade by coalitions of the private and public sectors.

The US health system has historically evolved in silos, with providers, health insurance, pharmaceutical, and medical device sectors each having unique financial incentives. There is growing support for a vision of optimizing health care that will integrate and coordinate the silos into a common goal of improving health care for each individual.

Health care is a knowledge industry. Tremendous advances have been made in the creation of knowledge, such as sequencing the genome and digitizing medical care through the HITECH Act of 2009. The current FFS payment model has been described by Ken Paulus as a "rifle shot" for payment.[1] That is, the health system is designed for a provider to perform a single procedure, such as a hip joint replacement, rather than coordinating the procedure within the context of the individual's overall health.

The challenge is for politicians, policymakers, providers, and insurers to engineer a transition from the current prevailing FFS model to one where delivery and financial incentives are aligned with individual convenience and preferences. COVID-19 has caused changes in health policy, such as changing the rules for telemedicine encounters to adjust the licensure requirements and pay for telehealth procedures. There will be short-term, medium-term, and long-term consequences of COVID-19 for federal and state policies. As President Barack Obama said, "Elections have consequences."[2] In this case, COVID-19 has consequences that will influence policy development throughout this decade.

The first three chapters of this book, health care politics, is inextricably linked with health policy, the subject of this section. Sections covering provider networks and data-driven personalization will follow. Chapter 4 provided the background, trends, and a review of key health policy issues. Chapter 5 presented the voice of the leaders in responding to COVID-19 and its influence on the issues discussed in chapter 4. This chapter consolidates the findings of chapters 4 and 5 and develops lessons for leaders (see figure 6.1) that will guide health care leaders during this decade.

Private-Public Leadership Is Shaping Payment Reform

COVID-19, with its self-isolating fundamentals, drove individuals to demand virtual and home care, and providers responded. Kevin Mahoney, CEO of the University of Pennsylvania Health System, indicated in a recent interview that the health system was going to offer a hospital-at-home program.

With today's technology, companies such as Dawnlight can install sensors in the home that feed real-time data to the provider that can become part of the patient's medical record. When asked whether Penn would be reimbursed for the hospital-at-home program, Mahoney focused on the fact that it was the right thing to do for the patient. In the end, with today's technology and

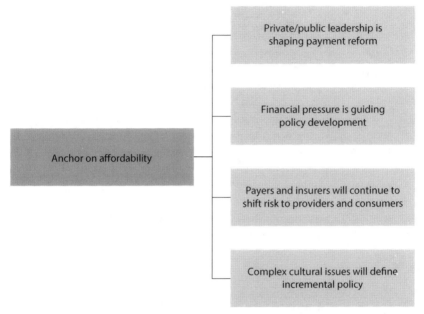

Figure 6.1. Ground rules for health policy and financing.

data systems, it makes sense to develop a payment model for a program that has strong support by patients and providers.

The ground rule outlined in chapter 3 applies to health policy and financing. Specifically, health care reform typically plays out over time. For example, ten years ago, a hospital-at-home model would not have been practical because there was no way to monitor or track the patient while at home. Now, with innovations and new technology, policymakers face a choice about whether expanding home-based services can be a tool for meeting patient preference and increasing affordability.

Financial Pressure Is Guiding Policy Development

We have discussed the fact that health care is the largest item in the federal budget. It is also the largest item in most state budgets. Consequently, health care is not only fully political, it is also highly visible. Health economy financial pressures will grow:

- We will see an increase of twenty-two million baby boomers during the 2020s, or a 44 percent increase from the current fifty-one million.

The average age of a Medicare recipient will increase, resulting in more beneficiaries with multiple chronic diseases and higher-intensity levels. As a result, the Medicare Trust Fund will be depleted in 2024 given the current projections.

- In addition, financial pressures associated with Medicaid are increasing. As of March 2021, COVID-19 led to significant growth in enrollment resulting in eighty-two million people receiving Medicaid and CHIP benefits, with nearly a quarter of states having yet to expand Medicaid.
- COVID-19–related debt in the multiple trillions of dollars will need to be retired, putting further pressure on health care as the largest item in the federal budget.

"Affordability in the Medicaid space means the more money Medicaid consumes, the less money is available for K–12 education."

—Tom Betlach, former Arizona Medicaid director

The conclusion to be reached from this discussion is that policymakers and all stakeholders will feel constant and growing pressure to moderate the increase in health care expenditures. What options exist? Broadly speaking, eligibility may be tightened, eliminating persons from coverage. A second alternative would be for services to be eliminated or trimmed back. But again, on a wide scale, this seems unlikely from the federal government.

A third and more likely option is a shift in the incentive structure from FFS to managed care. Depending on how the program is structured, there may be bipartisan agreement with this model. The affirmative case for change is the presumption that managed care would lower the use of expensive hospital care and certain surgeries, increase the use of ambulatory and telehealth care, and generally become more efficient.

Payers and Insurers Will Continue to Shift Risk to Providers and Consumers

What do we mean by risk? The term "risk" generally refers to both health risk and financial risk, since they can be directly related. Let's say that we have a $1,000 deductible before our health insurance kicks in. If we avoid treatment because we can't afford $1,000, we are bearing the health risk and may be causing future financial risk if avoiding care causes further complications and treatment.

As health care costs have risen, we have seen strategies to shift risk from payer and insurance company to consumer and provider. One example for managing that shift is the high-deductible health plan. This approach has been used extensively by employers. Medicare has also implemented cost-sharing provisions (e.g., deductibles and co-pays), as have some Medicaid plans. These cost-sharing provisions are useful for shifting risk to individuals, but they may not solve the problem of overuse of expensive procedures and admissions or readmissions.

Let's also discuss the term "payer." Payers are those organizations that are ultimately responsible for health care coverage: employers, governments, or the individual. As of January 2021, corporate health benefits are provided to approximately 155 million persons through their employers. Medicare provides coverage to 51 million baby boomers and 9 million other individuals. Medicaid programs cover 80 million persons. Health insurance plans are considered fiscal intermediaries. The payers (i.e., governments and employers) contract with them to administer, market, and provide additional services.

Home care is an example of a risk shift that may be preferable for the health insurer, the provider, and the individual. A growing number of patients would prefer to be at home rather than in a hospital. With today's technology, such as sensors and data monitoring capabilities, it is feasible to develop policies to cover hospital-at-home programs and other noninpatient services. As Terry Shaw, president and CEO of AdventHealth, explained, home care requires coordination across the care continuum and a business model shift. It fits the preferences of the consumer, and is an asset light approach that fits into AdventHealth's 2030 strategy.

Managed Care

Managed care is a payment and organizational model designed to consider the health of the individual rather than provide a rifle-shot service to receive payment (e.g., knee joint replacement), which is the profile of the FFS system. The managed care or "value" model is designed to align incentives between providers, insurers, payers, and consumers to increase the use of less expensive ambulatory or telemedicine services, lower the use of expensive hospital services, and increase preventive services.

Moving to one of several value or managed care models may allow more control of expenditures and provide care more aligned with consumers' interests of convenience and nonhospital location. During the 1980s, it was popular for health systems to create HMOs to provide insurance services on a per-member per-month basis. Many of those early HMOs were closed or sold to insurance companies because the health system was not experienced in operating them. Of those that remained, the largest include health plans operated by systems such as the University of Pittsburgh Medical Center, Providence, Intermountain Healthcare, Spectrum Health, and Sentara Healthcare.

ChristianaCare, a large health system located in Delaware, is a good example of a health system that formed an HMO during the 1980s and sold it. Recently, ChristianaCare and Highmark Health, a health insurer, formed a joint venture to redesign the relationship between a provider, an insurer, and the individual. ChristianaCare president and CEO Dr. Janice Nevin said, "We are rethinking the way care is delivered and the way it's paid for, creating a new health care ecosystem that will enable better health and more affordable, accessible, high-quality care that is continuous and data-driven."[3]

With today's low-margin hospital business, it is financially challenging for a health system to form a wholly-owned commercial health plan. Partnerships with insurers are the more opportune model, since starting a health plan de novo takes sustained commitment of capital that most health systems cannot commit.

The relationship between providers delivering services and insurers paying for services creates a natural conflict, in part because the two organizations have very different goals. The health insurer is tasked with slowing growth of health services, and the provider is incentivized to treat the individual, which increases the number of services. Creating a common goal of providing for the health of the individual may change the contentious dynamic between them.

Managed care models have at their core a narrow network, which is a defined group of physicians, hospitals, and services. One purpose of a narrow network is for the sponsor (health insurer or health system) to work closely with the physicians and hospitals so they understand and conform to a single set of rules and resources available to them.

Other forms based on narrow networks are ACOs and PPOs. Both are based on a narrow network. Their results have been mixed regarding the cost savings, although outcomes may be somewhat improved. A fully integrated model of prevention, the use of least expensive but necessary services, and a narrow network of providers is generally considered by policymakers as the most efficient and effective payment model.

Medicare Advantage

MA, sponsored by Medicare, is a managed care model that contracts with private insurers to operate the narrow network and manage care benefits. MA is popular among Medicare beneficiaries, with approximately half of newly eligible Medicare beneficiaries electing MA.

Dennis Murphy, president and CEO of Indiana University Health, during our recent interview spoke about the innovative approach to hip and knee joint replacement in Indiana University Health's MA program.[4] Rather than admit the patient post surgery to a rehabilitation facility or hospital, the procedure is performed as day surgery, and the patient is discharged to home with no overnight stay in a facility. Of course, there is an aggressive support and rehabilitation program conducted at the patient's home with the assistance of specialty experts and technology.

Larger health systems and private insurance companies frequently work together to sponsor and manage the MA plan. MA is a public-private partnership, with Medicare paying the premiums, a private insurance company administering the program, and private health systems or physician groups providing health care services.

Complex Cultural Issues Will Define Incremental Policy

Changing social and cultural issues require sustained attention and patience, since the issues have an emotional context and require redistribution of resources. Vaccination for COVID-19 is an example of a situation whereby the benefits to the individual and society are well documented, but some people refuse to take the vaccine. Changing the individual's perception requires continued education and patience.

We will discuss three issues in this section: social determinants of health, health equity, and end-of-life care. There are other social and cultural issues worthy of discussion, but the first two have gained public visibility and traction because of COVID-19.

Social Determinants of Health

SDoH are based on findings that good health is connected to where and how people live, work, learn, transport themselves, and eat. Historically, social service agencies and health systems operated in silos. A range of early-stage, venture-backed companies such as Unite Us have been formed to connect social and health services using the latest technology and networking strategies. This has provided a new comprehensive way to identify resources for those needing connection to social or health services or, as is frequently the case, both.

Intermountain Healthcare is participating in the Alliance for the Determinants of Health with community partners. This demonstration project is taking place in two counties in Utah. The project is defining health outcomes based on changes in social conditions. Early results are promising in finding that addressing gaps in social services improves health.

Social and health care communities have long-standing awareness of SDoH. The fundamental problem is that there has not been enough financial support allocated to addressing them. Increasingly, health systems and health insurers are defining their mission more broadly to address SDoH in advance of a medical encounter.

Health Equity

Health equity refers to the belief that all people have a fair and just opportunity to be healthy. Full health equity requires addressing poverty and racial and other forms of discrimination and providing access to jobs, quality education, affordable housing, and a safe environment. COVID-19 caused substantial visibility of the gaps in health equity when minority populations contracted COVID-19 at a higher rate than the general population and died at a faster rate.

As an example of a real-world program to address health equity is the Yale Medical School, which formed a program in 2010, the Yale Cultural Ambassadors Program, in which community leaders work closely with the Yale Medical School and the Yale New Haven Health System to encourage more members of minority communities to participate in clinical trials and learn more about health and science. "When we are in Washington, we tend to homogenize health care, and health care is too heterogeneous," according to Marna Borgstrom, former CEO, Yale New Haven Heath System.[5]

The Cultural Ambassador program has formed a new Youth Ambassadors program to attract younger members of the minority communities to learn more about health and science. The Cultural Ambassador program is working with other academic medical centers that are interested in replicating the model. The Yale Medical School has appointed the first associate dean of health equity, Dr. Marcella Nunez-Smith, to interact with and advance health equity with the community surrounding Yale University.

As a result of COVID-19, health equity has a much higher level of visibility among both the public and private sectors. Look for progress to be made on this difficult issue throughout the 2020s.

End-of-Life Care

As the baby boomers age and life expectancy increases, people are living longer and inevitably are more likely to develop multiple chronic diseases and confront end-of-life decisions. End-of-life decisions are highly personal; they will frequently involve the family, where all may not agree on a course of action, and in many cases religion may have rules that provide guidance. The United States has not had a broad national dialogue on the topic of resources provided at the end of life.

Currently, physicians are taught to provide a full and continuing range of services for patients. For example, when a person is admitted to an ICU with little or no chance of living, he or she may prefer not to be admitted, or the family might have preferences. Of course, these decisions are highly personal, and family and religious guidance are part of the equation. Hospice care focuses on the palliation of a terminally ill patient's pain and symptoms and attends to the patient's emotional and spiritual needs at the end of life. Hospice care is structured to prioritize comfort and quality of life by reducing pain and suffering.

Increasingly, people prefer end-of-life decisions to be made among the individual, the family (if involved), and the physician. This will be a difficult issue for governments to legislate, and there is no indication that governments are interested in discussing it in public forums. And yet, the issue will be addressed sooner or later in the context of costs, given estimates that one-third of Medicare expenditures are provided in the last days of a person's life. This is an issue to be aware of and prepare for, as it will surface at some point in this decade.

"End-of-life care is just yet another example of where we consume resources at the expense of future generations."
—Tom Betlach, former Arizona Medicaid director

International comparisons are useful when the countries are similar to the United States in socioeconomic status. We know that health care expenditures up until age fifty-five are similar for each country. Beyond age fifty-five, the United States shows a dramatic and exponential increase. Since life expectancy is increasing, people are living longer with chronic disease and multiple comorbidities, which is dramatically increasing expenditures.

What to make of this international comparison? Most Western countries discuss end-of-life issues more openly than the United States, and by some estimates end-of-life expenditures consume one-third of Medicare expenditures. End-of-life care may not lead to improved outcomes or life expectancy. There are cultural, religious, and family perspectives surrounding this issue. At some point during the 2020s, we as a country will need to begin to discuss end-of-life care.

Since World War II, health policy has been focused primarily on increasing access, primarily to acute care. The 2020s will see substantially more focus on affordability, health equity, and policies that are more responsive to the pref-erences of consumers while providing appropriate and quality care at lower cost. "We'll look back and remember with sadness the pain the country went through," notes Kevin Mahoney, CEO of the University of Pennsylvania Health System. "But as the next decade unfolds, we're going to see [these] dark years as a time when so many things that we had talked about turned into action and turned into small actions that led to larger actions and to a better health care system than we had before."[6]

Notes

1. Gary Bisbee, conversation with Ken Paulus, June 11, 2020. For a longer interview with Paulus, see Fireside Chat with Gary Bisbee, Ph.D., "Episode 42."
2. https://www.realclearpolitics.com/articles/2014/08/13/too_bad_obama_didnt _follow_his_own_advice_123650.html.
3. Janice Nevin, telephone conversation with author Gary Bisbee, December 14, 2020.
4. Dennis Murphy, telephone conversation with author Gary Bisbee, December 17, 2020.
5. Fireside Chat with Gary Bisbee, Ph.D., "Episode 81."
6. Fireside Chat with Gary Bisbee, Ph.D., "Episode 74."

PART III

Provider Networks

7

All Health Care Is Local

Background

Dr. Darius Rastegar a Johns Hopkins internist, in his 2004 book *Health Care Becomes an Industry*, observed that the delivery of health care is in the process of "industrialization" similar to other industries a century ago.[1] Increasing division of labor, role and task standardization, and consolidation promises more efficient and effective health care. Dr. Rastegar had it right. No sector within health care met his framing more than hospitals.

The oldest hospitals in the United States were founded in the mid-1700s. Bellevue Hospital, founded in 1736, is now part of New York City Health and Hospitals Corporation; Pennsylvania Hospital, founded in 1751, is now part of the University of Pennsylvania Health System; New York Hospital, founded in 1771, is now part of New York-Presbyterian; and Johns Hopkins Hospital, founded in 1773, is now part of Johns Hopkins Health System.

The fact that the four oldest hospitals in the United States are owned by large multihospital systems is no accident. Consolidation among the nation's hospitals began in earnest in the mid-1970s, largely among hospitals with religious affiliations. The religious sponsors were pursuing their missions to serve a broader set of communities, hospital revenues were growing, hospital finances became more complex, and increased size allowed the health systems to realize economies of scale, share resources and talent, and capitalize on shared infrastructure.

Historically, hospitals were autonomous and governed by local leaders.[2] Merging with other hospitals was a concept that grew slowly. Hospital leaders saw that larger hospital entities could attract higher-level talent, acquire technology, and increase ability to negotiate with larger health insurers and pharmaceutical and medical device companies. In addition, as Medicare and Medicaid grew from their introduction in 1966, regulations increased, creating much more complex reporting and operations.

As compared to hospitals founded three hundred years ago, health insurance companies in the United States are the new kid on the block, with the oldest, Blue Cross, being founded one hundred years ago. The health insurance business was given substantial tailwinds during World War II when the US Tax Board indicated that corporate health benefits would not be taxed. Health insurers grew rapidly and firmed up their roles as intermediaries between employers who paid for coverage and the providers who delivered the services.

The relationship between hospitals, doctors, and Blue Cross plans was relatively collegial through the mid-1900s. In fact, Blue Cross was affiliated with the American Hospital Association until 1972. The Blue Cross and Blue Shield organizations merged in 1982.

The inherently contentious relationship between health insurers and providers grew as financial pressures on health care increased. Margins on the hospital and health insurance businesses tracked down as government payments became a larger part of revenues. Both health insurers and hospitals valued increased scale to create operating efficiency as well as to gain leverage in negotiations.

Health care does not exist in a vacuum, of course, and consolidation was well under way in most other sectors of the economy—for example, commercial banking, automobiles, entertainment, energy, and media. Society had become more complex, and scale was seen both as a defensive and an offensive strategy.

The Advent of the Large Provider Health Systems and Health Plans

Amid shifting business model realities, mergers and acquisitions emerged as a key instrument in the tool kits of providers and insurance companies. Hospital consolidation began in the mid-1970s primarily with religious hospitals. In the 1990s, the promise of managed care led to a wave of consolidation. The 2010s brought a second far larger wave with a burst of activity following the Great Recession of 2008–9.

During the second half of the decade, merger and acquisition transaction volumes for hospitals consistently exceeded one hundred acquisitions per year starting in 2014.[3] And while the closing part of the decade saw deal count begin to flatten, transacted revenue volume skyrocketed, with the net patient revenue of the average seller exceeding $400 million.[4] The debates about whether scale matters and how, have clearly been answered by the need for health systems to negotiate with much larger health insurers, suppliers, and the biggest payer of all, the federal government. Northwell's Michael Dowling, who built one of the largest health systems in the country, wrote that the COVID-19 crisis and

Table 7.1. Revenues of large health systems compared to leading industry brands, 2020

	Health System	Industry Brands
	$10 billion	
Company revenue	Banner Health $10.4 billion	Marriott $10.5 billion
	$19 billion	
Company revenue	Trinity Health $18.8 billion	McDonald's $19.2 billion
	$26 billion	
Company revenue	Providence $26 billion	Kraft $26 billion

Source: Jain, *2021 Trends Shaping the Post-Pandemic Health Economy.* (Brentwood, TN: Trilliant Health, 2021).

requirements for scale in supplies, clinicians, and caregivers of all types unequivocally reinforced the benefits of a large integrated health system.[5] "Scale matters if you do it the right way," he said in an interview. "The idea of systemness during the COVID crisis was one of the keys to our success in dealing with it."[6]

These consolidation waves have created enormous health enterprises. In 2020, the largest not-for-profit health system was CommonSpirit at approximately $30 billion in annual revenues. HCA, an investor-owned hospital company, realized $51 billion, while Kaiser Permanente, a hospital, physician, and health insurance behemoth, recorded $85 billion. Forty large health systems would qualify for the *Fortune* 500 if they were listed companies. The average size of the largest one hundred health systems is over $7 billion in annual revenue. As a frame of reference, Providence realized around $26 billion of revenue, which is similar to annual revenue realized by Kraft (see table 7.1).

Consumer expectations, the increased percentage of government payments, and the sheer size of the opportunities and challenges together have influenced the evolution of health system business models. The core strategic rationale for provider mergers and acquisitions centers on three objectives. Consolidators believe that they can cut costs, increase productivity, and gain material economics of scale.[7]

There are, however, reasons to wonder if structural differences within provider health care complicate execution. In the early 1980s, the Hospital Research and Education Trust published a collection of essays under the title *Multihospital Systems: Policy Issues for the Future.* In it, now–Syracuse University professor

Carl Schramm wrote the essay "Hospital Consolidation: Lessons from Other Industries."[8]

After looking extensively at banking, trucking, passenger airlines, retail groceries, and automobile manufacturing, Schramm concluded that there were reasons to wonder if health care was different. The cultural differences of not-for-profit health care complicate integration efforts. Strategies around technology-driven standardization are far more challenging, particularly advancement of a clinical standard of care. State and local political sensitivities around postacquisition integration, ranging from head count reduction to facility closures, are real.

The durability of the Schramm analysis is striking. His writing is reinforced further by the forward march of federal spending in health care. Four decades later, US health care providers increasingly resemble public utilities in the core markets in which they operate. Industry-wide consolidation typically occurs when operating margins decline, and scale is a natural step to spreading fixed costs over a larger group of customers. Hospital and health system margins have been declining, and leaders expect this trend to continue as the percentage of revenue from governments increases.

The largest health insurers were formed in the 1970s and 1980s. United Health Group was founded in 1977; Anthem as a corporate entity was formed in 2004 and is made up of twelve Blue Cross plans that had been in business for fifty to sixty years or more; and Cigna predecessors had been in business for two hundred years, but the current Cigna health insurance business was formed in 1982. Blue Cross Blue Shield of America as a single entity was created in 1982. It owns thirty-five Blue Cross plans and covers fifty states.

Health insurance consolidation in many ways paralleled that of hospitals. Mergers and acquisitions picked up steam as operating scale and negotiating leverage became more important.

Scale matters in industries with low margins, as we have seen in both health insurance and health systems similarly bearing low single-digit margins. For health care providers and insurers, the shift in payer mix strained operating margins. Government programs such as Medicare and Medicaid pay hospitals less than employer-based payments. As the baby boomers reach the age of sixty-five, they retire, drop their commercial health plans, and pick up Medicare coverage. The effect on hospitals creates pressure on margins. The average annual operating margin for hospitals and health systems fell during the 2010s (see figure 7.1), with the decline for the largest one hundred health systems falling to less than 3 percent by 2017. Operating margins for health insurers, from the health insurance business, fell over the same time frame and to the same levels.

The inexorable decline in operating margin has left providers and health insurers searching for new revenue and margin opportunities, seeking expense-

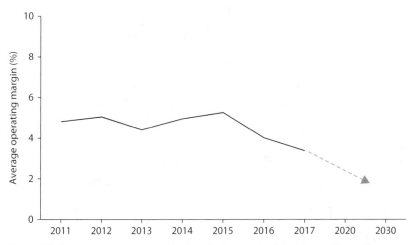

Figure 7.1. Average operating margins for the largest health systems. Operating margins have been steadily declining since 2015, with an average margin of 3.2 percent among the largest 150 health systems. Among the megahealth systems with total operating revenue of $5B or more, the average operating margin falls to 2.7 percent. *Source:* Authors' analysis of 2017 publicly available financial reports.

line efficiencies to make money at Medicare (and Medicaid) rates, and thinking far more expansively about what will be required to balance margin and mission in the decade to come.

Margin pressures can lead to novel business model approaches, such as the acquisition of Aetna by CVS in which CVS is betting on Aetna subscribers driving business to CVS retail pharmacies and health clinics.

Consolidation Strategy

On a comparative basis, the level of national consolidation within provider health care remains low. The American Hospital Association puts the total number of registered hospitals at more than 5,500.[9] Only four health systems (HCA, Ascension, CommonSpirit, and Community Health Systems) have more than one hundred hospitals.[10] Comparatively, the top four airlines control close to 80 percent of all domestic capacity.[11] The top four health insurers control about the same percentage of market share.[12]

For providers, the more telling view may be at the core-based statistical area (CBSA), or "zip code" level, of the market. Health care delivery is, of course, largely local. A look at the US Census Department's CBSA data set finds that almost half of provider mergers in the last decade have occurred within a defined geographic area.[13] Through that lens, the level of consolidation at the defined CBSA or market level rivals other regulated, heavily consolidated industries.

Broadly defined, consolidation tends to follow an established curve described by Deans, Kroeger, and Zeisel in *Harvard Business Review*.[14] The authors' research indicates that consolidation has four discrete stages: opening, scale, focus, and balance/alliance. Many of the largest US industries are now late in this consolidation curve ranging from telecommunications and banking to commercial aviation and health insurers.

The authors concluded that companies that evaluate each strategic and operational alternative as to how it will advance them through the four stages will be the most successful. Early movement and speed of decision making will add to success and lower risk of failure. Slower firms, or those that ignore the need underlying consolidation, eventually become acquisition targets and will likely disappear. "There is value to these kinds of crises in narrowing our priorities. It forces us to be crystal clear about what's important," noted Jim Skogsbergh, president and CEO of Advocate Aurora Health.[15]

As noted, health systems are comparatively early on in forming national level networks, but consolidation within discrete CBSA or zip codes is much more advanced. We can see those realities reflected in the balance and alliance strategies being pursued by top health systems within their core markets, ranging from joint ventures in the health insurance space to direct-to-employer collaborations with large self-insured companies. The large health insurers, however, are already national in scope and are actively expanding into health care delivery.

Given the trends in the health economy that we have discussed, such as margin pressures, demographics, and expectations of individuals for more convenient and affordable care, we expect to see horizontal and vertical consolidation continue at a strong pace, within the boundaries of the Federal Trade Commission and the Department of Justice.

The Emergence of Private-Sector Public Health Utilities

COVID-19 has increased visibility to the fact that health systems filled the role of public health infrastructure through vaccine administration and testing and, in effect, positioned them as a private-sector public health utility. A public utility, at the definitional level, "furnishes an everyday necessity to the public."[16] The utility provides capabilities that are essential and desirous for a community, ranging from water to telecommunication services to electricity. Utility rates are set by government, albeit usually by state and local governments. Public utilities carry a significant community obligation.

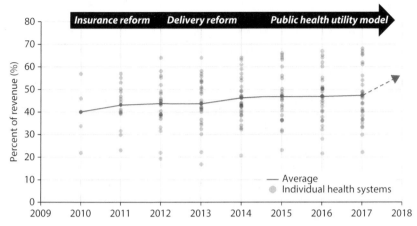

Figure 7.2. Proportion of health system revenue attributed to government payments. On average, nearly half of the largest health systems' revenue is tied to government sources (e.g., Medicare, Medicaid). This proportion grew by 17 percent from 2010 to 2017. While the percent of revenue attributed to government payments across health systems spans a large range, many health systems such as Montefiore in New York represent proportions as high as 70 percent. *Source:* Authors' analysis of data provided by publicly available financial reports (2018).

In our view many US health care systems have largely reached this status today, which has been accelerated by COVID-19. When Washington is responsible for half or more of the revenue of a given health system (see figure 7.2) and sets the terms of payment at a defined rate, we are describing a private-sector public health utility.

The day-to-day implications of this change in status are profound. For providers of care, it informs capital allocation. The status of private-sector public health utility impacts speed of decision making, including, as Schramm noted, in areas surrounding postacquisition integration. Efforts to rethink the practice and delivery of medicine are made more difficult as Washington payment models complicate organizational change and make it challenging to meet rising consumer expectations around price, convenience, and service. For the large health insurers, the change in status affects their strategies and business models.

Pursing the New Middle

As payment models continue to shift toward value-based care, the opportunity to engage the person will evolve with it. Both providers and health insurance plans face a key strategic choice around how they seek to define their community value proposition. Who will eliminate the cost inefficiencies and consumer frustrations that exist in the complicated administrative middle between consumer demand and health care supply?

We believe that there will be a New Middle built out in US health care in the decades ahead. By New Middle, we refer to the ultimate in person-centered health care. The models to deliver the New Middle are found at the intersection of delivery and financing, where services are delivered based on the patient's need without reference to the cost of a specific service, test, or procedure, as in an FFS model. These models are typically referred to as managed care, or value-based, models.

The natural evolution of the health care system toward a person-centric model was envisioned by the late Cerner CEO Neal Patterson, who coined the term "New Middle" in the present context. That is, a person-centric model requires doctors and other caregivers in an environment where incentives of providers, persons, and financing are aligned. The proper incentive structure changes the role of the health insurer, as utilization review and appropriateness are managed by aligned stakeholders. The traditional role of insurers as the intermediaries between payers and providers is shifting to a commodity-like status. In this case, providers will carry more of the member's health risk balanced by the opportunity to realize more financial margin and improve quality.

Some health insurers seeing this evolution occur are moving to add health services and providers. For example, United Health Group through its Optum Health subsidiary employs at least fifty thousand physicians. Humana has moved into home care and other services outside the hospital enhanced by its recent acquisition of Kindred.

The acceptance of the New Middle has been slow to evolve. The first reference to a managed care model in the United States was made in the Committee on the Cost of Medical Care report of 1932, which was the first national report on the organization and financing of health care. Reference was made to the value-based model financed by a per-member per-month payment. Kaiser Permanente, founded in 1945 to provide health care to workers on Kaiser projects, has a long history of success, primarily in California where Kaiser currently has over twelve million members. Kaiser's efforts at expansion outside of California have not gone well.

In the 1980s, newly formed health systems were encouraged to form HMOs in part because of the Health Maintenance Organization Act of 1973, which provided grants for building HMOs. There was also a belief by providers that the value-based model was superior to FFS for treating the whole patient.

Many of the health systems that formed an HMO underestimated the complexity of managing care, from actuarial foundation to databases to managing patients who traveled out of area. Development of a network of providers and social services agencies was not envisioned as a top priority and was a drag on growth of members and substantially inflated costs.

Many of these HMOs were sold to insurance companies or closed down. There are around a dozen of these early HMOs that are striving to provide a person-centric set of services.[17] The largest is the University of Pittsburgh Medical Center, with 3.5 million members, and Intermountain Healthcare, Spectrum Health, Sentara Healthcare, and the Oregon region of Providence each have nearly 1 million members. Many more health systems own or operate MA or Medicaid managed care plans.

The shining star for a managed care or value-based model at the national level is MA. This CMS-orchestrated business has attracted around 50 percent of newly Medicare-eligible individuals who select MA rather than Medicare FFS. The ACA provided a demonstration for ACOs that have had mixed success primarily because of structural and regulatory requirements. United Health is the largest health insurer sponsoring MA plans. Humana is the second-largest MA sponsor. Many health systems have formed their own plans or are in a health insurance–sponsored network.

The historical lines between provider health systems and health insurers is blurring as their roles and business models evolve. The core business of health systems is to deliver health care. The historical core business of health insurers is to provide insurance and associated administrative services. The overlap is caused by an important question: Who is best suited to provide person-centric care and manage the health of the individual?

> "Health plans and providers [will] align with incentives for the consumer/member to become healthier, and the total cost of care [will be] lower and the quality of care [will be] higher."
>
> —Craig Samitt, MD, former president and CEO,
> Blue Cross Blue Shield of Minnesota

Physicians have a special relationship with patients that is referred to as "a sacred trust."[18] As more health insurers pursue the development of care-providing structures and health systems pursue financing models, physicians are a key to success. The New Middle has been slow in coming, but the evolving health systems and insistent demands by consumers for convenient, affordable, and satisfying health services are creating more options by both health systems and some health insurers to merge the financing and delivery of health care.

As Dee Hock, the entrepreneurial founder of Visa, once opined, "The problem is never how to get new innovative ideas into your head; it is how to get the old ones out."[19]

Notes

1. Rastegar, "Health Care Becomes an Industry."
2. Koster, Bisbee, and Charan, $n = 1$.
3. Singh, "2019 Healthcare M&A in Review."
4. Singh.
5. Dowling and Kenney, *Leading through a Pandemic*.
6. Fireside Chat with Gary Bisbee, Ph.D., "Episode 55."
7. Weeks, Greene, and Weinstein, "Potential Advantages of Health System Consolidation and Integration."
8. Schramm, "Hospital Consolidation."
9. American Hospital Association, "Fast Facts on US Hospitals."
10. Dyrda, "100 of the Largest Hospitals and Health Systems in America."
11. Ben Mutzabaugh, "Era of Airline Merger Mania Comes to a Close with Last US Airways Flight," *USA Today*, October 16, 2015, https://www.usatoday.com/story/travel/flights/todayinthesky/2015/10/15/airline-mergers-american-delta-united-southwest/73972928/.
12. Dafny, "Evaluating the Impact of Health Insurance Industry Consolidation."
13. Gaynor, "Examining the Impact of Health Care Consolidation."
14. Deans, Kroeger, and Zeisel, "The Consolidation Curve."
15. Fireside Chat with Gary Bisbee, Ph.D., "Episode 57."
16. Jain, "Investment in Government Relations."
17. Jain, "Health System Revenue Attributed to Health Plan Premiums."
18. Harris, *A Sacred Trust*.
19. Waldrop, "Dee Hock on Management."

8

The Frontline Battle

Interviews

The adage "scale matters" played out immediately as COVID-19 surged from region to region throughout the United States. The immediate problem of not being able to predict the surge hit Seattle, the New York region, and Detroit with little warning. Health systems received no predictive guidance about timing of the surge from the CDC. Not wanting to be caught short again, each health system set up a command center that built a team of epidemiologists and data analytics experts to develop their own predictive models.

Each of these teams also built tracking mechanisms to monitor the progression of the surge and the evolution of patient outcomes during the surge. The level of sophistication of these activities far exceeded predictive and tracking models of the past. The large health systems had the resources in hand, in terms of talented experts, sophisticated software and hardware, and data collection capabilities. Although Dr. Darius Rastegar may not have envisioned the COVID-19 pandemic in "Health Care Becomes an Industry," he clearly referenced the capability of health systems to respond.

Almost immediately as the surge unfolded PPE was in short supply, with little assistance from the national stockpile. Efforts to obtain PPE were expensive and labor-intensive and required sophisticated international approaches. The efforts were well beyond the capabilities of an individual hospital or even small health systems. In short, those hospital leaders who initiated hospital consolidation and challenged the historical local governance model had it right. The larger health systems had the advantage of resources, talent, and expertise.

So little was known about COVID-19 in terms of transmission, testing, and treatment that calls were immediately placed to medical colleagues in Italy,

China, and other countries that were managing their own surges. As ventilators were in short supply, particularly in the first surge, and those obtained from the federal stockpile were of little use because they were outdated or not maintained, clinicians at New York-Presbyterian (NYP) developed a technique to use a ventilator for more than one patient, an innovation taking place on the other side of the country at Providence in Seattle. Tests were developed at health systems that shortened the turnaround time for results rather than sending to centralized laboratories that were overwhelmed with demand. Techniques were developed to clean PPE on site.

In short, health systems, clinicians, caregivers, and administrators were fighting a battle that few of them could ever imagine. As they championed curve-flattening containment, leaders were simultaneously advancing strategies around mitigation for a virus with a troubling level of silent spread. COVID-19 had a first-order impact on our communities, bringing durable second- and third-order effects ranging from renewed focus on diagnostics to increased virtualization of care to supply chain management. Underlying it all was widespread recognition of provider organizations as a vital national asset whose lifesaving impact was increasingly on full display.

For their part, health insurers were communicating with the CMS, employers, physicians, and health systems to monitor the progression of COVID-19. The explosion of telehealth as people stayed away from in-person contact with physicians and hospitals brought up questions of payment. Most of the health insurers followed the CMS's lead and paid for televisits, at least during the heat of the surge. Longer term, each health insurer worked through what its policy would be in paying for televisits going forward.

Since elective surgeries were postponed at the direction of state and local governments, hospitals lost substantial revenue and bore the expenses of maintaining the facility, the equipment, and people. Of course, the health insurers benefited financially by not having to pay for elective procedures that were budgeted but did not occur. As the initial COVID-19 surge tailed off in the early summer of 2020, patients who had put off surgery began to flood back.

The next challenge for the health systems was the administration of vaccines, with EUA for the Pfizer/BioNTech COVID-19 vaccine on December 11, 2020, and the Moderna vaccine shortly thereafter on December 18, 2020. The first step for health systems was to vaccinate their own employees and medical staff. Larger health systems have over one hundred thousand persons located in multiple states and locations. Since the public health infrastructure was not designed to administer the high volume of shots necessary, the health systems were called upon to administer vaccines to the community.

COVID-19 Interviews

In the discussions that follow, you will have the opportunity to hear firsthand from three CEOs, two from large health systems in the center of two of the hardest-hit areas, Detroit and the epicenter of New York City, and one from Blue Cross Blue Shield of Minnesota (BCBSM).

Dr. Steven Corwin leads NYP. Dr. Corwin and team increased ICU beds from four hundred to nine hundred almost overnight, scaled down elective surgery, repurposed and trained staff to treat COVID-19 patients, and guided frontline workers through an extremely stressful crisis likely leading to PTSD for some of them.

Wright Lassiter had been CEO of the Henry Ford Health System for four years when COVID-19 exploded. He immediately took steps to ensure that caregivers' safety and health were being quickly and clearly addressed. Lassiter shared with us that the frontline staff were handling a very stressful situation, in

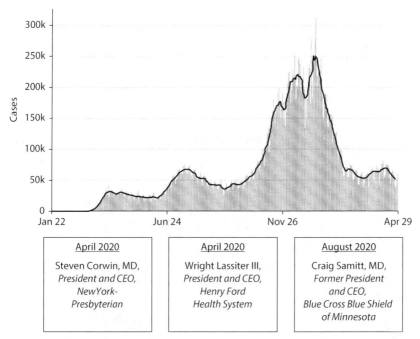

April 2020	April 2020	August 2020
Steven Corwin, MD, President and CEO, New York-Presbyterian	Wright Lassiter III, President and CEO, Henry Ford Health System	Craig Samitt, MD, Former President and CEO, Blue Cross Blue Shield of Minnesota

Figure 8.1. Featured case study interviews from a provider networks lens. *Source:* Data from Centers for Disease Control and Prevention, 2021. Figures are updated as of May 1, 2021, from the COVID Data Tracker and underlying data set available at https://covid.cdc.gov/covid-data-tracker/#datatracker-home.

part because they had seen 250 COVID-19 patients die in the space of three weeks, which was more than most staff had seen die in their entire careers.

Dr. Craig Samitt has been a leader in provider organizations and health insurers. He is using the COVID-19 crisis to attack gaps and structural challenges in the health care system. Dr. Samitt is outspoken about how we need to seek alignment between providers, payment models, and the person.

These leaders and others like them offered real-time thoughts over the course of 2020 (see figure 8.1) and into 2021 on how their organizations responded to the COVID-19 crisis and, amid response and recovery, what it might look like as they reimagine key aspects of how health care services are organized, financed, and delivered.

Getting Upstream with the Patient

Getting upstream with the patient becomes really important. So you think of yourself as a health system with a strong population health program, not an acute illness system.

—Steven J. Corwin, MD, president and CEO, NewYork-Presbyterian

NewYork City was the epicenter of the coronavirus pandemic and its COVID-19 crisis. We interviewed Dr. Steven Corwin first in January 2020 and then in mid-June 2020, around sixty days after the peak of the crisis on April 11, 2020.[1] We had the unique opportunity to gain Dr. Corwin's views before COVID-19 and after the peak of the first surge. The demands on NYP as an institution and for all frontline staff and support workers during the COVID-19 surge emphasized the fact that all health care is local.

Steven J. Corwin, MD

Dr. Steven Corwin joined NYP in 1979 and was its chief medical officer and chief operating officer before being appointed president and CEO in 2011. He is highly decorated and is viewed as one of the most strategic and successful CEOs in the nation.

NewYork-Presbyterian

NYP is an academic medical center founded nearly 250 years ago that provides integrated patient care, research, and teaching for the New York metropolitan area, the United States, and internationally. NYP records six million patient visits annually and has nearly fifty thousand employees and affiliated physicians. It is continuously ranked at the top of the annual lists of hospitals in the United States. NYP is unique as it collaborates with two medical schools, Weill Cornell Medicine and Columbia University.

The New Middle

NYP has considered directly integrating patient care delivery with the financing system through forming an NYP insurance company. Dr. Corwin's team has studied how a health system–owned insurance company has worked well in other markets and geographies. However, in New York there is plenty of competition among health insurance companies. Furthermore, successful models of health systems owning a health insurance company were created thirty to thirty-five years ago when the financial times were more conducive to the cash requirements of doing so. There have been high-profile failed experiments in recent years of health systems trying to get upstream on the payment system by having access to the flow of insurance payments.

Rather than organizing its own network to get upstream on the financing flow of funds, NYP is organizing to get upstream with the patient, that is, to provide integrated services through population health services inclusive of acute care. To provide population health services, NYP needs to be where the population is, and that has resulted in NYP building a network of local hospitals and expanding ambulatory and primary care footprints. A unified digital data system is an important foundation for the integrated health system so that each hospital and ambulatory clinic has access to the same data on each patient.

Scaling Up and Scaling Down

The exponential increase in COVID-19 patients began in early February 2020 and continued until early April before receding. The increase put dramatic pressure on facilities, staff, equipment, and supplies and required an unprecedented scaling up of each. The provider-person relationships were disrupted in unprecedented ways. For example, Dr. Corwin and his team relay the story of families that said, families watched their loved ones die on FaceTime because they could not be in the same room due to COVID-19.

During the first COVID-19 surge, a high proportion of cases were admitted to the ICU. NYP's ICU complement of around four hundred ICU beds quickly became insufficient and within a matter of days was expanded to nine hundred ICU beds. But where to find five hundred ICU beds? They were created out of high-intensity acute care beds, whether step-down, orthopedic, or other surgery rooms.

Finding beds was the first step, but organizing physicians, nurses, and other workers required the development of an immediate strategy and plan of execution. The approach was best characterized by the expression "building while flying." Dr. Corwin discussed the plan, which was to create a staffing pyramid with the most capable intensivists, respiratory therapists, and nurse leaders at the top. Physicians and nurses were layered below them. This pyramid structure allowed a nurse to take care of four patients and an intensivist to take care of six to eight patients. NYP deployed two thousand physicians and one thousand nurses to treat COVID-19 patients in the ICU and elsewhere. The training of these redeployed professionals was vitally important.

Dr. Corwin discussed the process of scaling down as the surge slowed and of rebuilding the facilities and staffing to treat the elective surgery patients who began to return. He noted that the lesson of flexibility of facilities and staffing is the most important learning. Scaling up and scaling down has become a necessary core competency. Throughout the COVID-19 surge, maintaining the physician-person relationship was a constant challenge.

Stress on Frontline Caregivers

The pressure that the frontline caregivers were under day after day, twelve hours a day, seeing an inordinate number of deaths caused elevated stress levels. It is generally agreed, after interviewing dozens of health system CEOs, that this will result in PTSD among some frontline caregivers postpandemic.

NYP provided substantial mental health resources and ongoing support and made a concerted effort to destigmatize reaction to the stress. As Dr. Corwin said, "Typically, health care workers will say, 'I can tough it out. I don't need help. I've been trained to do this.' But my response to them has been, nobody's been trained to do this. Because in my forty years of medicine, I've not seen this. And I've seen a lot."

Postpandemic Lessons for Leaders

The COVID-19 crisis in New York could have swamped many health systems. Dr. Corwin shared his view that NYP and any organization relies on its culture in a time of great crisis. The NYP culture is built on inclusiveness among its employees and medical staff whereby the caregiver-patient relationship has been sacred.

The COVID-19 crisis has further emphasized the fact that all health care is local. During the 2020 surge, the patients flooding into the NYP emergency rooms were from adjoining neighborhoods. The communication from NYP executives was to the communities in which their hospitals and ambulatory clinics were located.

Dr. Corwin referenced the large number of doctors and nurses who volunteered to come to New York and join NYP in its fight for COVID-19 lives. Other health system leaders reached out and offered supplies and support. Dr. Corwin came away from this experience with the conclusion that the US population are "good people" who rise to the occasion by rallying around each other in a crisis. He observed that "cooperating with each other is part of the public good that we represent."

"We developed protocols as we went along. We certainly did not know how to do it at the start. If you look at those types of things, how can I be more flexible? How can I ramp up? I think that it starts to lead to a planning process that's somewhat more robust than what we've typically done. There are mundane things like, what are the airway protocols across the system? What is the ICU staffing model across the system? Who are the best people that we can identify? How do you redeploy? What do you do with outside resources that have to be brought in? What are your pharmacy supplies? What are your PPE supplies? How do you deal with the supply chain under those circumstances? We had to arrange domiciles for three thousand employees, either people that were coming in to help us from the rest of the country, or employees who were afraid to go home and possibly infect their loved ones or infect somebody in their family who might be immunosuppressed.

We have to think in terms of flexibility. Flexibility of the physical structures within the hospital to accommodate issues like this, but also flexibility of training. We have become more and more specialized in medicine for good reasons. But specialization becomes limiting if you have a crisis like this."

—Steven J. Corwin, MD

Protecting the Community

Our frontline caregivers are tired. So clearly, they are stressed because they are seeing more deaths than they normally see in a career.

—Wright L. Lassiter III, president and CEO, Henry Ford Health System

Detroit was an early hotspot for the COVID-19 crisis. We interviewed Wright Lassiter in April 2020 when Detroit was third in the United States for COVID-19 cases and deaths, behind New York and Seattle.[2] We had the opportunity to speak with Lassiter as the Henry Ford Health System was "catching its breath" after the initial surge. Lassiter spoke about Henry Ford's commitment to the provider-patient relationship and its role in protecting the community.

Wright L. Lassiter III, President and CEO

Wright Lassiter joined the Henry Ford Health System in 2014 and was appointed president and CEO in 2016. He is an experienced executive of large health systems, having led health systems in Texas and California. He is well decorated and is the 2021 chair-elect of the American Hospital Association.

Henry Ford Health System

Henry Ford Hospital was founded over one hundred years ago, in 1915, by Henry Ford, the automotive entrepreneur. The hospital has grown to become an integrated health system with hospitals, ambulatory clinics, retail sites, a physician medical group, and a health plan. The Henry Ford Health System is a well-known and highly regarded health system in Michigan.

Fully Integrated Care Delivery

The Henry Ford Health System's primary service area is southeastern Michigan, where the bulk of the Michigan population resides. Henry Ford is a health system with 5 acute care hospitals, 250 ambulatory care and retail locations, a 1,900-physician medical group, 33,000 employees, and a 650,000-member health plan.

Providing health care services to a diverse community is facilitated by an integrated health system that emphasizes the importance of the provider-person relationship. Whether ambulatory care, home care, or acute care, tracking persons and their data across modes of care is necessary for comprehensive and high-quality services.

Henry Ford purchased HAP, a health insurance plan, in 1986, which Lassiter believes provides the opportunity for Henry Ford to integrate payment with service delivery and remove incentives for overordering that can exist in the FFS system.

Caregiver Safety and Health

This interview took place approximately five weeks after the first COVID-19 case was admitted to a Henry Ford facility. Lassiter spoke about treating the first wave of COVID-19 cases as a battle. It was ongoing with no let up, PPE was in short supply, and there was the ever-present risk of contracting the disease and possibly passing it on to families. Further, nearly 250 patients died in the first five weeks, which was more deaths than most caregivers had seen in their entire careers.

Lassiter and the board put the safety of caregivers as the highest priority along with patients. Henry Ford's position in the community is to recognize that all health care is local. This is inclusive of caregivers as well as patients.

The concern about stress felt by frontline caregivers at Henry Ford as well as all health systems affected by the COVID-19 surge included the possibility of PTSD. The use of the term "battle" by Lassiter and other health system leaders is not accidental or an overreach. Lassiter described a battle as requiring that all resources be marshaled; people think about working as a cohesive, tight-knit group pursuing similar goals, and the circumstances are known to be extraordinary.

Supply Chain

Adequate PPE is important for employees, medical staff, and patients. The phrase "all health care is local" is a core underpinning of the Henry Ford Health System's culture and represents the trust that Henry Ford has with its community.

At the same time that the hospitals were being prepared for an increasing growth in COVID-19 patients, the hunt for PPE was under way. The supply chain team was challenged to identify sources of PPE, much of which was manufactured internationally. The COVID-19 crisis slowed or shut down manufacturing and transport.

Lassiter concluded that the key finding was that the supply chain system must be resilient and diverse. Meeting those standards will acknowledge that we live in a globalized world and that some supply chain items will be made internationally. A solid foundation requires a focus on domestic manufacturing and not a dependency on one country outside the United States. The federal stockpile, which was understood to be a source of supply chain material that would fill in gaps, was clearly found to be inadequate and should be reevaluated.

Postpandemic Lessons for Leaders

By its very nature, a crisis is difficult to preemptively prepare for. The foundation of mission and values becomes the swim lanes for an organization to respond to the crisis. Lassiter and his team communicated with caregivers, employees, the board, and the community every day, seven days a week. Communications included critical updates such as emergency response and operational changes, real-time clinical learnings, policy and process improvements, expressions of gratitude to teams for their tireless service, and resources to help them care for themselves and each other. Lassiter and other CEOs we interviewed over the course of 2020 agreed that in-depth, straightforward, truthful informational updates were the bedrock of the approach to an intensive crisis.

Lassiter spoke about the speed of decision making during the COVID-19 crisis. In many cases, process was stripped away, individual accountabilities were sharpened, and the objectives were targeted and clear. Many CEOs strategized about how the speed of decision making could be maintained as the crisis receded. Approaches included discussing and gaining input from employees and medical staff, many of whom appreciated the faster response time to required decisions. Also, a common strategy was to form a task force to identify approaches to maintaining more rapid decision making.

"When you're in a battle, number one, you think about marshaling all your resources. Number two, you think about being a member of a cohesive, tight-knit group of individuals who are working toward a group purchase, and number three, you think about being in extraordinary circumstances that you're not normally asked to be in. I'm not a mental health practitioner, but the data would tell us that this is an extremely traumatic situation. You would expect some level of post-traumatic stress syndrome from workers who have been in the battlefield during this time.

Morale is about as high as you can expect when you have a set of individuals going through what is a battle. We get people working really, really hard, working overtime and double shifts and doing their best to ensure we have enough clinical resources available. They're tired; clearly they are stressed because they're seeing more death than they normally see in a career."

—Wright Lassiter III

Alignment of Interests between Health Plans and Providers

The more that we move toward the predominance of government payers, the more we're going to see private-sector payers and providers come together to align interests.

—Craig Samitt, MD, former president and CEO,
Blue Cross Blue Shield of Minnesota

During the COVID-19 crisis, many people lost their jobs, with many having shortfalls in paying for health care. These coverage dislocations have increased national and local discussions about moving to a value-based model whereby health insurers and providers integrate the payment and delivery systems and address gaps in coverage. Dr. Samitt has been an outspoken leader in creating a value-based model, and the COVID-19 crisis has served as an impetus for him to lead the discussion with actions. The interview took place in late August 2020 when Dr. Samitt could look back on the devastation of the COVID-19 surge in Minnesota.[3]

Craig Samitt, MD

Dr. Craig Samitt is a former president and CEO of BCBSM. For those who thought BCBSM should develop more value-based models, Dr. Samitt was an ideal leader, having served as a both a provider and a health insurance company executive.

Blue Cross Blue Shield of Minnesota

The history of BCBSM began in 1933, when seven St. Paul hospitals teamed up to form the Minnesota Hospital Association. It became the country's first prepaid health care network and the first health plan to become known as Blue Cross. Today, BCBSM is the largest health insurance plan serving Minnesota, with nearly three million members.

Value-Based Payment Models

Dr. Samitt refers to the FFS payment model as an "addiction." He summed it up by saying that "it doesn't reward better care in many respects; it rewards more care." This view has many proponents, and Dr. Samitt is committed to transforming care by eliminating volume-based payment models. In his role as CEO of the health insurer with the most Minnesota members, he was well positioned to work with provider health systems and lead change toward aligned financial models with provider health systems.

During our August 2020 interview, Dr. Samitt referenced discussions with large health systems in Minnesota to create alignment designed to reward both parties for "better care at lower cost." The punch line as stated by Dr. Samitt: "What if we all benefited when the patient was healthy and when health care was more efficient?"

One model that BCBSM is pursuing is a partnership model focused on increasing quality of care through restructuring incentives, which will lower the total cost of care. Dr. Samitt believes that these partnership models will allow the private sector to pursue transformation and not be mandated through federal legislation.

Dr. Samitt referenced MA as a government program that BCBSM considers a value-based model. In Minnesota, 56 percent of newly eligible Medicare recipients choose MA over FFS Medicare. Dr. Samitt expects to see that percentage grow, which will not only further solidify Medicare's commitment to a value-based model but also serve as a model for commercial health plans when they see the benefits of quality and efficiency.

Dr. Samitt observed that health plans and providers have historically had a contentious and transactional relationship and that the patient/member has suffered as a result. His vision is that the health plan and providers align with incentives for the consumer/member to become more healthy and the total cost of care is lower and the quality of care is higher.

Payments for Telehealth Visits

Dr. Samitt had been tackling the COVID-19 crisis for 40 percent of the time he had been CEO, working through a myriad number of COVID-19–related issues. Perhaps the largest issue on his plate when we interviewed him was whether or how much to pay for telehealth visits, which many insurers and the CMS had not been willing to do pre–COVID-19. Dr. Samitt said that BCBSM will definitely cover telehealth visits, but the bigger question is how much the payment rate will be.

The BCBSM position is that a telehealth visit does not cost the provider as much as an in-person visit, and therefore payment should be preconditioned on positive outcomes as a basis of the amount of payment. As Dr. Samitt knows from his time as a practicing physician and a health system executive, providers believe that the largest part of the cost of a visit is the physician's time; therefore, they expect similar payment for a telehealth visit.

This telehealth coverage issue is representative of the different points of view that lead to contention between health insurer and health provider. Samitt is seeking a middle ground where coverage of telehealth visits takes place within a broader value-based model.

Postpandemic Lessons for Leaders

Dr. Samitt commented on the trends under way pre–COVID-19 involving the intersection of politics, health policy, provider networks, and personalization. He believes that the COVID-19 crisis will accelerate those trends.

Commercial businesses have long been frustrated with the rising costs of health benefits. Dr. Samitt believes that the pandemic will change the way employers and consumers are thinking about health care. During our interview, he reflected on his view that a company external to health care, such as Amazon, Walmart, Target, and Apple, would be a major disruptor.

In fact, Dr. Samitt believes that these companies will have a transformative effect but that COVID-19 and the affordability gaps it has exposed will cause employers and consumers to lead. Much as Uber and Netflix have provided a way for consumers to change habits and cause suppliers to respond, he believes that a similar trend will occur in health care.

"If we just look at the impact that COVID-19 has had on health systems, it highlights the dangers of addiction with fee-for-service or volume-based health care. Many of the health systems are suffering because of the absence of elective procedures. If we were not volume companies and instead were population health companies, then provider-payer partnerships would flow over the peaks and valleys of health care utilization. We've historically seen several organizations that continue to thrive under one organizational structure. Kaiser Permanente is a gold standard in that. I don't necessarily say, though, that it has to be an organizational structure. It has to be alignment of interests, which could very well be population health coaccountability. That's the kind of relationship we want to drive, not just vertical integration.

In many respects, the reimbursement model that we've been under in a fee-for-service world has driven many of us to be commodities. When you look at the margins of both health plans and hospitals in particular, they're very lean. But when you look at the margins of population health companies, where they're no longer addicted to or beholden to the lean margins that come with volume, that's where the world is going to go. Less will be more in the future in a model that moves more toward government. Less in terms of utilization, more in terms of quality outcomes."

—Craig Samitt, MD

Notes

1. The content of this case study was gleaned from Steven J. Corwin's interview with author Gary Bisbee on June 25, 2020. A longer excerpt of the interview appeared in Fireside Chat with Gary Bisbee, Ph.D., "Episode 40."
2. The content of this case study was gleaned from Wright L. Lassiter III's interview with author Gary Bisbee on April 17, 2020. A longer excerpt of the interview appeared in Fireside Chat with Gary Bisbee, Ph.D., "Episode 19."
3. The content of this case study was gleaned from Craig Samitt's interview with author Gary Bisbee on August 25, 2020. A longer excerpt of the interview appeared in Fireside Chat with Gary Bisbee, Ph.D., "Episode 54."

9

Embrace the New Middle

Lessons for Leaders

Epidemiologists refer to the influenza outbreak of 1918 as a common reference point for the COVID-19 pandemic and its lack of understanding of the causal and transmission uncertainties and the havoc wreaked upon human life. Following the 1918 pandemic, significant changes occurred that advanced public health forevermore in the United States. The primary example is governmental initiatives to develop clean water supplies.

Compared to one hundred years ago, the federal, state, and local governments are substantially more involved in the payment, regulation, and provision of health care. Changes to health care delivery because of COVID-19 are already under way, and there is general agreement among those leaders we interviewed and interact with that we will see changes to health care over the short, mid, and longer term as a direct result of COVID-19.

Our conversations with CEOs during the pandemic indicated that the COVID-19 surge and the resulting demands on health systems and caregivers were uniformly described as a battle. Terms such as "fear," "courage," and "bravery" were freely used. In many cases, caregivers were afraid to go home after their shift because they might infect their families. Families used FaceTime to say goodbye to loved ones dying in the ICU because they could not enter.

The COVID-19 pandemic will fade into stories that most of us will tell our children and grandchildren after the vaccines are widely administered in 2021 and COVID-19 is brought under control. Those on the front lines who lived through the surges will never forget them.

We think of changes that have occurred to manage the crisis, such as the use of telemedicine and remote working. Changes that have begun and will unfold over the next several years include a rethinking of the national stockpile and supply chain. Longer-term changes will involve federal initiatives to the

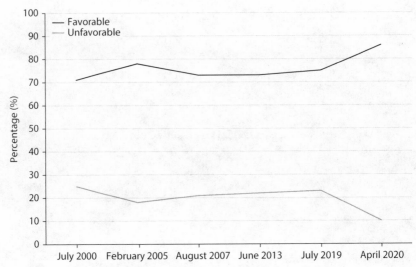

Figure 9.1. Reported public perception of favorability toward US hospitals. The image of hospitals is at its highest point over the past two decades. Survey respondents were asked to indicate whether they had a favorable or an unfavorable opinion of hospitals. As part of the same survey, respondents were presented with a list of several other stakeholders (e.g., government, insurers), and asked to indicate their favorability and unfavorability for each. Percentages do not sum to 100 percent due to "Don't Know/ Unsure" responses. *Source:* Public Opinion Strategies survey data. The most recent data collected was part of "Public Opinion Strategies/Jarrard Phillips Cate & Hancock National Survey of 1,000 Adults," conducted April 16–20, 2020. Used with permission.

organization and financing of health care, such as a national health care coverage floor. Forward-thinking leaders will not be lulled into assuming that COVID-19 will fade into history and we will return to the way things were. Every health care sector will be differentially affected.

During our short experience with COVID-19, we have learned yet again that Washington decision makers and the public have high levels of confidence and trust in doctors, nurses, and hospitals. In fact, public trust and favorability of hospitals reached its highest point in over a decade, with an increase from July 2019 to April 2020 of 15 percent (see figure 9.1). It is critical that our provider executive teams, boards of directors, frontline caregivers, and health insurance executives actively participate in the coming national conversation.

The leadership charter is about public health, care delivery, and person-centric payment models to address inequities. It also includes the related calculus of economic impact and community well-being. They are the many shades of uncertainty that health leaders must boldly tackle in the years to come.

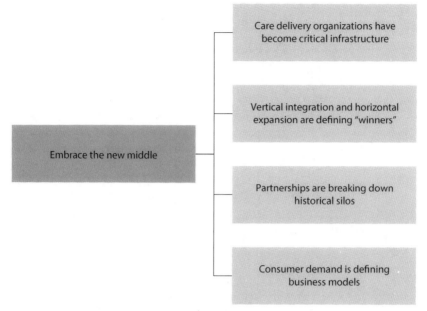

Figure 9.2. Ground rules for provider networks.

As leaders look to blend the pre–COVID-19 historical background, trends, and issues with the influence of COVID-19, they will consider heath care politics, health policy, the body of knowledge and directional trends of provider networks, and data-driven personalization, discussed in part IV. In this section on provider networks, chapter 7 presented the background and trends and a review of key issues. Chapter 8 brought the voice of leaders in responding to COVID-19 and its influence on the issues outlined in chapter 7. This chapter synthesizes the findings of chapters 7 and 8, which underlie lessons for leaders (see figure 9.2) that will define the post–COVID-19 landscape.

Care Delivery Organizations Have Become Critical Infrastructure

Prior to the pandemic, Washington was inextricably intertwined with how providers deliver on their mission and margin. The largest health systems and health insurers had anywhere from 50 to 80 percent of their revenues attributed to government payments.[1] With only about 70 percent of baby boomers old enough to qualify for Medicare, the percentage of revenues from governments will certainly increase.

In effect, governments setting rates for the majority of the health systems' and large health insurers' business equates them to critical infrastructures, much like a public health utility. Health care as a highly regulated industry draws further comparability to public utilities. As WellSpan's president and CEO Roxanna Gapstur shared, public health is part of the economic and health security of the nation.[2] That is top priority for governments, providers, and insurers.

In our view, the emergence of the large provider organizations as a public health utility has become even more true in the post–COVID-19 health economy. For starters, health systems, akin to how the Department of Homeland Security considers critical national infrastructure, are now touted as essential services underpinning American society. It became apparent that health security is national security, as public health continues to influence the economy and massive outflows of government money supported health care during the crisis. "Public health has been the stepchild of Western medicine for a long time," notes Dr. Joanne Conroy, president and CEO, Dartmouth-Hitchcock Health System. "COVID-19 really emphasized to people the value of public health."[3] Moreover, the prepandemic projections for Medicaid enrollment growth are compounded by millions of Americans who lost their employer-sponsored coverage due to unprecedented levels of unemployment.

A question that will provoke the discussion of how to define a public health utility is how the payment model evolves over the 2020s. Furthermore, what organizations are responsible for SDoH and health equity will further accelerate discussion about the large health system and health insurers as private-sector–led public health utilities.

"We will have to have a discussion as a country as to how the system finances itself. We currently finance it with commercial payments subsidizing Medicare and Medicaid. When you add to that the inequality of the virus for mortality in people of color and lower socioeconomic groups, but particularly people of color, that will also influence the discussion."

—Steven Corwin, MD, president and CEO, NewYork-Presbyterian

As the government tab for health coverage increases, more pressure is being applied to health systems to take responsibility for the consumer's health and prevent readmission for expensive hospitalizations. As large health systems continue to develop an expertise in population health and managing health risk in order to lower costs, increase affordability, and improve the health of the community, it is a natural next step to actively address social factors that lead to poor health. Timing is uncertain, but COVID-19 will in retrospect be viewed as a singular event that positioned the large health systems as private-sector public health utilities.

Vertical Integration and Horizontal Expansion Are Defining "Winners"

COVID-19 has created a consensus that there will be a New Middle. There may be uncertainty of timing and direction of change, but there is no uncertainty that there will be steady and substantial change in the 2020s. Consolidation and its influence on costs, either to increase or decrease, will be a continuing flash point. Consolidation, both horizontal and vertical, will accelerate as financial pressures continue, the government role in health care grows, and payment models continue to evolve.

As discussed, the Great Recession of 2008–9 spawned a wave of horizontal mergers approximately twenty-four to thirty-six months later. This consolidation in turn led to growing levels of regulatory review and scrutiny. As the Federal Trade Commission continues its focus on the effect on pricing caused by horizontal mergers in closely aligned markets, we will see mergers in noncontiguous markets. A pre–COVID-19 example is the 2017 merger of Advocate Health Care and Aurora Health Care to create Advocate Aurora Health, the tenth-largest nonprofit health system in the nation. We expect that the financial pressures caused by COVID-19 will similarly drive a forthcoming wave of horizontal mergers.

Beyond traditional provider organizations, COVID-19 is driving a set of high-profile nontraditional consolidations such as the acquisition by Teladoc of Livongo. As part of this transaction, the medical outcomes business of Livongo was merged with the telehealth business of Teladoc, creating a new company, Teladoc Health. Teladoc's CEO, Jason Gorevic, watched COVID-19 exponentially increase the demand for televisits, which created the opportunity for Teladoc to expand its business model through the acquisition. As Gorevic explained, Teladoc now can provide not only televisits but also the virtual delivery of outcomes-based health services.

Finally, the pre–COVID-19 acquisition of Aetna by CVS looks even smarter postpandemic. CVS is playing an important role in diagnostic testing

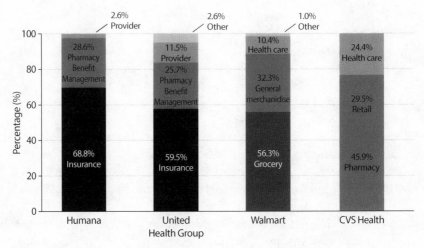

Figure 9.3. Percent of revenue dedicated to health care services for nontraditional provider entities. *Source:* Sanjula Jain, *2021 Trends Shaping the Post-Pandemic Health Economy* (Brentwood, TN: Trilliant Heath, 2021).

and vaccine administration and is now looking to expand its footprint in direct ambulatory clinics, further buttressing its position with consumers (see figure 9.3). The Aetna insurance products allow CVS-Aetna to create a first-dollar risk model.

As regulators further scrutinize consolidation across the new health economy, meaningful partnership is a critical prescription for delivering the integrated, seamless experience that consumers demand. Sophisticated acquirers will redefine the way they structure deals and share risk to elevate the scale advantage needed in a postpandemic health economy.

Partnerships Are Breaking Down Historical Silos

As the payment system evolves and moves toward a person-centric, risk-based, or value model, the blurring between health systems and health insurers will continue. COVID-19 will accelerate legislation, regulation, delivery, and financing of health care to a tighter coordination between health insurers and providers.

Partnerships spawned by COVID-19 are also contributing to breaking down historical silos. For example, the CARES Act provided $175 billion in appropriations to support hospitals—with essential relief for our provider supply-side infrastructure.[4] Many commercial insurers followed suit with the waiving of cost-sharing for COVID-19 tests and treatments, among other payment accommodations. Select plans, such as Blue Cross Blue Shield of California, took additional steps and expanded value-based arrangements to transition providers to a monthly revenue model to help offset some of the volume-based revenue declines.

Despite the leadership of the MA model and CARES Act partnerships, steps forward will be slow and cautious. Historical silos, incentive structures, and payment flows are hard to change. Moreover, digital platforms, such as those developed by start-ups DexCare and Omada Health, will disrupt by filling voids in care delivery and providing consumers more convenient care management services. As providers solely providing services virtually expand—a trend further highlighted by the recent formation of Teladoc Health mentioned previously—their relationships with providers and other third-party payers will break down historical silos.

> "The plans and the providers have historically had a more contentious and transactional relationship and I think the patient has suffered."
>
> **—Craig Samitt, MD, former president and CEO, Blue Cross Blue Shield of Minnesota**

As health insurers continue to seek cost efficiencies and ways to reclaim touch points at the front door of care, they may discover new synergies with health systems that are highly trusted by the patient. True paradigm shifts are hard. Regardless, providers and insurers are demonstrating by their actions a belief that the incremental financial pressures of increasing Medicare beneficiaries driven by the baby boomer population, Medicaid enrollments, gaps in coverage, mixed incentives, and a weak economy require new thinking.

Banner Health's president and CEO Peter Fine has multiple experiences developing partnerships with insurers. He concurred that it is not easy to align incentives. However, it is necessary to provide value-based services to the patient. The current partnership with Aetna, named Banner|Aetna, is a leader in the Phoenix market and designed to create New Middle incentives. "In this industry we spend way too much time fighting amongst ourselves," notes Jim Skogsbergh, president and CEO of Advocate Aurora Health. "We should be working together. There are other people that we could be competing with rather than ourselves."[5]

The New Middle battle is being played out in each of the 334 metropolitan statistical area–level markets. An uneasy truce will exist in certain markets and health systems, and health insurers will prevail in others. The underlying basis of health care is diagnosis and treatment. With the continued evolution of the health care system, a person-centric, New Middle option will certainly become available selectively if not universally during the 2020s.[6]

Consumer Demand Is Defining Business Models

Convenience and affordability for the consumer have challenged traditional business models and pressured operating margins. Facilitated by the growing availability of data, the fundamental gap between health system business models and expectations of governments, employers, and consumers has opened the door to myriad players disaggregating health care delivery and financing. Riding the wave of changing expectations, the growing number of new entrants and existing players is accelerating competition for higher-margin and less asset-intense services, further increasing margin pressures and disaggregating the health system's traditional care models.

> **"I hope with both traditional and nontraditional players coming in that health care gets as aggressive as we've seen the financial services industry getting around trying to create new consumer solutions."**
>
> **—Marcus Osborne, former senior vice president, Walmart Health**

As health systems deconstruct the traditional asset-intense brick-and-mortar model of care delivery, they will build on their ability to leverage human capital and talent in novel and dynamic ways. Compounded by the need to manage financial and health risk for their employees, patients, and communities, health systems are further embracing their expanded role as a steward of the community and will increasingly assume a parallel role to public health utilities.

The business models of providers, health insurers, and pharmaceutical and device companies are all challenged to keep pace with the speed of disruption and change in health care, which is due in large part to the increase in government payments and evolving consumer preferences. It should be no surprise that regulators are similarly challenged. Normally, the consequence is that health institutions and governments will experience a lag in responding to accelerating change. COVID-19 will provoke the norm, and change will likely come more quickly and be of greater magnitude. "The leadership moment is making sure that those people with deep health care knowledge—the physicians, the nurses, the respiratory therapists—have the business skills to make sure we are not locked into the models of what we have done, but to be willing to embrace the disruption we know we need to get the health care infrastructure to a much better place," said Dr. Amy Compton-Phillips, president of clinical care, Providence.[7]

COVID-19 has already begun to define a new business model for providers as a result of the following key dynamics:

- *Telehealth.* COVID-19 caused a six-to-eight-month bubble when 80 percent or more of contact with ambulatory patients was through telehealth technology. Some health systems such as AdventHealth are already in the process of delineating telehealth as its own business line.
- *Remote work.* Like much of business, health systems have encouraged remote working for those administrative workers who do not provide direct patient care. As Dr. Joanne Conroy, president and CEO of Dartmouth Hitchcock Health System, located in semirural Lebanon, New Hampshire, stated about remote working, she can now recruit nationally.
- *Ramp up and ramp down.* New York-Presbyterian expanded ICUs from four hundred to nine hundred beds in a few days. All health systems reorganized or eliminated waiting rooms to accommodate social distancing. Assuming future epidemics, a core competency in flexing physical and digital capacity has developed.
- *Facility planning.* With the combination of remote working, telehealth visits, and reconfigured or eliminated waiting rooms, Dennis Murphy, president and CEO of Indiana University Health, indicated that certain ambulatory buildings on the drawing boards were going to be dramatically redesigned.[8] Fewer examination and waiting rooms and more telehealth facilities will be part of postpandemic design.
- *Supply chain.* COVID-19 brought the nation's supply chain to its breaking point in terms of both quality and availability, with supplies critical to the health of US citizens fully dependent on other countries with their own outbreaks to manage. Health system CEOs agree that we have no choice but to minimize our dependency on a foreign supply chain. Going forward, we will need to build a reliable supply chain that can support a national infrastructure for health care.[9] "When you have a sole producer in the market or one country dominating the manufacture of a good that is a common good, you run into trouble," notes Dr. Redonda Miller, president of Johns Hopkins Hospital.[10]

Business model evolution is well under way and will pick up steam over the course of the 2020s. Those health system executive teams that recognize the pace of change and commit to meeting expectations of governments, employers, and consumers will strengthen the role of the health system in their communities.

Notes

1. Authors' analysis of publicly available financial statements for large insurers.
2. Roxana Gapstur, interview by author Gary Bisbee, October 13, 2020.
3. Fireside Chat with Gary Bisbee, Ph.D., "Episode 28."
4. Provider supply-side federal relief included payment accommodations for hospitals such as a 20 percent increase in Medicare payments for treatment of a patient with COVID-19 and expansion of the Medicare hospital Accelerated Payment Program to apply payment qualifications to more types of hospitals.
5. Fireside Chat with Gary Bisbee, Ph.D., "Episode 57."
6. "Payvider" is a term coined by ACA architect Nancy-Ann DeParle in reference to an entity that shares payment and delivery incentives.
7. Her Story with Sanjula Jain, "Episode 26."
8. Fireside Chat with Gary Bisbee, Ph.D., "Episode 30."
9. In this context we refer to national infrastructure with parallels to how the United States thinks about its national defense system. Similar to how 9/11 prompted the government to define and prioritize critical areas underlying US safety, we will need to adequately invest in and protect the lifesaving supplies deemed critical to the health and well-being of US citizens. To ensure reliability, we must consider health care as part of national security and build strategies comparable to how we manage our national defense assets. For more on this concept, refer to insights from Bob Kerrey's interview excerpts in chapter 2.
10. Fireside Chat with Gary Bisbee, Ph.D., "Episode 43."

PART IV

Data-Driven
Personalization

10

Individual as Decision Maker

Background

Every year, *Fortune* magazine ranks America's largest companies. It is, as *Fortune* describes, a ranking synonymous with business success. In 1955, the list featured names such as 3M, Boeing, and IBM. The list also included a set of companies that would be unrecognizable to us today, ranging from Armstrong Rubber to Cone Mills. As Marc Perry at the American Enterprise Institute detailed, there are "fewer than 12% of the Fortune 500 companies included in 1955 [that are] still on the list today."[1] Said differently, less than sixty enterprises were able to drive sufficient profitability to maintain a six-decade presence on the list. They are *Fortune*'s fortunate few.

For health care companies trying to deploy "time the market" calculus on the rate of change, the *Fortune* 500 data offers a sobering reminder. Market dynamism is real, and no one is immune. Jeff Bezos amplified the point in a 2018 meeting with employees, a recording of which was shared with CNBC: "Amazon is not too big to fail. . . . If you look at large companies, their lifespans tend to be thirty-plus years, not a hundred-plus years."[2] He concluded by arguing that if Amazon failed to focus its full energy on its customers, it would be "the beginning of the end. The collective ambition of Amazon leaders must be to delay that day as long as possible."

Health care organizations historically have had a different diffusion rate of change as compared to other industries. Health care is a basic need. The US population is growing, living longer, and aging, furthering demand for health care. The increased role of government in the economics of health care, coupled with growing political dysfunction in Washington, has introduced a complexity of health care that creates real barriers to entry and deepens moats.

Yet, we believe that the Schumpeterian destructiveness that has toppled categories such as media, telecommunications, consumer finance, and brick-and-mortar retail will begin to show itself in health care in the decade to come. Digitization offers the promise of profound opportunities to rethink strategies around conditions, roles, and venues. Democratic-led reform will shift the next wave of political positioning and policy debate to affordability over access, offering entrepreneurial oxygen for low-cost disruptors. Aging baby boomers will demand a very different level of experience than their Greatest Generation parents.

The Health Care Customer

As we navigate executive conversations across health care, we see a striking level of confusion about who the person at the center of these business model shifts actually is. Health systems are illustrative. For many years, leading health system CEOs frequently described physician practices within their catchments as the customer. Today, we hear the federal government and state governments described as outsized influencers on health systems operations. Infrequently do we hear CEOs describe a substantial resource commitment of their organization to reorient to the person as the central force for how their organizations invest, organize, and run their enterprises. "Differentiation is going to be around access, affordability, and ability to control one's own destiny," says Dr. Marc Harrison, president and CEO of Intermountain Healthcare. "The idea that each of us wants to be treated as an individual, both medically and personally will be something that people just expect and they should."[3]

Health care financing shifts from MA growth to out-of-pocket increases within commercial insurance also will bring increased consumer presence in health care. These shifts will require renewed focus on the person as the customer, a relationship that organizations work to create and keep. The failure to do so will bring the same ignominious fate as onetime icons of the *Fortune* 500 list.

The decade preceding the COVID-19 pandemic produced an amazing level of change in the tools available to understand the wants and needs of the customer, and there was also a revolution in the means available to companies to deliver on them. The last decade saw the rise of the smartphone, the ascent of social media, the scaling of Amazon, the fight-back of traditional retail, and an emergent collaborative economy as the five major drivers of personalization defining health care environment. Collectively, these prepandemic foundational drivers established the person as customer and the individual's growing demand for data-driven personalization. These trends toward catering to the personal needs of the customer will ultimately accelerate and, in some cases, dynamically change how we deliver health care in the years to come.

It is our view that the first-order impact of any crisis is an acceleration of macrotrends already playing out. The COVID-19 pandemic is no exception and powerfully reinforces the theory. As we discussed in earlier chapters, the federal government became the top regulator and top payer for health care in the 2010s. COVID-19 accelerated Washington's role with the multiple trillions of dollars it has pumped into the economy. Hospital consolidation has been a multiyear trend and will accelerate in the years to come. The home as venue to include the use of teleservices has been advancing at pace, accelerating through the crisis response. From scientific discovery to the deployment value of clinical data, acceleration of existing forces of change is the first known of any crisis.

Similarly, the pursuit of durable recovery after COVID-19 will continue to place the customer's need and expectation for convenient and affordable access to personalized health care at the center. In the next three chapters, we examine data-driven personalization, exploring patient, member, and consumer trends both inside and outside of health care. These contextual dynamics will critically inform how leaders shape the future of US health care as the demands for leadership continue to grow. Person-centric technologies can fundamentally redefine health and care. Having a redefining impact demands that leaders bring intersectional domain competence across not only health policy, health politics, and the provision of care but also data-driven personalization as consumerism takes hold. It is the sum of these parts that will truly create a first-time system of health and care.

The Foundation of Data-Driven Personalization

The Disruptive Impact of the Smartphone

The iPhone may be one of the most important pieces of technology in our lives. From the moment Steve Jobs lifted the curtain on the device at MacWorld it was a genre-bender, bringing together the phone, the iPod, and the internet. "It put the world in our pockets."[4]

While the iPhone launched in 2007, the size of the form factors of the screen, the e-commerce experiences that it offered, and its initial speed were limiting. But for all its alpha innovation, considering the iterative advancement is equally amazing. It was the introduction of the 3G network at a lower price point and the addition of the App Store that began to unleash the mobile disruption that we almost take for granted a decade later. The iPhone has changed how we engage in just about every aspect of daily life.

In iPhone's success, there is obvious learning. Just as Jobs slavishly focused on the consumer, health care leaders must focus tirelessly on the patient. In the

App Store, we see an exemplification of collective innovation that will be central to solving health care's most intractable problems.

The prolific Mary Meeker, Silicon Valley investor and analyst, further describes the ongoing dynamism of the smartphone technology. Mobility continues to have "aggressive momentum," with more than 3 billion smartphones in use.[5] There is a massive opportunity to drive further growth by converting the close to 4.5 billion current traditional mobile phone users to smartphone technology in the coming years. With the average smartphone user reaching for her or his device more than 150 times a day,[6] predominantly for messaging, voice calls, and time checking, this frequency represents a profound opportunity for ongoing smartphone-mediated personalization.

As Meeker notes in her annual Internet Trends reports, time will tell how it all plays out. From connectivity to smartphones to wearables, technology is being "re-imagined and uploaded at an accelerating pace."[7] Technology has significant implications for personalized medicine and for redefining provider models of care looking to deliver it.

The Rise of Social Media

Growing mobility in turn brought an evolution in social media. In many ways as the internet progressed beyond its initial military use cases, popular commercial adoption centered on the internet as a means of communication. The early entrants centered around the desktop from AOL to Friendster and MySpace. Then, players such as Facebook (founded in 2004) emerged in the 2000s. Not surprisingly, while Facebook (and likewise Twitter) became multichannel, many of the newer entrants in the last decade are highly tethered to smartphones. Instagram (now owned by Facebook) arrived in 2010. Snapchat made its debut a year later.

As Clay Christensen and others have framed, photos (and later video sharing) emerged as a way to communicate quickly and efficiently. The twin macros of smartphones and an evolving social media landscape slowly began to transform multiple industries to include the consumer category as a whole and thus shifted consumer expectation and influenced brand positioning.

The deeply rooted mainstay of social media in individual living will continue to usher in enriched population intelligence and decision support in the years to come. As we examine personalization in a crisis environment, the power of social media's platform will be brought to the forefront in the context of real-time COVID-19 data collection. This holds the promise for new tools for targeted health and wellness and for groundbreaking experience sharing personalized to the individual.

The Age of Amazon

The third major driver of change has been what some have called the "Age of Amazon." Indeed, the single biggest driver of corporate recalibration in the last decade has been the Seattle-based online book purveyor that became the "everything store." Jeff Bezos and his team have built a retail (and enterprise cloud) behemoth. The expansion of e-commerce, like so many other trends, was accelerated by the pandemic. A confluence of factors has driven the Amazon ascent. This started with customer focus. The company describes its mission as being the most customer-centric company on the planet. It is a world where customers can "find and discover anything they want to buy." As part of that mission Amazon brought a systems view, recognizing that last-mile fulfillment was a key part of the end-to-end customer experience and incurring billions of dollars of annual losses to make shipping transparent and efficient.

Beyond fulfillment innovation, Amazon also understood from its experience with online book selling that peer sentiment impacts buying behavior. In industries such as health care in which information asymmetry is high, this is a critical reminder. Amazon was one of the first companies in the mid-1990s to advance a review system on its site. Now these are commonplace. As customer trust in the ecosystem grew, Amazon's brand license expanded with it. A storehouse of customer preference data coupled with the power of machine learning allowed for more personalized shopping experiences with larger per-ticket economics as Amazon moved into virtually every category.

Yet, the impact of Amazon is arguably about much more than strong revenue growth and rising market share. The company's focus on selection, price, and convenience along with habits changed customer expectations across all categories. The shift in sentiment, we believe, can be seen clearly in growing frustration with parts of health care that seem to be stuck in a different era.

One place that Amazon clearly sees opportunities is in health care. In June 2018, Amazon won the contest to purchase online pharmacy company Pillpack. The asset gives Amazon a killer use case to health care—enable Alexa and begin to condition Prime members to the cost benefit and convenience of solving basic health care needs such as pharmacy refills in the home. Opportunities for scale growth beyond that strategic start are enormous.

Following the announcement of the Pillpack deal, the major brick-and-mortar retail pharmacies—Walgreens, CVS, and Rite Aid—lost $10 billion in combined market cap. Analysts have dubbed this the "Amazon effect." Rumblings of Amazon's entry into the prescription drug space was at least one reason CVS proactively moved to merge with insurer Aetna following the decision to call off the Aetna-Humana combination in late 2017. Working through the strengths, weaknesses, opportunities, and threats of individual deals across the health care ecosystem entails a threat analysis that starts with Amazon. Bezos and company are looking to disrupt the food industry with the purchase of Whole Foods. Amazon also is eyeing health care ranging from the private label Basic Care for over-the-counter medications to a primary and preventive care health services business called Amazon Care.

The role of online marketplaces such as Amazon has never been more critical. As consumer demand for convenience increasingly tethers to the individual's need for health and security, we can expect to see the continued impact of the Amazon effect on consumer behaviors. Change is coming. And when it comes, it will happen faster than we thought it could.

More Discrete Focus on Omnichannel Strategies

For all of the talk of the Amazon effect, the story of the decade before COVID-19 is also one in which a number of traditional companies reaffirmed their mission around the customer and advanced unique strategies around personalization. In doing so, they sought to engage consumers outside the parameters of the traditional shopping experience.

For every high-profile headline about the demise of traditional retailers from Blockbuster to FAO Schwartz to Borders Books, there also are stories about the successful multichannel fight-back of companies such as Walmart and Best Buy.

Beyond culling and reconfiguring stores, big-box retailers such as Walmart are investing in digital. "We will be the first to deliver a seamless shopping experience at scale," said Walmart CEO Doug McMillon. "No matter how you choose to shop with us, through your mobile device, online, in a store, or a combination, it will be fast and easy. Online retailers are testing physical store experiences because they recognize the same customer desire that we do. There's a race to do this right, but only Walmart can bring together a dense network of stores, supported by a supply chain and systems like ours, with an emerging set of digital capabilities to win with customers."[8]

Similarly, Best Buy offers a case study of another brick-and-mortar player successfully fighting back in the era of Amazon. At one point in time, the website Inc. described Best Buy as a retailer "dying a slow death."[9] Yet, under former CEO Hubert Joly, Best Buy has posted at least 3 percent growth for eight consecutive quarters. What can we learn from the Best Buy turnaround? Joly began with an emphasis on driving employee engagement, including increased training and "restor[ing] a beloved employee discount program." He created a culture focused on customer experience both in the store and online. Finally, he made the complexity of electronics a strength, creating new offerings such as home tech consultation. The Best Buy turnaround is a timely reminder of the power of centering any organization around the laser-focused delivery of customer value.

Brick-and-mortar retailers initially focused on becoming omnichannel centered on strategies to ensure that they were fully integrated. Over time, they came to overweigh their energies on multichannel, with the store and the phone at the core and brick and mortar no longer assumed as the point of purchase.

Conversely, Apple brought an appetite to innovate within retail. Jobs added Gap CEO Mickey Drexler to the Apple board and hired retail veteran Ron Johnson to inform design and execution. The Genius Bar was one of several innovations. Apple took a back-office function and placed it prominently in the store footprint to demystify its technology, decode key functionality, and drive ease of use. In 2017 at its flagship store in San Francisco, the Genius Bar was upgraded with a line of trees to replicate a town square feel, as then senior vice president of retail, Angela Ahrendts (the former Burberry CEO), explained on *CBS This Morning*.[10]

Convenience. Simplicity. Satisfaction. And now, we also see a hint of community. Health care customers will seek out brands that deliver this experience, and the eventual category leaders will deliver it. Demand will exponentially grow as individual expectations continue to evolve.

"Transformation will be led by the consumers who will get a taste of a higher value model. We don't have to look much past Netflix or Uber to realize that the purchasers of health care are very much going to expect something better in the future."

—Craig Samitt, MD, former president and CEO,
Blue Cross Blue Shield of Minnesota

The Sharing Economy

The final driver of personalization that sprinted into the US marketplace in the 2010s is the so-called sharing economy. These no-asset platforms emerged from the entrepreneurial premise that individuals can share value from an underutilized skill or asset to create a market. This may seem like a libertarian utopia. It is not.

Popularized by Uber and Airbnb, some third-party estimates suggest that the global sharing economy could exceed $300 billion by 2025.[11] Interestingly for health care, its origin story can be traced to players such as eBay and Amazon, which created a level of trust in online e-commerce. As customers grew increasingly comfortable with the digital world, their willingness to reimagine what a market might look like expanded. This led to something that academicians call "platform-mediated peer trust," distinct and different from institutional trust.

The rise of the sharing economy has not been without controversies. A failure to effectively manage Dr. Ron Adner's *Wide Lens* impacts made the rise of several of these companies a noisy ascent. If they were tackling market inefficiencies, they also were running askance of regulations and disrupting state and local tax revenues.

As Francis Fukuyama wrote in *Trust: The Social Virtues and the Creation of Prosperity*, trust is cultural.[12] It is about community expectations outside the family. These institutional trust reserves run deep in health care; we see the roles of physicians and nurses consistently cited as the most respected societal roles. At the same time, consumers are rethinking the parameters of caregiving across role, venue, and condition to include both medical and nonmedical services such as food and transportation. And in a world in which health and care are centered around—and increasingly driven by—the individuals, the pace of that reconsideration will accelerate. The intersectional dynamics underpinning the health care ecosystem bring a complicated reality of required policy change, polarized politics, evolving provider delivery models, and increasingly vocal person-centric demand for better prices, services, and convenience.

Notes

1. Perry, "Fortune 500 Firms 1955 v. 2016."
2. Kim, "Jeff Bezos to Employees."
3. Interview with author Gary Bisbee, April 10, 2020.
4. Pierce and Goode, "The WIRED Guide to the iPhone."
5. Meeker, "Internet Trends 2018."
6. Naftulin, "Here's How Many Times We Touch Our Phones Every Day."
7. Meeker, "Internet Trends 2013."
8. Waldron, "How Walmart Is Leading the Omnichannel Charge."
9. Bariso, "Amazon Almost Killed Best Buy."
10. "Angela Ahrendts Talks Apple Store Makeover, Why Tim Cook Hired Her," *CBS This Morning*, April 25, 2017, https://www.cbsnews.com/news/angela-ahrendts-apple-svp-of-retail-redesign-today-at-apple/.
11. Marchi and Parekh, "How the Sharing Economy Can Make Its Case."
12. Fukuyama, *Trust*.

11

Focus on the Whole Person

Interviews

The articulation of a future state in which health care organizations retain deep institutional trust as they strive to match the customer-obsessive focus of Jeff Bezos will take more than a better understanding of the 2010s and the decade's implications for health care. It will take courageous leadership.

Health care leaders must decide who is the primary customer they want to serve. We believe that business strategies with the person at the center will be best positioned to deliver the personalization that health care customers will demand. Johns Hopkins's Paul Rothman has it right. Combining the intellectual capabilities of a world-class medical center with the commitment to the individual has resulted in a project to develop personalized medicine centers of excellence—all with the goal of redefining patient care.

The consumerization of health care is rising. As Walmart's Sam Walton once said, "There is only one boss. The customer."[1] The person's emergence as the primary economic decision maker in health care will be a defining feature of the 2020s. The smart players are investing today for that very different tomorrow.

When it comes to health care, consumers are interested in convenience, price, and satisfaction. Providers are getting the message, but it is a heavy lift for them to change the culture, approach, and facilities to become more person-centric.

COVID-19 was an instant shift for providers (and insurers) as customers "voted with their feet," to use the political expression, by substantially increasing their use of televisits during the COVID-19 crisis rather than in-person visits to physicians, hospitals, and ambulatory care centers. Patients adapted to the technology and the opportunity to have their encounters more conveniently from home. Similarly, many of the CEOs we interviewed indicated that previously skeptical physicians and caregivers saw the benefit of televisits and became supporters.

While some of the marketplace euphoria (and utilization rates) have calibrated down as the crisis has progressed, it is clear that televisits will be part of the health services solution suite in the decade ahead. Televisits are too convenient for certain categories of services. Telehealth's value proposition is too high at point of access for certain patient profiles, and its comparative cost advantage versus in-person visits is too compelling.

Affordability has become a flash point issue during the pandemic. A *Health Affairs* article published before COVID-19, discussing the health care financial burden on working families, referenced survey results from the West Health Institute and NORC of the University of Chicago, noting that "40% of individuals have foregone a recommended test or treatment in the last year due to health care costs."[2] As leaders we shouldn't need another study to know that affordability is the challenge of the decade and will require intense and ongoing focus and both the public and private sectors working collaboratively to improve affordability.

To be successful in the decade that is now advancing, health care leaders must understand the forces of data-driven personalization afforded by the foundational growth in data and technology. Technology-mediated platforms deliver continuity around consumer health journeys. We believe that these platforms move us closer to the digital front door consumers are seeking for health and care. For all of the disruptive promise of data-driven personalization, the best leaders will not just study the lessons they offer but will also rapidly apply them in their strategies to fundamentally redefine health care around the unique needs and preferences of the person.

COVID-19 Interviews

In the case discussions that follow, you will have the opportunity to hear from three leaders who offered real-time thoughts over the course of 2020 and into 2021 on how their organizations responded to the COVID-19 crisis.

Dr. Albert Bourla discusses what motivated Pfizer to commit itself to developing a vaccine in a time frame never before imagined. He also equated Pfizer's commitment to being responsive to the need of the individual.

Carolyn Witte shared why she formed a company directed toward women's health and well-being. The COVID-19 crisis presented organizational hurdles but also created a significant opportunity to address women's satisfaction as well as convenience and price.

Marcus Osborne shared Walmart Health's strategy of organizing around the person who is treated as a decision maker. Walmart Health believes that people

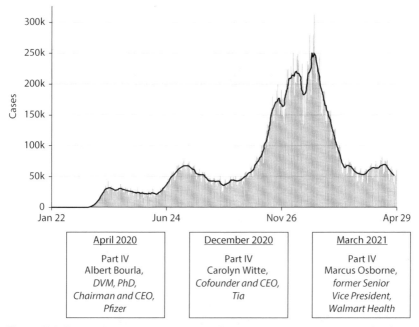

Figure 11.1. Featured case study interviews from a data-driven personalization lens. *Source:* Data from Centers for Disease Control and Prevention, 2021. Figures are updated as of May 1, 2021, from the COVID Data Tracker and underlying data set available at https://covid.cdc.gov/covid-data-tracker/#datatracker-home.

are interested in affordability, convenience, and satisfaction and addresses these objectives through its omnichannel strategy.

These three leaders, amid COVID-19 response and recovery (see figure 11.1), shared what it might look like to reimagine key aspects of how we organize and deliver health care services around the whole person.

Special Circumstances Call for Special Decisions

Staying focused on what matters most has been essential to serve as we are living our values and supporting our employees and communities. We know that as an industry, we can change the face of global public health, and there's no challenge that we cannot overcome.

—Albert Bourla, DVM, PhD, chairman and CEO, Pfizer

Before COVID-19, vaccines took years to develop from the laboratory before going into patients' arms. But in the spring of 2020 with an unprecedented pandemic threatening to kill millions and upend normal life around the world, pharmaceutical companies including Pfizer saw the necessity of curbing the pandemic through an effective vaccine in record-breaking time. In a public-private partnership with Operation Warp Speed, Pfizer was successful in developing its vaccine and bringing it to market in an unimaginably short time frame.

Albert Bourla, DVM, PhD

Over the course of his more than twenty-five years with Pfizer, chairman and CEO Dr. Albert Bourla, has held a wide range of senior positions, including group president of Pfizer's Global Vaccines, Oncology, and Consumer Health-care business, where he led the company's work on oncology and heart drugs, among others. His experience prepared him to push the company toward a bold goal beginning in the spring of 2020: developing and delivering an authorized vaccine against COVID-19 to reach Americans by the end of the year. This goal was achieved in mid-December, when the first shipments of Pfizer and BioN-Tech's BNT162b2 vaccine were delivered after the FDA issued it the first EUA for a COVID-19 vaccine on December 11, 2020.

Pfizer

Pfizer Inc. is a multinational pharmaceutical corporation headquartered in New York City. Since its inception in 1849, it has grown into one of the largest pharmaceutical companies in the world and was ranked sixty-fourth on the 2020 *Fortune* 500 list of the largest corporations in the United States by total revenue. Pfizer's product portfolio includes blockbuster drugs for chronic diseases, antibiotics, and vaccines.

Pfizer's Ambitious Goal

Our interview with Dr. Bourla took place in April 2020 during the height of the first surge of COVID-19 cases and deaths in the United States, which were concentrated largely in urban areas including Pfizer's home base of New York City.[3] Amid fears of hospital overcapacity and massive disruption to the economy, it was becoming evident that the fight against the virus would need more than public health measures such as physical distancing; a vaccine represented the surest bet to prevent infection and death. Dr. Bourla referred to vaccines as "one of the greatest public health interventions of all time," noting their role in eliminating smallpox and making polio a distant memory in most countries. "Effective vaccines can be one of the most final and reliable steps that can happen to address this crisis," Dr. Bourla said, explaining why Pfizer was moving quickly to deliver a vaccine by the end of 2020.

Moving quickly became Pfizer's mission in the spring and ensuing months as it worked in partnership with the German biotechnology company Bio-NTech to collaborate on developing the world's first mRNA-based vaccine against SARS-CoV-2. Pfizer expanded its manufacturing capabilities to ensure it could rapidly scale up production of an eventual vaccine while not disrupting the supply of its other products. Aside from overseeing the laboratory development and testing of vaccine candidates, Dr. Bourla pushed Pfizer to submit data to the FDA in real time for feedback without the typical lag time between trials. Because of the parallel phases of development, Pfizer invested hundreds of billions of dollars in capital, equipment, and materials to advance this novel vaccine platform without the guarantee that any candidate would eventually work or be approved, but, as Dr. Bourla said, "special circumstances are calling for special decisions."

Data-Driven Personalization

Dr. Bourla spoke passionately of Pfizer's business strategy as a person-centered one, keeping focus on maintaining its stable supply of medicines and vaccines to patients around the world as well as developing new drugs and vaccines to address the crisis. When we spoke, Pfizer was concurrently testing four vaccine candidates on the precipice of entering phase one clinical trials, which Dr. Bourla noted was an "atypical" strategy but one that aimed to maximize the chances of at least one of them eventually proving successful. The rapid pace of discovery and testing exemplified the urgency that Dr. Bourla felt was necessary to bring these vaccines to patients as soon as possible. Data resulting from the clinical safety and effectiveness trials were used to identify the most efficacious candidate and submit it for FDA authorization, eventually fulfilling Dr. Bourla's goal of delivering vaccine doses by the end of the year.

Dr. Bourla emphasized that the life sciences industry has achieved medical breakthroughs in other fields, such as therapies for HIV and cancers, proving that "we can change the face of global public health and there's no challenge that we cannot overcome" when skilled scientists work with a drive to deliver better outcomes for patients and society. He spoke of the importance of sharing scientific knowledge across institutions to benefit the broader scientific community and mentioned Pfizer's commitment to offering its "clinical development and regulatory expertise to support the most promising companies."

Beyond Personalization

As early as April 2020, Dr. Bourla recognized that gaining regulatory clearance would be a key hurdle to getting shots in arms. His team laid the groundwork with the FDA and its European counterpart, the European Medicines Agency, for the regulatory bodies to quickly move on submitted data "so that we can kill all this downtime that exists between trials and be able to start the next trial," he explained. Still, the process was not insulated from the political context, as President Donald Trump accused Pfizer and the FDA of delaying the release of positive vaccine data until after the presidential election.

Throughout the course of the pandemic, Pfizer ensured flexibility for its medical professional employees who wished to work on the front lines of the crisis with "support from Pfizer and with a job waiting for them once they want to go back," Dr. Bourla said. He also discussed areas of collaboration between Pfizer and integrated delivery networks, which had been in the works even before the pandemic. While the two have differing financial incentive structures, they have similar goals, making them a natural fit to work together to address SDoH, enact value-based care or population health initiatives, and share digital technology and data analytics solutions. "I think those partnerships, particularly when they focus on shared priorities, can lead to breakthroughs in transformational change in ways that neither Pfizer nor doctors can do independently," Dr. Bourla explained.

Postpandemic Lessons for Leaders

Pfizer's bold actions since the start of the pandemic show how it is possible to respond more adeptly to a crisis, starting by setting clear priorities for the leadership team early on. For Pfizer, these were the well-being of its employees, the continued supply of medicines and vaccines internationally, and the commitment to working together to discover tools to address the crisis. Dr. Bourla shared the specifics of Pfizer's five-point plan to "connect all members of the innovation ecosystem," which he hopes can improve rapid responses to any global health threats that may arise in the future. While it was developed with COVID-19 in mind, its emphasis on drawing in key players—from large pharma companies and small biotech innovators to government entities and academic institutions—can be applicable far beyond the current crisis.

"As one of the world's largest pharmaceutical companies, our focus in this crisis is dual. On the one hand, we are focused on protecting the safety and well-being of our colleagues while maintaining the continued supply of our medicines to patients around the globe. But also on the other hand, and more specifically, we are working with experts, both within and outside of Pfizer, to contribute medical solutions to this pandemic.

We know that as an industry, we can change the face of global public health and there's no challenge that we cannot overcome. Right now, we want to work as one team with our interested people and partner closely with federal agencies to more rapidly bring forward variants of options. Typically, it takes a very, very long time. And the only reason why we can bring it earlier is because you are doing things very atypically. First of all, we collaborate with the FDA in an expeditious manner. We are submitting papers to them and they are giving us feedback in no time so that we can kill all this downtime that exists between conducting the trials and being able to start the next trial. Usually you will do phase one, and then you will do phase two, then you'll do phase three, and then you will start thinking about manufacturing. We are going to do it in parallel."

—Albert Bourla, DVM, PhD

Personalization Is the Future of Health and Care

COVID-19 has accelerated the need for recognizing why different populations have different access issues, experience disease differently, and how we might think about having people-specific approaches to health.

—Carolyn Witte, cofounder and CEO, Tia

The COVID-19 crisis shifted Tia's tactics and also validated the founders' belief in a person-based health care model that meets patients where they are to deliver personalized care and education. By blending physical and digital care modalities and capitalizing on the virtual interests of many, Tia fostered an integrative care relationship between providers and patients and positioned itself as a one-stop shop where women can easily access information and care is delivered by a variety of providers ranging from primary care to gynecology to mental health.

Carolyn Witte

Carolyn Witte, cofounder and CEO of Tia, describes herself as a "design-thinker and storyteller," applying the principles of user-centeredness she learned from her time at Google's Creative Lab to make women's care more personalized, preventive, and integrative.[4] Witte hopes that Tia, by offering a trusted front door to health care, can help women avoid the siloed care, dehumanizing experiences, and difficult navigation that had characterized her previous experiences with the health care system. The rationale for creating Tia specifically for women arose from her realization that "if you are designed to serve everyone, then you're kind of designed to serve no one"; in contrast, "tailored approaches are better understood and more authentic."

Tia

Born out of the founders' frustrating experiences with the health care system, Tia is the developer of a network of digital wellness apps, clinics, and telehealth services focused on holistically treating women's health and well-being. Initially launched in 2016 as a text-based chatbot app for women to receive sexual health and wellness advice, Tia has since expanded its services to in-person and virtual clinics with a mission to "enable every female to achieve optimal health, as defined by herself."

Tia's Principles Validated by the Pandemic

We spoke with Witte in December 2020, when the United States was experiencing a surge in COVID-19 cases around the holidays. Reflecting on how Tia's strategy evolved during the pandemic, Witte noted that COVID-19 had validated the company's core views on where health case is going, as people became even more averse to receiving care in the hospital setting out of fear of infection. Tia sees itself as a new front door to the health care system that allows patients to access care in a comfortable clinic or from their own homes. The patterns of disproportionately worse COVID-19 outcomes among people of color reinforced Tia's belief in a population-specific approach to health care that delves into the drivers of health care disparities. Simultaneously, the uptake of telehealth seen during COVID-19 encouraged Tia to invest in telehealth as a valuable service offering and to expand its COVID-19–related and behavioral health services available virtually. Witte estimated that the pandemic has accelerated the use of telehealth by about three to five years, transforming virtual care into a major revenue driver.

While many health care companies paused expansion or even shuttered in-person clinic sites during the pandemic, Tia took a more aggressive approach and opened physical locations in two new markets, which Witte attributed to women's needs and preferences to receive certain health services in person. The leadership team launched the virtual care component ahead of the brick-and-mortar opening, which Witte called "a playbook that we didn't have nine months ago" before the pandemic.

Data as a Connector

Data, according to Witte, represents "the moat that will keep patients in our ecosystem and is the key to personalization." Tia uses a structured EHR that is controlled by patients and hopes to expand its use to integrate with other data sets, such as from tracking apps, and clinical and laboratory data to build predictive models and move into the realm of precision medicine. Tia's data platform connects providers in disparate settings and contexts, enabling them to connect the dots in a patient's care. Witte noted that instead of providers being treated like data-collection machines, they should be empowered to interpret and synthesize the vast quantity of data available to them and put those actions into the practice of medicine.

Tia's emphasis on personalization extends to the tone of messaging it uses to communicate with patients. For instance, Witte feels that one-size-fits-all messaging about the COVID-19 vaccines coming from an organization such as the CDC won't be as effective as messaging that is designed by and for women. "I think that's a huge opportunity that we have with these people-specific health care models to be the right messenger, if you will, about something that is intended to be for everyone," Witte said.

With its focus on women and their whole health, Tia brings together different provider specialties to provide personalized care. Witte noted that the need for integrated care is especially pronounced in women, for whom the care specialties of fertility and mental health are often interwoven. "We think there's a huge need clinically and then as well experientially to have integrated your therapist or psychiatrist and your PCP or gynecologist to manage your mental health in the context of your reproductive journey, wherever you are," Witte said as an example.

Beyond Personalization

Witte explained Tia's belief that women want vertically integrated care that connects both virtual and in-person services, joining together the formerly siloed parts of the health care ecosystem for both patients and providers and reducing the risks of fragmented care. One of these silos is mental health, a core focus for Tia and an area that Witte says needs to be integrated into primary care instead of standing on its own as a "niche" service. The 400 percent increase in mental health–related messages pouring into Tia's platform during the pandemic created a "clinical imperative for us to roll out more robust mental health services," as the company heard both patients and providers asking for more support.

The boom in telehealth during the pandemic has given rise to a proliferation in virtual-only telehealth start-ups, which Witte feels "treat the practice of medicine more like this commoditized transaction." She drew a contrast between Tia, which employs its health care providers and built its platform around the providers and patients, versus virtual-only platforms that simply connect patients to providers without employing the providers.

From a policy perspective, Witte spoke about the "financial and moral imperative to rebuild a health care system that works with women at the center of it," as she noted that women are often considered a "niche" population even though they make up half the population and control more than 80 percent of US health care dollars.

Postpandemic Lessons for Leaders

Witte envisions Tia as a test case for the viability of people-based care models, predicting that if Tia's playbook works, "we'll see a lot of activity in new people-based care models built for different populations that used to be considered niche." She drew a parallel between Tia's focus on women and personalized care delivery companies built for elderly populations, such as ChenMed and Oak Street. By cultivating trust in a period of crisis, next-generation companies will be in a better position to succeed in the post–COVID-19 world. For Tia, that success is defined as being "the trusted, digital/physical front door for women for the long-term health care system."

> "We're still doing exactly what we set out to do. Sure, COVID-19 has shifted our tactics a bit, but by and large, the pandemic just further validated our thesis. Our thesis is the need to shift from a one-size-fits-all approach to health care to a people-based health care model. COVID-19 accelerated the need for recognizing why different populations have different access issues, a different sort of clinical issue, experience disease

differently, and how we might think about having population specific approaches to health.

Pre-COVID-19, people had to choose between virtual-only players or traditional incumbents that were in person. There's going be a race to the bottom, and telehealth will become much more commoditized. You're seeing all these point solutions explode, and it's going to be interesting to think about who can connect those dots. We have to be able to connect the experience for patients and for providers and account for preferences from a price and access point perspective."

—Carolyn Witte

Setting a High Bar for Consumer Experience

Walmart Health would like to be the local family doc who took care of everything.

—Marcus Osborne, former senior vice president, Walmart Health

The first Walmart Health Center opened in September 2019. Plans are to have twenty-two centers opened by the end of 2021. As the largest retailer in the world, Walmart could substantially disrupt health care if it expands its health centers across the United States. We sat down with Osborne to learn more about why Walmart is entering the direct provision of health care, how it intends to organize around the person, what is its health strategy, and what are the postpandemic lessons for leaders. We interviewed Osborne in March 2021.[5]

Marcus Osborne, Former Senior Vice President, Walmart Health

Osborne was at Walmart since he left Harvard Business School in 2007 through late 2021. He has worked in Walmart's health care strategy and execution business since starting. Osborne is highly versed in health care and has the objective view of an outsider as well as the knowledge and understanding of an insider.

Walmart

Walmart is the largest retailer in the world, with 4,800 stores and 3,500 Supercenters in the United States. It had 2020 revenues of around $525 billion and a market capitalization of $375 billion as of March 2021. Walmart is acknowledged to have a supply chain and distribution system that is among the best in the world. Walmart provides pharmacy and vision wear services in its Supercenters, but Walmart Health is the first formal and widespread entry into the direct provision of health care.

Walmart Health

Osborne and Walmart Health leaders have studied the health care system, its strengths and gaps. Walmart Health is organizing around the person, whom it believes is an important decision maker. Walmart Health believes that people are interested in affordability, convenience, and satisfaction across the continuum of necessary health and social care.

The term "omnichannel" was pervasive in our conversation with Osborne. What does omnichannel mean in the context of health care? At its core, omnichannel is a type of retail that integrates different methods of shopping available to consumers, such as online, storefront, or by digital means (e.g., phone or video). Walmart Health executives believe that an integrated continuum of care with all types of coordinated delivery, such as facilities, clinics, phone, and video, will increase access to care, convenience, and affordability for the patient.

Walmart Health has studied consumer and provider preferences and has concluded that both consumers and providers would find a true omnichannel experience rewarding. Further, Walmart Health believes that neither consumers or providers have had the opportunities to participate in a fully coordinated omnichannel experience similar to what it is providing.

The bulk of the visits that Walmart Health Centers have seen to date are for people with chronic diseases. Walmart Health is staffed to provide services to people with strains, sprains, pinkeye, sinus infections, and the flu. Since the centers are equipped with radiology and heart monitoring equipment, they can treat most primary care and many urgent care needs.

Primary care in the Walmart Health model includes behavioral and social health as well as ancillary services such as dental, vision, and hearing. The omnichannel experience allows Walmart Health physicians and caregivers to choose the best mode of care for the particular patient's needs and to do so in an affordable and convenient way.

Affordability is an important piece of the Walmart Health strategy. Currently, an initial workup is $60 and a follow-on adult visit is $40. If a person has health insurance coverage, it will be accepted. If they do not, according to Osborne, the price is low enough that most people can afford it. Interestingly, we found a 1991 quote from Sam Walton, founder of Walmart, who said, "We've got to get the hospitals and doctors in line. We've got to get those charges under control."[6] The marching orders for Walmart Health turn out to have been issued thirty years ago.

Relationships with Providers and Health Insurance Plans

Walmart Health has directly employed primary care physicians, nurses, and other practitioners for the first centers. Going forward, Walmart Health is considering opportunities to work with health systems and physician groups in a coordinated way. For example, perhaps a physician group would serve both a health system and a Walmart Health Center. Osborne indicated that developing relationships with existing provider groups will be a focus as Walmart Health expands its centers.

In terms of relationships with health insurers, Walmart Health is pursuing two pathways. One is to work with health insurers that have a Medicare or Medicaid plan so that there is reimbursement for covered persons and an integrated coordinated approach to care. The second path will be for Walmart Health and health plans to develop a fee-for-value program for commercial groups and employers of all sizes. Learnings from this type of fee-for-value plan will be integrated into the full service that Walmart Health provides its customers.

Postpandemic Lessons for Leaders

Osborne states that Walmart Health's goal is to improve the health of Americans. The first step in that goal is to help people feel more engaged in their health. Engagement leads to control, empowerment, and action, which is directed at seeking contact with a provider or center that results in improving health.

Walmart Health is in the consumer experience business. Osborne believes in setting a high bar for consumer experience. For example, he thinks about using the standards that Four Seasons and the Montage deliver to its customers for hospitality and the standards that Apple uses in its Apple stores. The lesson to be learned from Walmart Health is to focus on the consumer experience, set high standards, and aim to have an impact on people by improving the health of the population.

"There's a little too much noise at the moment about telehealth. I just don't believe in telehealth in and of itself. I believe in telehealth solutions as part of an integrated omnichannel experience for consumers that combines more accessible care that's physical in nature, telehealth, digital health, AI-driven care, care in the home, care in the community. If anything, COVID created an accelerant to that movement into an omnichannel care environment, certainly for consumers.

The other thing that we're not talking a lot about here is it also accelerated the desire of providers and professionals to want to participate in that omnichannel environment. There were a lot of physicians, for example, who were skeptical of working in a telehealth environment or working in a digital environment and then got exposed, and now all of a sudden, they themselves are more convinced. You're seeing a lot of these providers and professionals raise their hand and say, 'I want to now be part of this new omnichannel experience that we can create for patients for consumers.' That's what COVID did. It accelerated our belief of what is possible, taking something that might have been five or seven years out and saying now it might be two or three years out."

—Marcus Osborne

Notes

1. Robert Reiss, "How Top CEOs Transform Companies around the Customer," *Forbes*, April 21, 2014. https://www.forbes.com/sites/robertreiss/2014/04/21/how-top-ceos-transform-companies-around-the-customer-like-the-new-kentucky-derby-video board/?sh=21fa3a3432ac
2. McCarthy-Alfano et al., "Measuring the Burden."
3. The content of this case study was gleaned from Albert Bourla's interview with author Gary Bisbee on April 10, 2020. A longer excerpt of the interview appeared in Fireside Chat with Gary Bisbee, Ph.D., "Episode 20."
4. The content of this case study was gleaned from Carolyn Witte's interview with authors Gary Bisbee and Sanjula Jain on December 21, 2020.
5. The content of this case study was gleaned from Marcus Osborne's interview with Gary Bisbee on March 6, 2021.
6. "Sam Walton's Vision for the Future, of Retail Healthcare," YouTube, March 6, 2017, https://www.youtube.com/watch?v=iNs6cDUKl7Y.

12

Organize around the Person

Lessons for Leaders

A recurring theme of this book is that crisis accelerates trends already under way, which is embodied by COVID-19. Access to information accelerates the desire of the individual to act, behave, and be treated as unique. In many other areas of their lives, individuals have choices and options.

> "COVID was more of an accelerant, meaning there
> were already these things that were occurring;
> it just [added] rocket fuel."
> **—Marcus Osborne, former senior vice president, Walmart Health**

There was no better role model for customer focus than Walmart's Sam Walton. In more recent times, Jeff Bezos and the late Steve Jobs have become the modern exemplars of providing customers with useful information and convenient access to it. Both exhibited a singular commitment to the customer experience from the very beginning of their companies.

Amazon puts the customer first, with undivided attention to price, selection, and convenience. A review of a company's shareholder letter is an excellent way to learn about the culture and priorities of a company. A review of Amazon's annual shareholder letters offers a consistent reminder of the company's "customer obsession."

Likewise, Jobs was a leader who was obsessive about the customer experience. He was a notorious perfectionist and slavishly focused on the consumer. Both Bezos and Jobs were willing to disrupt their companies in the interest of the consumer even as they were growing them. Most importantly, they were unconfused about who the customer was as they sought to scale their companies.

Dating back decades, the health care delivery and financing system has been oriented toward the physician as customer. Historically this made economic sense, since the physician referred patients to the hospital. The 2010s began the evolution from the physician to the customer who was armed with newfound data and data liquidity and growing expectations for convenience, satisfaction, and price. Notably, as innovations such as next-day delivery disrupt other non–health care businesses, they also work to elevate expectations inside health care. How does a seven-day wait for a physician visit feel compared to a next-day delivery to your doorstep?

Terminology is important: A *consumer* consumes a product or service, while a *customer* purchases goods and services. It is a subtle, important difference. In the coming years, leading health systems and other providers will become increasingly customer-focused. This will require not just a willingness to listen to customers but also the creation of a customer-oriented culture across the enterprise.

There was a customer effect taking hold before COVID-19, and the outbreak dramatically accelerated it. Former Nebraska governor and US senator Bob Kerrey made the point repeatedly that we will see substantial changes in response to the COVID-19 pandemic: "This virus is not going to disappear. There's not going to be a signing ceremony, unconditional surrender. It's going to be with us."[1] Dr. Mark McClellan makes a similar point, unequivocally stating as early as March 2020 that there will be a new normal. The winners among health organizations will be those that solidify the depth of the customer connection.

The essential takeaway for health care leaders is that the individual is the most influential decision maker (see figure 12.1). We see it in the macrotrends that have advanced in the decade outside of health care. We hear it from leaders ranging from Walmart Health to Pfizer to Tia looking to innovate inside health care. We will watch the consumer as decider unfold with increasing pace across every facet of health care in the 2020s.

Digitization and Scientific Innovation Are Expanding Personalization

The COVID-19 outbreak of 2020 demonstrated once again that medicine is both art and science. Health care implies healing, which is based on a "sacred trust" between clinicians and patients.[2] Digitization and scientific innovation facilitate diagnosis and treatment, but a relationship between caregiver and patient is a core part of the healing process. For those persons with a higher

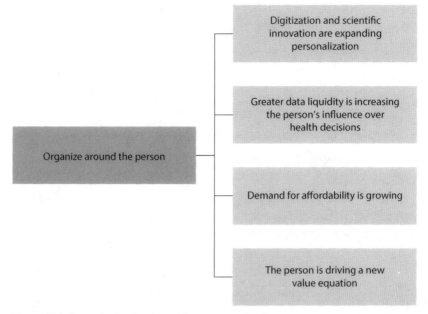

Figure 12.1. Ground rules for data-driven personalization.

perception of illness, this relationship is even more necessary. "Patients will have a lot of the data. They'll have their whole genome on their iPhone," according to Dr. Paul Rothman, dean and CEO of Johns Hopkins Medicine.[3] "One of the roles of a physician is to interface between the data and the patient, either interpreting the data for the patient or working with the patient to use that data to better their case."

Most of us have been impressed and in some cases amazed by the scientific discoveries and innovations of recent years, including genetic profiling, new medicines, and treatments designed for the unique individual. With all of this innovation, we found that we knew very little about COVID-19—how it spreads, how we contract it, why it affects some persons and not others, and what the chemical and genetic composition is—and needed to know more so that a useful vaccine and treatment paradigm could be developed.

The COVID-19 crisis reminds us that you can't fool Mother Nature. We will plan much better for the next crisis and assume a thought process of continued scientific innovation. The framework is one of respect for what we don't know or understand about how our bodies react to environmental challenges.

A conversation with Dr. Albert Bourla, Pfizer chairman and CEO, during the height of the COVID-19 surge provided him an opportunity to announce that Pfizer was entering four vaccine candidates into testing and concurrently modifying and ramping up existing manufacturing facilities to meet the needs of clinical trials and beyond.

"Special circumstances call for special actions."

—Albert Bourla, DVM, PhD, chairman and CEO, Pfizer

As referenced by the *Wall Street Journal*, Pfizer was pushing scientific innovation to the limit in the interest of developing the much-needed vaccine in less than a year. According to Bourla, we will learn and become more adept at responding to a crisis because of COVID-19.

As the Great Recession unfolded in the late 2000s and early 2010s, the federal stimulus package included tens of billions of dollars for the HITECH Act. The Meaningful Use regulations it spawned in 2010 drove pervasive EHR adoption. An underappreciated second order impact is the first-time digitization of health care data. The early seeds of its second order disruptive potential are starting to emerge.

For example, let's consider the Johns Hopkins inHealth initiative for developing Precision Medicine Centers of Excellence. During a discussion with Dr. Rothman, he emphasized the importance of digitizing medical care to facilitate scientific innovation.

Dr. Rothman referred to the Center of Excellence for Multiple Sclerosis, which gathers information from "sources such as DNA, family history, imaging, lifestyle, and environmental conditions to create prevention and treatment plans tailored for the individual."[4] Prior to the passage of the HITECH Act, the breadth and depth of data required by the Center would not have been available or affordable, the EHR would not have had its current breadth of data, and genetic data would not have been available or easily integrated.

Another example of the progress of digitization and scientific innovation is chimeric antigen receptor T cell therapy, a groundbreaking treatment in which a patient's T cells (a type of immune system cell taken from a patient's blood) are reengineered in the laboratory to recognize and attack cancer cells and reinfused into the patient's bloodstream. There are multiple examples of such individualized treatments available or in development that will change the delivery, financing, and organization of medicine and health care.

A complete model for personal diagnosis and treatment includes retrospective, concurrent, and prospective data. An early example, the acute physiology and chronic health evaluation (APACHE) outcomes methodology for assessing critical care patients, has at its foundation a database of retrospective information from millions of critical care patients. To that database is added concurrent information generated by the EHR. The APACHE algorithms, developed by researchers over many years, provides prospective (predictive) information about when the patient can be transferred to a less intensive unit, proving to be of less risk to the patient and reducing the cost of care. Information is also provided to the treating physician, conveying the likelihood of mortality in the ICU.

The APACHE example is one of many applications developed or under development that combine large databases, sophisticated technology, and medical research incorporating the individual's unique characteristics. These applications provide real-time information to the treating physician.

Digitization underlies the capability to quantify leading or informed practices and has made it more possible to quantify the variation in medical practice. Medical science research has prided itself on developing innovations in diagnosis and treatment, but the introduction in practice is complicated by the patient's unique biologic nature, large geographic variations that are not well understood as documented in the Dartmouth Atlas Project,[5] and physicians' experience and financial incentives.

Greater Data Liquidity Is Increasing the Person's Influence Over Health Decisions

"Real time" is the learning postpandemic. As we saw from the onset of COVID-19, we did not have time to pull together disparate databases to examine the effects of COVID-19 on the individual. Real-time and concurrent data are necessary to monitor a patient when the course of the disease is uncertain.

Of course, the value proposition of real-time data is both broad and deep. The diagnostic testing efforts by Dr. Tony Allen and Delaware State University tell the story. Dr. Allen, the university president, embarked upon building a real-time data infrastructure during the early days of COVID-19 to facilitate diagnostic testing and an innovative campus-influencer model to shape public health behaviors of students, faculty, and staff. The level of safety that Delaware State achieved was well beyond what would have been possible without real-time data. The postpandemic lesson is clear. As Dr. Amy Compton-Phillips, president of clinical care, Providence, noted, "How we use data and understand how to take this incredible volume of information in and then leverage it to change what we do is the task we have ahead of us."[6]

While Americans are generally supportive of real-time tracking of health risk for contact tracing purposes, when individuals learn that such initiatives would involve their phone (i.e., downloading an app) there is more resistance. And yet, we see that consumers are relatively comfortable self-reporting potential virus symptoms on social media platforms, such as Facebook, to identify potential COVID-19 hotspots. The use of personal health information as a critical component of national surveillance will magnify the role of both clinical data as a key asset and customer concerns about data privacy and security.

Generating and acting on intensely private information brings front and center the safety of the individual's data. Cybersecurity has leaped to the forefront of risk for providers and other organizations with access to an individual's data, such as payers, insurers, and employers. Another critical endeavor is to ensure that the data being generated by the EHRs are accurate, as new treatments require individual-specific data.

Many scientists and politicians support a national sentinel surveillance system that could include point-of-care testing, serological testing, and contact tracing. A country- or state-wide database balances the health of the population with the privacy rights of the individual. This balance will be at the heart of scientific and political debate, health policy development, provider engagement, and financing during the 2020s.

Providers will not have the resources or time (as discovery is moving faster than any one organization or individual can keep pace with) to develop an expertise in delivery and treatments such as chimeric antigen receptor T cell therapy and genetic applications. Partnering with those organizations that have expertise in database technologies is a strategy that providers will increasingly prioritize.

The late Steve Jobs's well-chronicled perfectionism drove his teams to iteratively enhance the iPhone with each and every release. Similarly, health care leaders have been reminded from the COVID-19 experience that they must better plan for the unexpected and push unstintingly for continuous improvement as Jobs demanded of his Silicon Valley engineers.

One opportunity in health care is both obvious and frustrating. Remember the last time you visited a physician or were admitted to a hospital? How many forms did you fill out? One for the physician, one for the insurance company, a waiver of your rights, a waiver for use of your data. Following completion of the battery of forms, your visit to the radiology department required completion of another form or two, just for good measure.

Can you imagine passing out clipboards in the emergency department while it is flooded with COVID-19 patients? We have learned from COVID-19 that we cannot control the flow of patients during a crisis. Data liquidity is the first step to adapting to an onslaught of patients. Neal Patterson, the late cofounder and former CEO of Cerner, was fond of saying, "We need to get rid of the clipboard and, while we're at it, let's get rid of the waiting room."[7]

At its core, health care data liquidity refers to the sharing of secure, trusted health care data concurrently with the needs of the patient. You might think that this is a matter of convenience for the individual. However, using the example of Johns Hopkins's precision medicine centers of excellence, genetic data comes from one source, clinical data from another, sociodemographic data from a third, and so on. Gathering these data from different sources takes time, and the interface must be as accurate as banking data and vectoring information for your forthcoming airline flight.

Common sense suggests that we should only need to fill out a form once or maybe not at all, since the information likely is available elsewhere. Filling out forms once is more convenient, less costly, and more satisfying for the individual. And it is critical in the heat of a crisis.

When combined with big data and analytical capabilities such as artificial intelligence and machine learning as popularized by Amazon, the prospects of liquidity and data-driven personalization in health care are becoming a reality. Unfortunately, the HITECH Act did not require interoperability. Sharing of data from one EHR, financial, or administrative system to another has been a major challenge. Why? At a high level,

- Health care information technology organizations structured their information systems and data repositories differently, and the benefits of interoperability have relatively recently become of high priority;
- Personalized data are precious, and interoperability requires trust in the security and purpose of sharing data;
- The cost of sharing data is not directly reimbursed by the payer; and
- Organizations do not want to lose control of data.

Each of these reasons has importance to the organization holding the data, but when data-driven personalization is the goal, the use of the data will come to outweigh the interests of the organization.

As Meaningful Use–stage progression continues and payment models continue their inexorable shift, the opportunities are obvious. Mobile health holds the promise of shaping clinical workflow, redesigning treatment paradigms and moderating costs in areas such as primary and chronic disease care, and extending care to rural and underserved populations.

Yet, more data sharing will introduce new questions for leaders (see table 12.1). Will greater sharing of data deepen the relationship between caregiver

Table 12.1. Public opinion perceptions regarding sharing of personal medical data

	Likely	Not Likely
There will be more data breaches and attempts by hackers to steal patient data.	82%	11%
Health insurance companies will try to influence where patients receive care.	82%	10%
Health care costs will increase for unhealthy patients.	76%	14%
Medical providers such as doctors and hospitals will try to influence where patients receive medical care.	73%	18%
The federal government will monitor patients' medical history.	67%	23%
Health care providers and the government will be able to identify disease outbreaks faster.	52%	35%
Patients will become more involved in their personal health and wellness.	49%	41%
There will be more medical breakthroughs, and more diseases will be cured.	40%	47%
Health care costs will decrease for healthy patients.	24%	65%

Note: By and large, Americans believe that increased sharing of medical data will result in more negative implications. Respondents were asked to respond to the following question: "How likely do you think each is to happen as a result of a personal medical data being shared more?"

Source: Public Opinion Strategies Analysis based on their own national survey of 1,010 registered voters, conducted August 5-7, 2019. Used with permission.

and customer/patient? Will it allow a more individualized therapeutic relationship? Will the clinician know more about the patient's genetic profile and possible solutions to health challenges? All signs are that digitization and scientific innovation will fundamentally increase the capability of the clinician.

The COVID-19 outbreak caused fundamental concern for individuals about visiting hospitals or doctor's offices for fear they would be exposed to the virus. The use of telemedicine visits grew exponentially in response. In April 2020, Ascension CEO Joe Impicciche shared that during the initial surge, telehealth visits jumped from five hundred visits per day before the crisis to ten thousand per day during it.[8] This experience was replicated in health systems throughout the country. "What we had planned to do in forty-eight months, we did in three weeks," said Carillion Clinic president and CEO Nancy Howell Agee.[9] And there will be no looking back.

COVID-19 made it abundantly clear that use of health facilities was not necessary and was arguably wasteful in costs. Home as venue for patients was loudly trumpeted as individuals preferred the comfort and familiarity of home over the risk of COVID-19 exposure in a health facility. New approaches to data liquidity and sensor technology designed for monitoring those in homes further facilitates home as a venue and will become the standard.

There is universal agreement among large provider health system CEOs that the new health economy will include greater use of telehealth to screen, monitor, and treat patients. However, the true breadth of telehealth's postpandemic impact is still playing out. A range of intersectional forces across the 4Ps will determine this modality's scale impact. Key policy issues such as state licensure for telehealth providers remain unresolved. Critical payment decisions surrounding reimbursement are being addressed by Washington policymakers.

Notwithstanding these policy (and political) uncertainties, it is clear that some categories of consumers will gravitate toward telehealth. Jason Gorevic, CEO of Teladoc Health, is deeply committed to building a virtual connection between patient and caregiver. "It's all about the patient experience," Gorevic said, "and we do a lot of work in order to coach physicians on a webside manner, not just a bedside manner, because there are differences."[10]

Demand for Affordability Is Growing

Companies often forget to ask what customers value and that this is the most important question companies can ask. As health insurance premiums continue to rise and out-of-pocket expenses grow, a first-time shopper is coming to health care. Decisions more deeply influenced by price will increase, and demands for elevated transparency will become a deafening shout.

Affordability is a second-order impact of health care costs and transparency. Access to health care rather than cost or price has been a focus years since corporations added employee health benefits during World War II and took responsibility for payments. As costs continue to increase, the customer is demanding more value.

During COVID-19, many Americans experienced a double hit—that is, they lost their jobs and incurred costs of COVID-19 illness. In response, most insurance companies expanded their policies to cover COVID-19 testing, and some covered the cost of hospitalizations. The CMS relaxed certain payment policies for Medicare and Medicaid beneficiaries. We have gone through similar affordability challenges in past crises. As a country we can do better, and the COVID-19 crisis has galvanized the political and health policy process to do just that.

Employers, for their part, have reacted to cost increases by the introduction of high-deductible health plans. Governments are seeking to constrain expenditure growth, and more costs are being shifted to the consumer by increasing the price of health coverage. The consumer is bearing an ever-greater percentage of health care costs, leading to health care becoming increasingly unaffordable for many in the population. The chorus of demands for value continues to increase. "We've learned from the pandemic that we need to accelerate the move toward a value-based health care system," affirmed Dr. Vivian Lee, MD, president of health platforms, Verily Life Sciences.[11]

Affordability and economic equality have become a flash point in the COVID-19 outbreak. At the height of the initial surge, approximately one-third of the population, those who have jobs that allow them to do so, sheltered at home. About one-third of the population continued to report for work because they did not receive pay when they did not work. They were forced to choose between possible exposure to COVID-19 and their paycheck. This was exacerbated for minorities, who suffered higher mortality rates and lost jobs and income at a greater rate than Caucasians. This troubling trend has accelerated and amplified an already growing dialogue among health care leaders around not just affordability but also health equity.

How will the COVID-19 outbreak affect affordability of health care? Those without income will not be able to spend for their health care. Medicaid roles have increased to accommodate them, which puts financial pressure on the federal government, state governments, and providers that are reimbursed at a rate less than costs.

Before the COVID-19 crisis, affordability was growing as an important health challenge of the 2020s. Following the onset of COVID-19, affordability vaulted into the lead as the largest challenge that the health system and our political and health policy institutions will face.

How can we make health care more affordable? Most experts point to a combination of lower costs, increased price transparency, changing incentives for providers and consumers to use less expensive services, and more efficiency in health care organization and delivery. The COVID-19 crisis will result in changes for all health care stakeholders.

The forces of digitization and disruptive scientific innovation, as in many industries, is transforming health care and offers promise for increased administrative efficiencies. For example, many health systems' use of robotic process automation in areas such as revenue cycle and supply chain leads to greater efficiencies. Also, the innovation in personalization of diagnosis and treatment allows more precision and efficiency.

Many Americans have access to the finest health care in the world. Work needs to be done to ensure that all citizens are included. Health care is more expensive in the United States than in other countries. Costs are high, and annual increases typically exceed inflation. Successful efforts to lower costs will likely result in lower paychecks for health care workers unless we can alter incentives and lower economic friction points such as overlapping and unnecessary services.

The pressure for transparency is being heeded by health systems, albeit slowly, and transparency will soon be so routine that health systems will post prices for common procedures, providing choice for price shoppers. Since health care is fully political, legislators and regulators will play an increasingly active role. The 2020 election served as a referendum on handling of the COVID-19 pandemic.

The Person Is Driving a New Value Equation

The customer is increasingly demanding more value from the health care system. The dramatic growth in information, a greater amount shaped for people and their circumstances, provides individuals with the power to influence and make health care decisions. Yet, when we consider the critical nexus between provider and person, nobody owns the relationship with the person. As Ken Paulus, CEO of Prime Therapeutics, highlights, there is no "clear advocate or air traffic control for the patient."[12] There is a gap to be filled in regard to who can help guide the person in making decisions about where and when to seek care.

Hospitals, doctors, and nurses have traditionally ranked at the top of "most trusted" polls. The health care establishment has considered that a given. With exponentially increasing amounts of data parsed into information shaped to personal interests and characteristics, traditional loyalty has been shifting. Are we more loyal to the doctor or hospital or to the information generated and presented on our smartphones?

In fact, engagement surveys reveal that consumers are strongly loyal to their regular physicians, but convenience, satisfaction, and price could override loyalty.[13] Carolyn Witte, cofounder and CEO of Tia, speaks to the importance of platform-mediated trust as the front door to the health care system. When consumers don't know where to go and have various options from virtual to urgent care, there are increased risks of fragmented care. Those organizations that can connect these settings and experiences in a simplified manner for the consumer will be those that become the first-stop shop.

An important variable typically not included in public opinion surveys is the perception of illness at the point of making a health-related decision—a fact brought into stark relief by the COVID-19 outbreak, when there was a paucity of information and a high risk if the virus was contracted. The COVID-19 crisis has reminded us that when our perceived illness is life-threatening and our information is limited, our local physician or nurse is our trusted source. Information about less threatening illness, such as the common cold, can be gathered from many different sources.

During a March 2020 interview, Dr. Julie Gerberding, former CDC director and currently senior executive of Merck, shared her experience that during a national public health crisis, local physicians were the most trusted source of information about the crisis. As noted, doctors and nurses were the most trustworthy sources of information about the COVID-19 crisis. The trust reserve is high for traditional providers of care. The business question is how these traditional providers will leverage this trust in a differentiated manner.

Much has been made of the similarities of big-box retailers and health systems with their big-box–like hospitals that are highly reliant on facilities, people, and technology. Large health systems can learn from big-box retailers, such as Walmart, that have been disrupted by Amazon and responded with substantially upgraded digital and in-person conveniences.

In a matter of weeks, COVID-19 dramatically disrupted the US retail industry as states began issuing shelter-in-place orders, forcing nonessential businesses to close their doors. Despite these conditions, the big-box retailer Walmart focused on providing value to the customer and hired more than one hundred thousand new employees to support the surge in demand during the pandemic. By taking a community-first approach across both its online and physical channels, the company managed to set itself apart. While other retailers were focused on promoting discounts to encourage online sales, Walmart focused on informative messaging around grocery delivery. While Walmart's grocery app sales grew, the company was a first mover in implementing measures such as contactless payment methods, customer traffic control, and glass barrier protection for employees and customers to create a personalized and safe experience.

The challenge is captured by referring to the competitive strategy of the seamless shopping experience including both in-store and online shopping. We have asked the question of the large health systems, "Are you making muscular investments in e-commerce to offer the individual seamless experience that is convenient, simple and price competitive?"

Tia, a platform for providers and patients, is illustrative. After closing its in-person clinic in New York with the onset of COVID-19, Tia made the rapid shift to virtual appointments. The positive response from its customers led to an expansion of COVID-19–related and behavioral health services. In tandem, Witte and her team further made the decision to open physical clinics in two new markets during the pandemic in light of exponential growth in virtual care services across the country. She attributes this decision to defining value for the customer and to the need and preferences of Tia's target customer, women, to seek certain women's health services in person.

An interview with Dr. Rod Hochman, president and CEO of Providence, provided him the opportunity to discuss Providence's strategy to move closer to the consumer by self-disrupting through deconstructing Providence's care delivery. By that he meant that Providence created homogeneous units within the company with similar incentives to deliver health and care to individuals within respective markets.

As we discussed in part I, the decade of the 2010s solidified that health care is now fully political. Adult patients and health care consumers vote. What better way to gain advocates for health care preferences than a happy customer?

The term "value" has become a watchword among stakeholders in health care. The risk is that value is defined in the eye of the beholder. In other words, providers might see value differently than the insurer or the consumer. Pursuing a culture of disruption from the vantage point of the individual will place value in the right position for leaders to act on.

There is an emerging new health economy, with the consumer as an influential decision maker. The COVID-19 outbreak has transformed health care economics, which is coming faster than many in the political, health policy, and provider delivery sectors are anticipating.

Notes

1. The content of this case study was gleaned from Bob Kerrey's interview with author Gary Bisbee on April 21, 2020. For a longer excerpt of the interview, see Fireside Chat with Gary Bisbee, Ph.D., "Episode 24."
2. Koster, Bisbee, and Charan, $n = 1$.
3. Fireside Chat with Gary Bisbee, Ph.D., "Episode 5."
4. Fireside Chat with Gary Bisbee, Ph.D., "Episode 5."
5. Dartmouth Atlas Project, "The Dartmouth Atlas of Health Care."
6. Her Story with Sanjula Jain, "Episode 26."
7. During the 2000s, Cerner Corporation drove a series of innovation efforts around employer health. The development efforts centered around several design mantras, including "no more clipboards" and "medical records are redundant and they repeat themselves." These sentiments were shared in a series of conversations between Patterson and authors Donald Trigg and Gary Bisbee, Ph.D., throughout that decade.
8. Fireside Chat with Gary Bisbee, Ph.D., "Episode 22."
9. Fireside Chat with Gary Bisbee, Ph.D., "Episode 15."
10. Fireside Chat with Gary Bisbee, Ph.D., "Episode 50."
11. Her Story with Sanjula Jain, "Episode 28."
12. Fireside Chat with Gary Bisbee, Ph.D., "Episode 42."
13. Francis and Rastogi, "The RBC Capital Markets Consumer Health & Information Technology Survey."

Conclusion

A Call to Action

At the outset of this book, we told the story of Dr. Rod Hochman and Providence, at ground zero in Seattle, as they managed the first patient who had contracted COVID-19. Several weeks later, we spoke with Dr. Steven Corwin at New York-Presbyterian as New York began to emerge as the COVID-19 epicenter.

As the Delta variant surged forward over the course of 2021, the United States continued to reach a series of new milestones. Hospitalizations climbed. Lives lost soared. The numbers tell a tough and tragic story. They will drive profound health economy–level change in the decade ahead.

As Dr. Corwin shared with us, health care workers at New York-Presbyterian often tell him that they have been trained to take on the challenges of the moment. Amid the tumult and tough realities of COVID-19, he noted, "I tell them nobody has been trained to do what you are doing. Because in the forty years that I have been in medicine, I haven't seen this, and I have seen a lot."[1]

Providence's Dr. Hochman built a strategic scaffolding to organize his thinking surrounding the disorderly events of COVID-19. His BC (before COVID), DC (during COVID), and AC (after COVID) framework helped us as we sought greater clarity on the crisis and its postpandemic implications.

Why is knowledge of history important? Whether referencing the report of the Committee on the Cost of Medical Care published in 1932 or understanding the importance of the legislation of 1982 regarding diagnosis-related groups (DRGs), we believe that the starting point for thinking about the future is a thoughtful inspection of the past.

Our review of the 2010s, coupled with hundreds of real-time conversations with leaders amid the pandemic, have us excited about the coming decade in health care. For all of the Rumsfeldian known unknowns, the one thing that is certain is that our postpandemic tomorrow will be different than today.

The last decade (2010–19) represented one of the most consequential periods in US health care since the passage of Medicare and Medicaid in the 1960s. A critical combination of digitization, Democratic reform, and demographics launched a multidecade transformation in how we finance, organize, and deliver health and care. These macroforces placed Washington, D.C., squarely in the role of both top regulator and top payer in US health care.

The straight party-line passage of the ACA, followed by an equivalent GOP-led push to repeal and replace it, made the modern politics of health care utterly toxic. Nancy-Ann DeParle joked to President Barack Obama that some of the eventual opponents of the ACA had more provisions in the law than the president himself. She also reflected that the near-term impact of the ACA "would have been so much stronger if it had been bipartisan."[2]

In the absence of bipartisan support, the health care politics of the ACA were a white-hot flash point in every election cycle in the 2010s. Indeed, the issue would dominate four of the five election cycles in 2010–18 and would play out amid a larger wave of overall political polarization that some contend has reached its highest level since the American Civil War.

If the health politics fisticuffs were big, so too were the health policy reach and impact of the ACA. The law massively improved the level of access to health insurance, particularly for the individual. The expansion of coverage meant that there was a new center of gravity in health care policy: the challenge of increasing health care costs and its traveling companion, affordability. The crisis of affordability, accelerated by COVID-19 dislocations, will be the issue that will define the 2020s.

Washington, in its role as top regulator and payer, increasingly set the terms for how the health economy operated. For provider delivery models, Washington drove an important shift in business model, with the 2010s resulting in the most significant period of consolidation and pursuit of systemness since the 1990s.

Finally, in addition to a dynamic and evolving provider supply side, the before COVID-19 period also saw an increased level of personalization. The person, in the always-changing role as patient, member, caregiver, and consumer, thought increasingly about cost, convenience, and service. The health and care implications of COVID-19 will only accelerate this trend.

We have been privileged to conduct hundreds of interviews with health care leaders over the last quarter century. We also have had additional discussions across the health economy in our entrepreneurial efforts to define and lead it. In

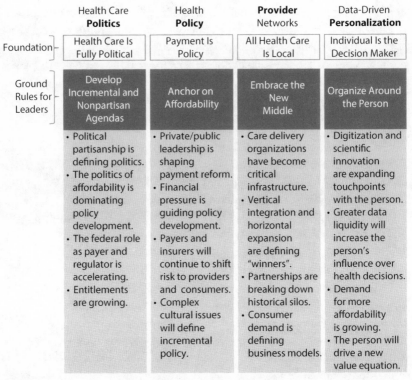

Figure 13.1. Ground rules for leaders.

our estimation, there is no more valuable skill set for a leader than active listening. It is the discipline of truly hearing what is said.

During COVID-19, the necessity of communicating with employees, medical staff, and the community surfaced time and time again in our conversations with leaders. Peter Fine at Banner spoke of hunger in the community for a wise guide that could be a trusted source of truth about the pandemic, safety, testing, social distancing, masks, and vaccines. Merck's Dr. Gerberding discussed the need to deliver tough messages and the essential role of voices such as the CDC. Former Indiana governor Mitch Daniels reflected on the credibility of local and state officials closer to essential facts on the ground. J&J's Alex Gorsky voiced the need to acknowledge challenges and, at the same time, give your associates a reason to believe in the future beyond the crisis.

Figure 13.1 presents each of the 4Ps that we think of as pillars of the health economy. Each P has a foundational term that characterizes it. We have developed ground rules (basic principles) for each P. The ground rules will guide strategy and action relating to that P. Let's consider the framework outlined in figure 13.1 and briefly review what we have discussed in depth in earlier pages.

Health Politics: Health Care Is Fully Political

The US health economy consumed 18 percent of the GDP. Health care spending is the largest single line item in the federal budget. Moreover, rising costs and declining affordability placed health care as a top-of-mind issue for voters, including in the 2020 election, when COVID-19 took center stage. As a result, health care demanded the attention of elected officials in their role as policymaker and politician alike.

If health care is visible, it is also complex. This correlated reality means that every health care leader has a responsibility to educate and advocate in Washington, D.C. As Providence's Dr. Hochman said, health care leaders simply aren't investing enough time in Washington. He is right. Health care leaders need to invest more time ensuring that their voices are heard in Washington.

While the early days of COVID-19 saw a brief period of bipartisan, bicameral collaboration, the political scars of Hillarycare, Obamacare, and repeal and replace were just below the surface. The 2010s saw health care make a final, fatigued shift away from the bipartisan policymaking it enjoyed for most of the post–World War II period. Health care is now fully political.

Affordability is a concern that is widely shared across the industry and, like many trends, was accelerated by COVID-19. Inside the Beltway, lowering the age of eligibility for Medicare and eligibility for Medicaid is a policy unknown amid ongoing debate. Outside the Beltway, players such as Walmart are also looking to tackle the health care cost curve. Walmart Health's Marcus Obsorne says that affordability is both a disappointed systems-level gap and a material opportunity for private sector innovation.

Health Policy: Payment Is Policy

As we wrote in part II, we noted that the true definition of a payer within the US health economy is a source of funding for health and care services. Government, employers, and individuals are the predominant source of those funds. Today, Washington is the largest percentage source of funding predominantly through Medicare and the federal share of Medicaid.

There is no rule that we see more consistently missed in health care than understanding that the role of how things are regulated and paid for has a disproportionate impact on how supply and demand operate (or operate differently) in health care. The ascent of Washington to the role of top regulator and payer has never made this rule a more critical one for current and aspiring leaders. Payment is policy.

Payment reform requires both public and private leadership. MA is a notable example, as discussed by former Blue Cross and Blue Shield of Minnesota's CEO Dr. Craig Samitt. He believes that partnerships between insurance companies and health providers is a business and operational framework that will be increasingly visible in the new health economy.

Payers (governments, employers, and individuals) and insurers, acting on behalf of the payers, have been shifting risk to providers and consumers for the last twenty years. This shifting of risk runs headlong into the affordability issue.

The pandemic showed clearly that unevenness and gaps exist in health insurance and access to care by diverse populations. Social/health programs such as SDoH became much more visible during the pandemic, and there is an opportunity to apply more resources and attention to increase their priority.

Provider Networks: All Health Care Is Local

During the 2010s, providers responded to the anticipated payment shifts framed by the ACA with a major consolidation wave. In addition to horizontal integration, they also consolidated vertically through the acquisition of care venues beyond the hospital. This zip code–level consolidation was coupled with a significant push to build out integrated delivery systems.

During the COVID-19 pandemic, health provider CEOs have talked consistently about the failure of the current payment model. Dr. Steven Corwin at NewYork-Presbyterian said there will be a coming conversation about how we finance health care. Wright Lassiter at Henry Ford noted the differential impacts of the crisis on provider and insurer, commenting that everyone should be pitching in. Dr. Marc Harrison at Intermountain Healthcare spoke of the need to treat people who are sick and be in the "keeping people well business."[3]

Incentives are not aligned today among health economy stakeholders. In the 2020s, we will see an evolution toward the New Middle as person-centered care redefines the delivery and payment models. Progress will be made on New Middle models for all people, including minorities, low-income people, and the uninsured. The payment model will be defined at the federal level but will be actioned at local and regional levels. The New Middle will define a provider delivery model at the zip code level that is increasingly centered on the person and will entail health systems taking on a role in the community similar to public utilities.

Data-Driven Personalization:
The Person Is the Most Influential Decision Maker

The 2010s brought amazing growth in the number of technologies available to the individual ranging from an explosion in mobility to a radical rethinking of e-commerce to the rise of social media. Within health care, the decade also saw the first-time digitization of the content of the industry, laying the foundation for data-driven personalization, and increasingly health care consumers cited the importance of cost, convenience, and experience in their expectations and preferences.

During COVID-19, many of these nascent person-centric trends accelerated. Health system leaders such as Terry Shaw at AdventHealth pushed forward on whole-person care models beyond the hospital. Jason Gorevic at Teladoc sought to define a new physical–digital care model he calls the "webside experience."[4]

As we move into the 2020s, the person will become the most influential decision maker in the new health economy. An emerging digital tool kit, coupled with ongoing growth in the availability of data, will offer the potential of a more informed and active consumer. The implications for key areas of the health economy ranging from MA to commercial payers will be significant.

Our Call to Leadership

Our extended time in the health economy marketplace has afforded us a chance to listen and to learn. It drove our belief that a reinvention of US health care requires us to think across the breadth and depth of health care politics, health policy, provider networks, and data-driven personalization.

Before COVID-19, our strategic framework was tested repeatedly in interactions with health economy leaders. During COVID-19, we further refined our thinking, concluding that many of the secular forces of change set forth in the 2010s would be accelerated in meaningful ways by the pandemic. This is our call to leadership in the decade ahead.

COVID-19 will be remembered as a flashbulb moment in the long arc of US history. We will recall it vividly for generations to come. For all of their diversity across health care, the leaders who feature in *The New Health Economy: Ground Rules for Leaders* are a splendid display of what it means to make a daily impact. Our caregivers and communities have rallied to serve both the sick and the economically challenged.

As leaders who have spent our professional lives at the heart of the health economy, we didn't need a crisis to know that health care is too important to stay the same. And in the postpandemic wake of COVID-19, we will see a generational opportunity to build a new health economy that is more caring, affordable, resilient, and equitable.

Notes

1. Fireside Chat with Gary Bisbee, Ph.D., "Episode 40."
2. Her Story with Sanjula Jain, "Episode 2."
3. Fireside Chat with Gary Bisbee, Ph.D., "Episode 17."
4. Fireside Chat with Gary Bisbee, Ph.D., "Episode 50."

Appendix

COVID-19 Timeline of Key Events

Note: The events reflected are representative of key activities that played out during the time in which the authors were writing this book, which primarily reflect the first twenty months of the COVID-19 pandemic.

January 9, 2020	**WHO Announces Coronavirus-Related Pneumonia in Wuhan, China** The World Health Organization (WHO) says the illness has infected at least 59 people, but the Chinese government has not yet made an official statement on the cause.
January 21, 2020	**CDC Confirms First US Coronavirus Case** A Washington state resident who returned from Wuhan on January 15, 2020, becomes the first person in the United States with a confirmed case of what is then called the 2019 novel coronavirus.
January 31, 2020	**WHO Issues Global Health Emergency** With a worldwide death toll of more than 200 and a jump to more than 9,800 cases, the WHO declares a public health emergency.
February 3, 2020	**US Declares Public Health Emergency** The Donald Trump administration declares a public health emergency due to the coronavirus outbreak.
March 11, 2020	**WHO Declares COVID-19 a Pandemic** In declaring COVID-19 a pandemic, the WHO expresses deep concern around the "alarming levels of spread and severity" of the outbreak.
March 13, 2020	**Trump Declares COVID-19 a National Emergency** President Trump declares the novel coronavirus a national emergency, thus unlocking billions of dollars in federal funding to fight the spread of the disease.
March 17, 2020	**CMS Temporarily Expands Use of Telehealth** The Center for Medicare and Medicaid Services (CMS) allows Medicare to reimburse telehealth visits the same as it would in-person visits, in hopes of protecting patients from possible exposure to the virus.

March 19, 2020	**First State Issues Stay-at-Home Order** California becomes the first state to issue a stay-at-home order, which requires all residents to stay at home except to go to an essential job or shop for essential needs.
March 27, 2020	**Trump Signs CARES Act Into Law** The Senate passes the Coronavirus Aid, Relief, and Economic Security (CARES) Act, providing $2 trillion in aid to hospitals, small businesses, and state and local governments. This marks the largest economic recovery package in history.
March 30, 2020	**FDA Authorizes Use of Hydroxychloroquine** The Food and Drug Administration (FDA) issues an emergency use authorization (EUA) for "hydroxychloroquine sulfate and chloroquine phosphate products" to be donated to hospitals to treat patients with COVID-19.
April 14, 2020	**Trump Orders a Halt on $400 Million in Funding for the WHO** In a press conference, the president announces that he is halting US funding of the WHO pending a review of its response to COVID-19.
May 28, 2020	**US COVID-19 Deaths Pass the 100,000 Mark** The Centers for Disease Control and Prevention (CDC) calls this milestone a "sobering development and a heart-breaking reminder of the horrible toll of this unprecedented pandemic."
June 10, 2020	**US COVID-19 Cases Reach 2 Million** Confirmed cases hit 2 million, and new infection numbers are on the rise in twenty states as some ease restrictions.
June 30, 2020	**Oklahoma Expands Medicaid** Oklahoma's Medicaid expansion passes by a majority vote, expanding eligibility to adults with incomes up to 138 percent of the federal poverty level.
July 2, 2020	**States Reverse Reopening Plans** States including California and Indiana postpone or reverse plans to reopen their economies, as the United States records 50,000 new cases of COVID-19—the largest one-day spike since the pandemic's onset.
July 7, 2020	**CMS Proposes Paying More for Home Dialysis Equipment** The CMS proposes a rule aimed at keeping patients outside of dialysis centers for treatment amid rising case counts. The transitional add-on payment for new and innovative equipment and supplies would allow greater access to home dialysis machines for Medicare beneficiaries.

July 15, 2020

HHS Announces New Hospital Data Reporting Protocol
The Department of Health and Human Services (HHS) announces a mandate that all hospitals must bypass the CDC and send COVID-19–related information to a central database run by HHS Protect. Previously, data were sent to the CDC's National Healthcare Safety Network website.

July 22, 2020

HHS and the DOD Announce Vaccine Distribution Agreement with Pfizer and BioNTech
HHS and the Department of Defense (DOD) strike a deal with Pfizer and BioNTech for a December delivery of 100 million doses of their COVID-19 vaccine candidate.

July 27, 2020

Moderna Vaccine Begins Phase 3 Trial, Receives $472 Million from Trump Administration
Moderna begins the first phase 3 clinical trial to examine a vaccine candidate against COVID-19 and announces that the Trump administration has increased funding by $472 million to expand the trial to 30,000 US participants.

August 5, 2020

Missouri Expands Medicaid
Voters in Missouri approve a state constitutional amendment that will open Medicaid eligibility to include healthy adults starting on July 1, 2021.

August 11, 2020

Trump Administration Reaches Deal with Moderna
Despite still waiting on final data, the Trump administration reportedly agrees to pay $1.5 billion to Moderna for 100 million doses of its vaccine candidate.

August 15, 2020

FDA Approves Saliva Test
The FDA issues an EUA for SalivaDirect, a test developed by researchers at the Yale School of Public Health. The saliva test is less invasive than the current standard nasal swabs.

August 25, 2020

CDC Changes Testing Guidance but Later Reverses Itself
The CDC quietly changes its guidance on who should get tested for COVID-19, saying that individuals who are asymptomatic but have been exposed do not need testing. The changes are reversed after it is revealed the decision had bypassed CDC's usual scientific review process and was without internal review.

August 26, 2020

FDA Grants EUA to Abbott's Rapid Test
The FDA clears, via an EUA, a portable rapid COVID-19 test that can deliver results in under fifteen minutes.

September 14, 2020

Pfizer/BioNTech Expand Phase 3 Trial
Pfizer and BioNTech announce the phase 3 trial of their COVID-19 vaccine candidate will include 44,000 participants, up from the original target of 30,000, in hopes of recruiting a more diverse population and yielding more data.

September 21, 2020

J&J Begins Phase 3 Vaccine Trial
The clinical trial aims to test Johnson & Johnson's (J&J) vaccine candidate in 60,000 participants, the most in all currently ongoing phase 3 vaccine trials.

October 2, 2020

Trump Tests Positive for COVID-19
President Trump announces that he and First Lady Melania Trump have tested positive for COVID-19. After experiencing reportedly mild symptoms of the disease, Trump was taken to Walter Reed National Military Medical Center.

October 22, 2020

FDA Approves Remdesivir as First COVID-19 Treatment
Gilead's remdesivir is the first drug to receive FDA approval to treat COVID-19 after three randomized trials found that it decreased the length of hospital stays and reduced the likelihood that patients will require oxygen.

October 28, 2020

CMS Issues Vaccine, Treatment Coverage Rules
The CMS provides new rules for insurance coverage, increasing what Medicare pays hospitals for COVID-19 treatments. The new rules waive co-pays and deductibles on vaccines for seniors with Medicare.

November 7, 2020

Former Vice President Joe Biden Determined to Be President-Elect
After days of counting votes, Joe Biden wins the presidency thanks to the battleground state of Pennsylvania.

November 9, 2020

President-Elect Biden Announces COVID-19 Transition Team; Pfizer Publishes Vaccine Results
President-elect Biden announces the names of the scientific, medical, and public health professionals who will serve on his Transition COVID-19 Advisory Board. Also, Pfizer releases data from its COVID-19 vaccine trial showing that the vaccine was 90 percent effective.

November 16, 2020

Moderna Reveals Vaccine Efficacy Results
Moderna announces that its experimental vaccine reduces the risk of COVID-19 infection by 94.5 percent in participants who received it.

November 18, 2020

Pfizer/BioNTech Vaccine Is 95 Percent Effective
The results of a nearly 44,000-person trial demonstrate that the COVID-19 vaccine from Pfizer and BioNTech is 95 percent effective.

November 23, 2020

AstraZeneca Reports Vaccine Is 90 Percent Effective
When AstraZeneca's COVID-19 vaccine is administered as a half dose followed by a full dose at least a month later, it can be approximately 90 percent effective.

December 11, 2020   **FDA Issues EUA for Pfizer/BioNTech's COVID-19 Vaccine**
After an advisory panel endorses the vaccine, the FDA grants an EUA for Pfizer/BioNTech's vaccine, making it the first vaccine to receive authorization.

December 14, 2020   **First COVID-19 Vaccine Doses Administered to Essential Health Workers**
Shipments of the first vaccine reach health care workers, and vaccinations begin.

December 18, 2020   **FDA Issues EUA for Moderna's COVID-19 Vaccine**
Shipments of the Moderna COVID-19 vaccine begin after it is given an EUA by the FDA.

December 21, 2020   **Congress Passes COVID-19 Relief Bill**
The $900 billion package includes a new round of stimulus checks, an extension of unemployment benefits, and more money for vaccines and education.

January 20, 2021   **President Joe Biden Inaugurated**
Joe Biden is inaugurated as the forty-sixth president of the United States and pledges to distribute at least 100 million doses of the COVID-19 vaccine within the first one hundred days of his presidency.

February 27, 2021   **FDA Authorizes J&J's COVID-19 Vaccine**
The FDA authorizes the country's first single-shot vaccine, which begins shipping within forty-eight hours, making it the third option available for Americans.

March 10, 2021   **Congress Passes the American Rescue Plan Act**
Congress passes a $1.9 trillion pandemic relief bill that builds on many of the measures within the CARES Act of March 2020.

March 25, 2021   **President Biden Announces Updated Vaccination Goal**
President Biden announces a revised goal of administering at least 200 million doses of the vaccine within his first one hundred days of the presidency.

April 13, 2021   **Federal Authorities Recommend Pause on Administration of the J&J Vaccine**
Upon report of six cases of blood clots among individuals receiving the J&J vaccine, the government issues a pause in administration to review the data and safety implications.

April 23, 2021   **FDA and CDC Lift Pause on Administration of J&J Vaccine**
Upon completing a thorough safety review of the J&J COVID-19 vaccine, the agencies determine that the risk of blood clots is rare and that the benefits outweigh the potential risks.

April 30, 2021 **President Biden Achieves First One Hundred Days Goal**
On day ninety-two, the Biden administration reaches its goal of administering at least 200 million vaccine shots in American arms within the first one hundred days of taking office.

July–August 2021 **Delta Variant Concerns Grow**
Just as President Biden had announced his goal to have at least 70 percent of all Americans vaccinated with at least one dose, the delta variant wave of the coronavirus was simultaneously leading to a surge in COVID-19 cases and hospitalizations.

September 9, 2021 **President Biden Announces Federal Vaccine Mandate**
President Biden issued an order to employers with one hundred or more workers to ensure that their workforce is entirely vaccinated or face weekly COVID-19 testing. This announcement would later result in several hospitals firing unvaccinated clinicians and prompted mass resignation, with a number of nurses in particular leaving their institutions.

September 22, 2021 **FDA Authorizes Booster Vaccine Dose for Select Populations**
The Emergency Use authorization for the Pfizer/BioNTech COVID-19 vaccine was amended to allow for a single booster dose at least six months after initial vaccination series within certain high-risk individuals, notably those sixty-five years of age or older and those working in occupations with high exposure.

September 30, 2021 **Congress Temporarily Averts Government Shutdown**
Congress passed legislation that would avoid a partial federal shutdown and keep the government funded through December 3, 2021.

Sources used to compile the appendix are as follows:

- AstraZeneca.com
- Ca.gov
- CDC.gov
- CMS.gov
- Defense.gov
- FDA.gov
- HHS.gov
- In.gov
- JNJ.com
- JoeBiden.com
- Modernatx.com
- Mo.gov
- Oklahoma.gov
- Pfizer.com
- WhiteHouse.gov
- WHO.int

Bibliography

ABC123. "The Failed Launch of www.HealthCare.gov." Technology and Operations Management, November 18, 2016, https://digital.hbs.edu/platform-rctom/submission/the-failed-launch-of-www-healthcare-gov/.

Adner, Ron. *The Wide Lens: A New Strategy for Innovation.* London: Penguin, 2012.

AJMC Staff. "A Timeline of COVID-19 Developments in 2020." *American Journal of Managed Care,* January 1, 2021, https://www.ajmc.com/view/a-timeline-of-covid19-developments-in-2020.

Alonso-Zaldivar, Ricardo. "White House Wins Ruling on Health Care Price Disclosure." APNews, June 24, 2020, https://apnews.com/article/politics-donald-trump-ap-top-news-health-courts-987f0144285d5f0fa4bf989a651706a7.

American Hospital Association. "Fast Facts on US Hospitals." January 2017, https://www.aha.org/system/files/2018-01/fast-facts-us-hospitals-2017_0.pdf.

Aubrey, Allison. "Trump Declares Coronavirus a Public Health Emergency and Restricts Travel from China." National Public Radio, January 31, 2020, https://www.npr.org/sections/health-shots/2020/01/31/801686524/trump-declares-coronavirus-a-public-health-emergency-and-restricts-travel-from-c.

Bariso, Justin. "Amazon Almost Killed Best Buy. Then, Best Buy Did Something Completely Brilliant." Inc., March 4, 2019, https://www.inc.com/justin-bariso/amazon-almost-killed-best-buy-then-best-buy-did-something-completely-brilliant.html.

Blendon, Robert J., and John M. Benson. "Implications of the 2020 Election for US Health Policy." *New England Journal of Medicine* 383, no. 18 (2020): e105.

Blendon, Robert J., Mollyann Brodie, and John Benson. "What Happened to Americans' Support for the Clinton Health Plan?" *Health Affairs* 14, no. 2 (1995): 7-23.

Brownstein, Ronald. *The Second Civil War: How Extreme Partisanship Has Paralyzed Washington and Polarized America.* New York: Penguin, 2008.

Bureau of Labor Statistics. "Employment Situation News Release." June 5, 2020, https://www.bls.gov/news.release/archives/empsit_06052020.htm.

Business Group on Health. "Large Employers Double Down on Efforts to Stem Rising U.S. Health Benefit Costs Which Are Expected to Top $15,000 per Employee in 2020." August 13, 2019, https://www.businessgrouphealth.org/who-we-are/newsroom/press-releases/large-employers-double-down-on-efforts-to-stem-rising-us.

Buttorff, Christine, Teague Ruder, and Melissa Bauman. "Multiple Chronic Conditions in the United States." RAND Corporation, 2017, https://www.rand.org/pubs/tools/TL221.html.

Callaway, Ewen, David Cyranoski, Smriti Mallapaty, Emma Stoye, and Jeff Tollefson. "The Coronavirus Pandemic in Five Powerful Charts." *Nature* 579 (2020): 482–83.

Cancryn, Adam. "Is Trump on Track for an October Vaccine Surprise?" Politico. July 22, 2020, https://www.politico.com/news/2020/07/22/trump-october-vaccine-surprise-coronavirus-379278.

Castele, Nick. "Meet the Republican Governors Who Don't Want to Repeal All of Obamacare." National Public Radio, January 23, 2017, https://www.npr.org/2017/01/23/510823789/meet-the-republican-governors-who-dont-want-to-repeal-all-of-obamacare.

Center on Budget and Policy Priorities. "Policy Basics: Where Do Our Federal Tax Dollars Go?" April 9, 2020, https://www.cbpp.org/research/federal-budget/where-do-our-federal-tax-dollars-go.

Centers for Disease Control and Prevention. "Transcript for the CDC Telebriefing Update on COVID-19." February 26, 2020, https://www.cdc.gov/media/releases/2020/t0225-cdc-telebriefing-covid-19.html.

Centers for Medicare and Medicaid Services. "National Health Expenditure Data: Projected." April 15, 2020, https://www.cms.gov/Research-Statistics-Data-and-Systems/Statistics-Trends-and-Reports/NationalHealthExpendData/NationalHealthAccountsProjected.

———. "Speech: Remarks by Administrator Seema Verma at the 2018 Medicaid Managed Care Summit." September 27, 2018, https://www.cms.gov/newsroom/press-releases/speech-remarks-administrator-seema-verma-2018-medicaid-managed-care-summit.

———. "Trump Administration Announces Historically Low Medicare Advantage Premiums and New Payment Model to Make Insulin Affordable Again for Seniors." September 24, 2020, https://www.cms.gov/newsroom/press-releases/trump-administration-announces-historically-low-medicare-advantage-premiums-and-new-payment-model.

———. "Trump Administration Puts Patients over Paperwork by Reducing Healthcare Administrative Costs." September 26, 2019, https://www.cms.gov/newsroom/press-releases/trump-administration-puts-patients-over-paperwork-reducing-healthcare-administrative-costs.

Chen, Caroline, Marshall Allen, Lexi Churchill, and Isaac Arnsdorf. "Key Missteps at the CDC Have Set Back Its Ability to Detect the Potential Spread of Coronavirus." ProPublica, February 28, 2020, https://www.propublica.org/article/cdc-coronavirus-covid-19-test.

Congressional Research Service. "U.S. Health Care Coverage and Spending 2020." January 26, 2021, https://fas.org/sgp/crs/misc/IF10830.pdf.

Corlette, Sabrina, Linda J. Blumberg, and Kevin Lucia. "The ACA's Effect on the Individual Insurance Market: An Assessment of How Individual Health Insurance Markets Evolved between 2014 and 2019, Using Metrics Such as Premium Changes, Insurer Participation, and Enrollment." Health Affairs 39, no. 3 (2020): 436–44.

Cox, Jeff. "Trump Is on His Way to an Easy Win in 2020, According to Moody's Accurate Election Model." CNBC, October 15, 2019, https://www.cnbc.com/2019/10/15/moodys-trump-on-his-way-to-an-easy-2020-win-if-economy-holds-up.html.

Dafny, Leemore S. "Evaluating the Impact of Health Insurance Industry Consolidation: Learning from Experience." The Commonwealth Fund, November 20, 2015, https://www.commonwealthfund.org/publications/issue-briefs/2015/nov/evaluating-impact-health-insurance-industry-consolidation.

Dartmouth Atlas Project. "The Dartmouth Atlas of Health Care." 2021, https://www.dartmouthatlas.org/.

Deane, Claudia, Kim Parker, and John Gramlich. "A Year of US Public Opinion on the Coronavirus Pandemic," Pew Research Center, March 5, 2021, https://www.pewresearch.org/2021/03/05/a-year-of-u-s-public-opinion-on-the-coronavirus-pandemic/.

Deans, Graeme K., Fritz Kroeger, and Stefan Zeisel. "The Consolidation Curve." *Harvard Business Review* (December 2002): 20-21.

Department of Health and Human Services. "What Is the Affordable Care Act?" August 4, 2017, https://www.hhs.gov/answers/affordable-care-act/what-is-the-affordable-care-act/index.html.

DeSilver, Drew. "Turnout Soared in 2020 as Nearly Two-Thirds of Eligible U.S. Voters Cast Ballots for President." Pew Research Center, January 28, 2021, https://www.pewresearch.org/fact-tank/2021/01/28/turnout-soared-in-2020-as-nearly-two-thirds-of-eligible-u-s-voters-cast-ballots-for-president/.

Doherty, Tucker. "Medicare's Time Bomb, in 7 Charts." Politico, September 12, 2018, https://www.politico.com/agenda/story/2018/09/12/medicare-baby-boomers-trust-fund-000694/.

Dowling, Michael, and Charles Kenney. *Leading through a Pandemic: The Inside Story of Humanity, Innovation, and Lessons Learned during the COVID-19 Crisis.* New York: Simon and Schuster, 2020.

Dyrda, Laura. "100 of the Largest Hospitals and Health Systems in America: 2019." Becker's Hospital Review. Updated January 15, 2020, https://www.beckershospitalreview.com/largest-hospitals-and-health-systems-in-america-2019.html.

Federal Reserve. "Report on the Economic Well-Being of U.S. Households in 2019, Featuring Supplemental Data from April 2020." May 2020, https://www.federalreserve.gov/publications/files/2019-report-economic-well-being-us-households-202005.pdf.

Fehr, Rachel, Cynthia Cox, and Larry Levitt. "Data Note: Changes in Enrollment in the Individual Health Insurance Market through Early 2019." Kaiser Family Foundation. August 21, 2019, https://www.kff.org/private-insurance/issue-brief/data-note-changes-in-enrollment-in-the-individual-health-insurance-market-through-early-2019/.

Fireside Chat with Gary Bisbee, Ph.D. "Episode 5. Precision Medicine: Digitization and Scientific Innovation with Dr. Paul Rothman, Dean and CEO, Johns Hopkins Medicine." February 28, 2020, https://www.firesidechatpodcast.com/5-precision-medicine-digitization-and-scientific-innovation-conversation-with-dr-paul-rothman-dean-and-ceo-johns-hopkins-medicine/.

———. "Episode 7. High Tolerance for Ambiguity and a Passion for Complexity: Peter Fine, President and CEO, Banner Health." March 13, 2020, https://www.firesidechatpodcast.com/7-high-tolerance-for-ambiguity-and-a-passion-for-complexity-with-peter-fine-president-and-ceo-banner-health/.

———. "Episode 8. COVID-19: The Importance of Trust at the Local Clinical Level, with Dr. Julie L. Gerberding, EVP and Chief Patient Officer, Merck & Co., Inc. and former Director, CDC." March 20, 2020, https://www.listennotes.com/podcasts/fireside-chat-with/8-covid-19-the-importance-of-7c1DAt4-zj_/.

———. "Episode 9. COVID-19: There Is Going to Be a New Normal, with Dr. Mark McClellan, Director and Professor, Duke's Margolis Center, Former FDA

Commissioner and CMS Administrator." March 23, 2020, https://www.listennotes
.com/podcasts/fireside-chat-with/9-covid-19-there-is-going-to-rAE0RHD9Itn/.

———. "Episode 13. COVID-19: The Financial Stress on Our Sector Is Going to Be
Profound, with Dr. Rod Hochman, President and CEO, Providence." March 30, 2020,
https://www.firesidechatpodcast.com/13-covid-19-the-financial-stress-on-our-sector
-is-going-to-be-profound-with-dr-rod-hochman-president-and-ceo-providence/.

———. "Episode 15. COVID-19: This Is What We Do, with Nancy Howell Agee,
President and CEO, Carilion Clinic." April 3, 2020, https://www.listennotes.com
/podcasts/fireside-chat-with/15-covid-19-this-is-what-we-TDLSVzf2_mq/.

———. "Episode 17. COVID-19: Enormous Community Spirit, with Dr. Marc
Harrison, President and CEO, Intermountain Healthcare." April 10, 2020, https://
www.theacademytable.com/17-covid-19-enormous-community-spirit-with-dr-marc
-harrison-president-and-ceo-intermountain-healthcare/.

———. "Episode 19. COVID-19: We Strongly Encourage CMS to Continue Waivers,
with Wright Lassiter, President and CEO, Henry Ford Health System." April 17, 2020,
https://www.listennotes.com/podcasts/fireside-chat-with/19-covid-19-we-strongly
-kos9vChjnE2/.

———. "Episode 20. COVID-19: Special Circumstances Call for Special Decisions, with
Albert Bourla, Chairman and CEO, Pfizer." April 20, 2020, https://www.listennotes
.com/podcasts/fireside-chat-with/20-covid-19-special-cEBNArzxd5P/.

———. "Episode 22. COVID-19: Normal Does Not Return until Confidence Is
Restored, with Joseph Impicciche, JD, President and CEO, Ascension." April 24, 2020,
https://www.listennotes.com/podcasts/fireside-chat-with/22-covid-19-normal-does
-not-y8vI1OK54f3/.

———. "Episode 24. COVID-19: There Are Times When 'Nothing' Is the Right
Answer, with Bob Kerrey, Former Governor and Senator, Nebraska and President,
The New School." April 29, 2020, https://www.listennotes.com/podcasts/fireside
-chat-with/24-covid-19-there-are-times--g3stWqxm_c/.

———. "Episode 28. COVID-19: How We Look at the Future Has Changed Dramatically, with Dr. Joanne Conroy, President and CEO, Dartmouth-Hitchcock Health
System." May 12, 2020, https://www.listennotes.com/podcasts/fireside-chat-with
/28-covid-19-how-we-look-at-2bZ1sCYRhHI/.

———. "Episode 30. COVID-19: How Much of the Place Can We Change? Dennis
Murphy, President and CEO, Indiana University Health." May 19, 2020, https://
www.firesidechatpodcast.com/30-covid-19-how-much-of-the-place-can-we
-change-with-dennis-murphy-president-and-ceo-indiana-university-health/.

———. "Episode 31. It's Our Duty to Find a Way, with (Former) Governor Mitch
Daniels, President, Purdue University." May 21, 2020, https://www.listennotes.com
/podcasts/fireside-chat-with/31-its-our-duty-to-find-a-sXIx_8UKZHh/.

———. "Episode 33. Goal: One Billion Doses by the End of 2021, with Alex Gorsky,
Chairman and CEO, Johnson & Johnson—COVID-19 Series." May 28, 2020,
https://www.listennotes.com/podcasts/fireside-chat-with/33-goal-one-billion
-doses-by-EyU5bLxBdKc/.

———. "Episode 38. Times of Stress Amplify Weaknesses and Strengths, with Terry
Shaw, President and CEO, AdventHealth." June 16, 2020, https://www.listennotes
.com/podcasts/fireside-chat-with/38-times-of-stress-amplify-Qg-XLyhOrVF/.

————. "Episode 40. We Exist for the Public Benefit, with Dr. Steven Corwin, President and CEO, New York-Presbyterian." June 23, 2020, https://www.listennotes.com/podcasts/fireside-chat-with/40-we-exist-for-the-public-1tjrlUwVZD7/.

————. "Episode 42. Do Something to Make a Difference, with Ken Paulus, President and CEO, Prime Therapeutics." June 30, 2020, https://www.listennotes.com/podcasts/fireside-chat-with/42-do-something-to-make-a-16l_z-OgAvF/.

————. "Episode 43. They Rally and They Get It Done, with Redonda Miller, M.D., President, The Johns Hopkins Hospital." July 2, 2020, https://www.listennotes.com/podcasts/fireside-chat-with/43-they-rally-and-they-get-yjRiQLzMCDr/.

————. "Episode 50. Single National Platform with Jason Gorevic, CEO, Teladoc Health." August 4, 2020, https://www.listennotes.com/podcasts/fireside-chat-with/50-single-national-platform-wYdcsPiRQVT/.

————. "Episode 54. Alignment of Interests, by Dr. Craig E. Samitt, President and CEO, Blue Cross and Blue Shield of Minnesota." September 1, 2020, https://www.listennotes.com/podcasts/fireside-chat-with/54-alignment-of-interests-by-svuC7lNQfnd/.

————. "Episode 55. A Culture of Preparedness with Michael Dowling, President and CEO, Northwell Health." September 8, 2020, https://www.listennotes.com/podcasts/fireside-chat-with/55-a-culture-of-preparedness-Yvrljm_R28-/.

————. "Episode 56. Tune Out the Static, with Peter Fine, President and CEO, Banner Health." September 15, 2020, https://www.listennotes.com/podcasts/the-academy-table/56-tune-out-the-static-with-8V-IcBjwEy7/.

————. "Episode 57. Calm over Chaos, Faith over Fear, with Jim Skogsbergh, President and CEO, Advocate Aurora Health," September 22, 2020, https://www.listennotes.com/podcasts/fireside-chat-with/57-calm-over-chaos-faith-e5C9F7qbj3A/.

————. "Episode 74. Stay Safe and Look Out for One Another with Kevin B. Mahoney, CEO, University of Pennsylvania Health System." December 15, 2020, https://www.firesidechatpodcast.com/69-stay-safe-and-look-out-for-one-another-with-kevin-b-mahoney-ceo-university-of-pennsylvania-health-system/.

————. "Episode 81. We've Created a Vaccine Buddy System, with Marna Borgstrom, President and CEO, Yale New Haven Health System." February 23, 2021, https://www.listennotes.com/podcasts/fireside-chat-with/81-weve-created-a-vaccine-_P95zN2egk4/.

Francis, David, and Himanshu Rastogi. "The RBC Capital Markets Consumer Health & Information Technology Survey." RBC Capital Markets, February 20, 2015, https://research.rbccm.com/sellside/EmailDocViewer?encrypt=f13dd195-f647-42ef-84fa-2f107f463ada&mime=pdf&co=rbcnew&id=david.francis@rbccm.com&source=mail.

Freed, Meredith, Anthony Damico, and Tricia Neuman. "A Dozen Facts about Medicare Advantage in 2020." Kaiser Family Foundation, January 13, 2021, https://www.kff.org/medicare/issue-brief/a-dozen-facts-about-medicare-advantage-in-2020/.

Friedberg, Mark W., Peggy G. Chen, Chapin White, Olivia Jung, Laura Raaen, Samuel Hirshman, Emily Hoch, Clare Stevens, Paul B. Ginsburg, Lawrence P. Casalino, Michael Tutty, Carol Vargo, and Lisa Lipinski. "Effects of Health Care Payment Models on Physician Practice in the United States." RAND Corporation, 2015, https://www.rand.org/pubs/research_reports/RR869.html.

Fukuyama, Francis. *Trust: The Social Virtues and the Creation of Prosperity*. New York: Free Press, 1996.

Gary Bisbee Show, The. "Episode 3. Payment Is Policy with Nancy-Ann DeParle, Managing Partner & Co-founder, Consonance Capital Partners; -ormer Deputy Chief of Staff to President Barack Obama; Proud ACA Architect; former CMS Administrator." April 1, 2021, https://healthpodcastnetwork.com/episodes/the-gary-bisbee-show/03-payment-is-policy-with-nancy-ann-deparle-managing-partner-co-founder-consonance-capital-partners-former-deputy-chief-of-staff-to-president-barack-obama-proud-aca-architect-former-cms-ad.

Gaynor, Martin. "Examining the Impact of Health Care Consolidation: Statement before the Committee on Energy and Commerce, Oversight and Investigations Subcommittee, US House of Representatives." SSRN, February 14, 2018, https://papers.ssrn.com/sol3/papers.cfm?abstract_id=3287848.

Gee, Emily. "Less Coverage and Higher Costs: The Trump's Administration's Health Care Legacy." Center for American Progress, October 6, 2020, https://www.americanprogress.org/issues/healthcare/news/2020/09/25/490756/less-coverage-higher-costs-trumps-administrations-health-care-legacy/.

Goldsmith, Jeff C. "Relatively Modest Health Reform May Create More Value Than 'Medicare for All.'" Health Affairs, September 5, 2019, https://www.healthaffairs.org/do/10.1377/hblog20190828.273499/full/.

Halperin, Mark, and John Heilemann. *Double Down: Game Change 2012*. New York: Penguin, 2013.

Harris, Richard. *A Sacred Trust*. Baltimore: Penguin Books, 1969.

Her Story with Sanjula Jain. "Episode 2. A Seat at the Table with Nancy-Ann DeParle." September 22, 2020, https://www.thinkmedium.com/her-story/ep-2-a-seat-at-the-table/.

———. "Episode 26. Clinically Led and Professionally Managed, with Amy Compton-Phillips, M.D." April 7, 2021, https://www.thinkmedium.com/her-story/ep-26-clinically-led-and-professionally-managed/.

———. "Episode 28. The 'Not So' Long Fix, with Vivian Lee, M.D., Ph.D., MBA." April 21, 2021, https://www.thinkmedium.com/her-story/ep-28-the-not-so-long-fix/.

Hibbs, Douglas A. "Bread and Peace Voting in US Presidential Elections." *Public Choice* 104, no. 1–2 (2000): 149–80.

Hillestad, Richard, James Bigelow, Anthony Bower, Federico Girosi, Robin Meili, Richard Scoville, and Roger Taylor. "Can Electronic Medical Record Systems Transform Health Care? Potential Health Benefits, Savings, and Costs." *Health Affairs* 24, no. 5 (2005): 1103–17.

International Churchill Society. "About the Society." https://winstonchurchill.org/about-the-society/.

Jain, Sanjula. "Health System Revenue Attributed to Health Plan Premiums." Academy Insights, January 31, 2019, https://www.linkedin.com/pulse/health-system-revenue-attributed-plan-premiums-sanjula-jain/.

———. "Investment in Government Relations: Are Health Systems on Par?" Academy Insights, July 31, 2019, https://www.linkedin.com/pulse/investment-government-relations-health-systems-par-sanjula-jain/.

———. *2021 Trends Shaping the Post-Pandemic Health Economy*. Brentwood, TN: Trilliant Health, 2021.

Jeffrey, Terence P. "U.S. Median Age Hits All-Time High of 38; Record 86,248 Are 100 or Older." CNSNews, June 22, 2020, https://www.cnsnews.com/news/article /terence-p-jeffrey/us-median-age-hits-all-time-high-38-record-86248-are-100-or -older.

Jost, Tim. "President Biden Announces Priorities for Medicaid, the Affordable Care Act, Women's Health, and COVID-19." The Commonwealth Fund. February 4, 2021, https://www.commonwealthfund.org/blog/2021/president-biden-announces -priorities-medicaid-affordable-care-act-womens-health-and-covid.

Kaiser Family Foundation. "Health Insurance Coverage of the Total Population." 2019, https://www.kff.org/other/state-indicator/total-population/?currentTimeframe= 0&sortModel=%7B%22colId%22:%22Location%22,%22sort%22:%22asc%22%7D).

———. "2019 Employer Health Benefits Survey." September 14, 2020, https://www.kff .org/health-costs/report/2019-employer-health-benefits-survey/.

Keith, Katie. "HealthCare.gov Enrollment Rises; More Enrollment Data." *Health Affairs*, December 21, 2020, https://www.healthaffairs.org/do/10.1377/hblog20201221.49 9996/full/.

Kellerman, Arthur L., and Spencer S. Jones, "What It Will Take to Achieve the As-Yet-Unfulfilled Promises of Health Information Technology," *Health Affairs* 32, no. 1 (2013): 63–68.

Kelly, Heath. "The Classical Definition of a Pandemic Is Not Elusive." *Bulletin of the World Health Organization* 89 (2011): 540–41.

Kim, Eugene. "Jeff Bezos to Employees: 'One Day, Amazon Will Fail' but Our Job Is to Delay It As Long As Possible," CNBC, November 15, 2018, https://www.cnbc.com /2018/11/15/bezos-tells-employees-one-day-amazon-will-fail-and-to-stay-hungry .html.

Koster, John, Gary Bisbee, and Ram Charan. *n = 1: How the Uniqueness of Each Individual Is Transforming Healthcare.* Westport, CT: Easton Studio Press, 2015.

Lafley, A. G. "What Only the CEO Can Do." *Harvard Business Review* 87, no. 5 (2009): 54–62.

Legal Information Institute. "Gregory v. Ashcroft, 501 U.S. 452 (1991)." June 20, 1991, https://www.law.cornell.edu/supct/html/90-50.ZO.html.

———. "New State Ice Co. v. Liebmann." March 21, 1932, https://www.law.cornell.edu /supremecourt/text/285/262.

Marchi, Alberto, and Ellora-Julie Parekh. "How the Sharing Economy Can Make Its Case." McKinsey & Company, February 9, 2018, https://www.mckinsey.com/business -functions/strategy-and-corporate-finance/our-insights/how-the-sharing-economy -can-make-its-case.

Martin, Anne B., Micah Hartman, David Lassman, Aaron Catlin, and National Health Expenditure Accounts Team. "National Health Care Spending in 2019: Steady Growth for the Fourth Consecutive Year." *Health Affairs* 40, no. 1 (2020): 14–24.

McCarthy-Alfano, Megan, Aaron Glickman, Kristen Wikelius, and Janet Weiner. "Measuring the Burden of Health Care Costs for Working Families." *Health Affairs*, April 2, 2019, https://www.healthaffairs.org/do/10.1377/hblog20190327.999531/full/.

Medicaid and CHIP Payment and Access Commission. "Medicaid's Share of State Budgets." 2017, https://www.macpac.gov/subtopic/medicaids-share-of-state-budgets/.

Meeker, Mary. "Internet Trends 2018." Kleiner Perkins, May 30, 2018, https://www .kleinerperkins.com/perspectives/internet-trends-report-2018/.

———. "Internet Trends 2013." Kleiner Perkins, May 29, 2013. https://www.bondcap .com/report/itl3.

MSNBC. "Trump: Coronavirus Will Disappear One Day 'Like a Miracle.'" February 28, 2020, https://www.msnbc.com/deadline-white-house/watch/trump-coronavirus -will-disappear-one-day-like-a-miracle-79636549723.

Murray, Mark. "Poll: At 100 Days, Biden's Approval Remains Strong. Can the Honeymoon Last?" NBC News, April 25, 2021, https://www.nbcnews.com/politics/meet-the -press/poll-100-days-biden-s-approval-remains-strong-can-honeymoon-n1265199.

Naftulin, Julia. "Here's How Many Times We Touch Our Phones Every Day." Business Insider, July 13, 2016, https://www.businessinsider.com/dscout-research-people -touch-cell-phones-2617-times-a-day-2016-7.

National Archives. "Health Care Task Force Records." 2006-0885-F, https://clinton .presidentiallibraries.us/collections/show/81.

———. "2020 Electoral College Results." https://www.archives.gov/electoral-college /2020.

Oberlander, Jonathan. "Long Time Coming: Why Health Reform Finally Passed." *Health Affairs* 29, no. 6 (2010): 1112–16.

Office of the National Coordinator for Health Information Technology. "Office-Based Physician Electronic Health Record Adoption." January 2019, https://dashboard .healthit.gov/quickstats/pages/physician-ehr-adoption-trends.php.

O'Neill, Thomas P., Jr., and William Novak. *Man of the House: The Life and Political Memoirs of Speaker Tip O'Neill*. New York: Random House, 1987.

Patel, Neel V. "Why the CDC Botched Its Coronavirus Testing." MIT Technology Review, April 10, 2020, https://www.technologyreview.com/2020/03/05/905484 /why-the-cdc-botched-its-coronavirus-testing/.

Perry, Mark J. "Fortune 500 Firms 1955 v. 2016: Only 12% Remain, Thanks to the Creative Destruction That Fuels Economic Prosperity." American Enterprise Institute, December 13, 2016, https://www.aei.org/carpe-diem/fortune-500-firms-1955-v-2016-only -12-remain-thanks-to-the-creative-destruction-that-fuels-economic-prosperity/.

Peterson, Peter G. "Gray Dawn: The Global Aging Crisis." *Foreign Affairs* 78, no. 1 (1999): 42–55.

Pew Research Center. "Election 2020: Voters Are Highly Engaged, but Nearly Half Expect to Have Difficulties Voting." August 13, 2020, https://www.pewresearch.org /politics/2020/08/13/election-2020-voters-are-highly-engaged-but-nearly-half -expect-to-have-difficulties-voting/.

———. "In a Politically Polarized Era, Sharp Divides in Both Partisan Coalitions." May 30, 2020, https://www.pewresearch.org/politics/2019/12/17/in-a-politically -polarized-era-sharp-divides-in-both-partisan-coalitions/.

Pierce, David, and Lauren Goode. "The WIRED Guide to the iPhone." WIRED, December 7, 2018, https://www.wired.com/story/guide-iphone/.

Pradhan, Rachana. "CDC Coronavirus Testing Decision Likely to Haunt Nation for Months to Come." Kaiser Health News, March 23, 2020, https://khn.org/news/cdc -coronavirus-testing-decision-likely-to-haunt-nation-for-months-to-come/.

Pramuk, Jacob. "Senate Passes $1.9 Trillion COVID Relief Bill, House Democrats Plan Final Approval Tuesday." CNBC, March 6, 2021, https://www.cnbc.com/2021/03 /06/covid-stimulus-update-senate-passes-1point9-trillion-relief-bill.html.

Rastegar, Darius A. "Health Care Becomes an Industry." *Annals of Family Medicine* 2, no. 1 (2004): 79–83.

Robison, Peter, Dina Bass, and Robert Langreth. "Seattle's Patient Zero Spread Coronavirus Despite Ebola-Style Lockdown." Bloomberg Businessweek, March 9, 2020, https://www.bloomberg.com/news/features/2020-03-09/how-coronavirus-spread -from-patient-zero-in-seattle.

Sabato, Larry, Kyle Kondik, and Geoffrey Skelley, eds. *Trumped: The 2016 Election That Broke All the Rules.* Lanham, MD: Rowman & Littlefield, 2017.

Schramm, Carl J. "Hospital Consolidation: Lessons from Other Industries." In *Multi-hospital Systems: Policy Issues for the Future*, ed. Gerald E. Bisbee Jr., 111–37. Chicago: Hospital Research and Education Trust, 1981.

Selin, Jennifer. "How the Constitution's Federalist Framework Is Being Tested by COVID-19." Brookings, June 8, 2020, https://www.brookings.edu/blog/fixgov/2020 /06/08/how-the-constitutions-federalist-framework-is-being-tested-by-covid-19/.

Singh, Anu. "2019 Healthcare M&A in Review: In Pursuit of the New Bases of Competition." KaufmanHall, January 2020, https://www.kaufmanhall.com/2019-health care-mergers-acquisitions-in-review.

Summers, Juana. "Timeline: How Trump Has Downplayed the Coronavirus Pandemic." National Public Radio, October 2, 2020, https://www.npr.org/sections /latest-updates-trump-covid-19-results/2020/10/02/919432383/how-trump-has -downplayed-the-coronavirus-pandemic.

Technology and Operations Management. "The Failed Launch of www.HealthCare .gov." November 18, 2016, https://digital.hbs.edu/platform-rctom/submission/the -failed-launch-of-www-healthcare-gov/.

United Nations. "Launch of Global Humanitarian Response Plan for COVID-19 Secretary-General." March 25, 2020, https://www.un.org/sg/en/content/sg/press -encounter/2020-03-25/launch-of-global-humanitarian-response-plan-for-covid-19.

Valverde, Miriam. "Donald Trump's Wrong Claim That 'Anybody' Can Get Tested for Coronavirus." Kaiser Health News, March 12, 2020, https://khn.org/news/donald -trumps-wrong-claim-that-anybody-can-get-tested-for-coronavirus/.

Waldron, John. "How Walmart Is Leading the Omnichannel Charge." eTailwest, n.d., https://etailwest.wbresearch.com/blog/how-walmart-is-leading-the-omnichannel -charge.

Waldrop, M. Mitchell. "Dee Hock on Management." Fast Company, September 8, 2017, https://www.fastcompany.com/27454/dee-hock-management.

Walter, Amy. "Will Impeachment Reshape the 2020 Race?" The Cook Political Report, September 26, 2019, https://cookpolitical.com/analysis/national/national-politics /will-impeachment-reshape-2020-race.

Weeks, William B., Robert A. Greene, and James N. Weinstein. "Potential Advantages of Health System Consolidation and Integration." *American Journal of Medicine* 128, no. 10 (2015): 1050–51.

Wellstone, Paul D., and Ellen R. Shaffer. "The American Health Security Act—A Single-Payer Proposal." *New England Journal of Medicine* 328, no. 20 (1993): 1489–93.

West, Darrell M., Diane Heith, and Chris Goodwin. "Harry and Louise Go to Washington: Political Advertising and Health Care Reform." *Journal of Health Politics, Policy and Law* 21, no. 1 (1996): 35–68.

White House. "Inaugural Address by Joseph R. Biden Jr." January 20, 2021, https://www
.whitehouse.gov/briefing-room/speeches-remarks/2021/01/20/inaugural-address
-by-president-joseph-r-biden-jr/.

———. "Remarks by President Biden in Address to a Joint Session of Congress." April 28,
2021, https://www.whitehouse.gov/briefing-room/speeches-remarks/2021/04/29
/remarks-by-president-biden-in-address-to-a-joint-session-of-congress/.

White House Archives. "Barack Obama's Inaugural Address." January 21, 2009, https://
obamawhitehouse.archives.gov/blog/2009/01/21/president-barack-obamas-inaugural
-address.

Williams, Jackson. "3 Legal Challenges Could Derail Surprise Medical Bills." STAT,
January 6, 2020, https://www.statnews.com/2020/01/06/3-legal-challenges-derail
-surprise-medical-bills/.

Witters, Dan. "50% in U.S. Fear Bankruptcy Due to Major Health Event." Gallup, September 1, 2020, https://news.gallup.com/poll/317948/fear-bankruptcy-due-major
-health-event.aspx.

Wolff-Mann, Ethan. "'Our Uniquely Expensive Healthcare' System Will Catch Up with
Us." Yahoo Finance, September 26, 2018, https://finance.yahoo.com/news/powell
-uniquely-expensive-healthcare-system-will-catch-us-212627406.html.

Wucker, Michelle. *The Gray Rhino*. New York: St. Martin's, 2016.

Yglesias, Matthew. "It's Good That You Can't Keep Your Insurance Plan; Obama Was
Wrong to Mislead People but Right to Scrap Dysfunctional Insurance Products."
Slate, November 12, 2013, https://slate.com/business/2013/11/obama-said-you-can
-keep-your-plan-an-unwise-promise-that-the-president-was-right-to-break.html.

Index

About the Authors

Gary Bisbee Jr., PhD, MBA, is founder, chairman, and CEO of Think Medium, which explores leadership through peer-to-peer conversations. His leadership positions have spanned Wall Street, academia, health policy, and entrepreneurial ventures. Bisbee is a frequent speaker and facilitator for executive teams and boards of directors. He is well published and most recently coauthored, *n=1: How the Uniqueness of Each Individual Is Transforming Healthcare*. Bisbee's weekly video interviews are found on *The Gary Bisbee Show* and YouTube. Prior to founding Think Medium, Bisbee was cofounder, chairman, and CEO of The Health Management Academy. He has been a member of multiple public and not-for-profit boards and currently sits on three boards and is an adviser to investment funds and entrepreneurs. Bisbee holds an MBA in finance and health care from the Wharton School of the University of Pennsylvania and a PhD in chronic disease epidemiology from Yale University.

Donald Trigg is the former president of Cerner Corporation, a *Fortune* 500 supplier of health care information technology. As president, he had P&L responsibility for the breadth of Cerner's business ranging from its electronic medical record and revenue cycle management solutions to emerging growth areas focused on value-based care and data. His earlier roles at Cerner included executive vice president of Cerner's Strategic Growth businesses, president of Cerner Health Ventures, and managing director of UK operations. Trigg has experience scaling early-stage health care information technology start-ups, including Natural Language Processing leader CodeRyte. Trigg served extensively in the federal government, working in senior policy roles in the US Senate and US House of Representatives. He spent four years working for George W. Bush on his 2000 presidential campaign in Austin, Texas, and during his first term in Washington, D.C. Trigg earned a bachelor's degree from St. Lawrence University in Canton, New York.

Sanjula Jain, PhD, is a health services researcher and strategic adviser working with health care organizations including *Fortune* 500 health care companies, health systems, and venture-backed start-ups. She is currently the senior vice president of market strategy and the chief research officer at Trilliant Health, a predictive analytics company that transforms how organizations maximize growth and engage individuals around their health care needs, just as the largest consumer brands in the world engage with their customers. Jain also serves on the faculty of the Johns Hopkins University School of Medicine, teaching courses in digital health entrepreneurship and population health. Jain's research, which is largely focused on delivery systems, has been published in prominent journals such as *Health Affairs*, the *American Journal of Managed Care*, and the *Journal of Healthcare Management*. Her work is frequently cited by industry publications such as *Business Insider* and the American Hospital Association's *Market Scan*. Jain holds a BA in psychology and ecology and evolutionary biology with a distinction in research and creative work from Rice University and a PhD in health services research and health policy, with a concentration in economics, from Emory University.